RED

RED

THE TEMPESTUOUS LIFE OF *Susan Hayward*

Robert LaGuardia
&
Gene Arceri

MACMILLAN PUBLISHING COMPANY   New York

Macmillan Publishing Company
866 Third Avenue, New York, N.Y. 10022
Collier Macmillan Canada, Inc.

Library of Congress Cataloging in Publication Data
LaGuardia, Robert.
Red : the tempestuous life of Susan Hayward.
Filmography: p.
Includes index.
1. Hayward, Susan.   2. Moving-picture actors and
actresses—United States—Biography.   I. Arceri, Gene.
II. Title.
PN2287.H378L3   1985   791.43′028′0924 [B]   85-4878
ISBN 0-02-567230-4

Macmillan books are available at special discounts for bulk purchases for sales promotions, premiums, fund-raising, or educational use. For details, contact:

Special Sales Director
Macmillan Publishing Company
866 Third Avenue
New York, N.Y. 10022

10 9 8 7 6 5 4 3 2 1

Designed by Jack Meserole

Printed in the United States of America

With love, to my mother, Dolly LaGuardia.

For those in spirit—my father Charles,
my mother Jennie, my brothers Bob and Jay.

ACKNOWLEDGMENTS

The research on this book, which spanned a decade, began only days after the afternoon Susan Hayward died, March 14, 1975. Since then, so many individuals were approached and interviewed that it would require many pages to give each one proper thanks. However, a certain core group of people was of such enormous help, pouring out, usually in multiple interviews, their recollections of the complex and clearly evolving Hayward character, making possible the full scope of this volume, that we would be remiss if we did not mention them.

Wally Marrenner, Susan Hayward's brother, was especially generous. He had spoken to other writers about Susan but never at such length or in such depth, and we are most grateful to him.

In Susan's last years, all roads, one continually learned from interviews, led to Ron Nelson, nominally her best friend, but much more. He was always enthusiastic and graciously helpful, and we wish now to express our deep appreciation to him.

From the beginning of our collaboration, Gene and I agreed on the importance of locating Florence, Susan's estranged sister, and eventually found her through Benny Medford, Susan's first agent in Hollywood. He was seventy-eight and couldn't have been more charming and direct. He was then handling Moira Dietrich, a young actress, the daughter of Florence. We went to see her in a play and spotted her mother and half-brother, Larry Zaenglin, in the audience. (Moira, by the way, bears a striking resemblance to her late aunt.) Florence was extremely candid about the Marrenners and her relationship with Susan. She did indeed unlock secrets about Susan's deepest self and for that we wish to thank her extravagantly.

For their contributions, we would like to thank Graham Kislingbury, Cleo Miller June, Ed Montgomery, Stan Musgrove, Bob Sidney, Henry Hathaway, Daniel Mann, Helen Rackin and Nolan Miller.

We would also like to thank so many of the inhabitants of Carrollton, Georgia, in particular Mary Williams and Ann Moran, as well as Mrs. Hollingsworth, the librarian, and a dozen or so of the town's shopkeepers who were not shy on the subject of their most famous patron. Monsignor Regan, pastor of Our Lady of Perpetual Help, Father Richard Morrow and Father Thomas Brew were most helpful.

Thanks also to the following generous individuals for talking with us: Martin Emslie, Mrs. Robert Emslie, John Engstead, Eddie Bracken, Jack Marta, Jesse Lasky, Jr., Evelyn Lane Dankner, Bill Williams, Richard K. Webber, Marsha Hunt, Larry Zaenglin, Moira Dietrich, Robert Cummings, Howard W. Koch, Del Armstrong, Carroll Righter, Tom Tuttle, Helen Turpin, Ben Nye, Buck Hall, Herman Boden, Rory Calhoun, Ben Chapman, Leonard Doss, Gerd Oswald, Cameron Mitchell, Stan Hough, Joseph L. Mankiewicz, Rose Steinberg Wapner, Helen Rose, Carmen Dirigo, Edie Adams. For helping us detail Susan's *Mame* experience, we thank— besides Ron Nelson—Helen Rackin, George Tregre, Onna White, John Bowab, Diana Baffer, Ruth Gillette, Betty McGuire, and Jerry Herman. And for aiding the narrative of Susan's last three years, we thank, aside from those already mentioned, Noreen Siegel, Dr. Lee Siegel, Janie Boxer, Walden Welch.

On a more personal level, Gene Arceri wishes to thank, for their assistance and encouragement, Ann Marchese, Fern Leiber, Sue Binder, Irene Manning, Jean Martin, Maureen Salaman, Jean Garceau, Countess Vivianna de Blonville, Bob Lawallen, Carl Palangi, Bartalini, Les Suter, Richard Frewen, Stan D'Arcy, Barry Brown of the BBC, Colin Briggs, Jean Cook, William Holland (most especially), and I wish to thank Leslie Sirro, David Yarnell, Tom O'Mara, Ron Durkop—and Hugh J. Lynch, Jr., for reading the entire manuscript while it was in progress and making valuable suggestions. From both of us: thanks to our editor, Arlene Friedman.

A final note now on the matter of accuracy. During the course of the research, we attempted, whenever possible, to establish cross-checks for major interviews by seeking more than one source for facts. When this was impossible, we tried to establish a sense of veracity about individuals who supplied information. Using both techniques, often in concert, we were usually able to cut through the many rumors which surrounded Susan's life and reveal its actual structure. Our emphasis upon corroboration always gave us an added sense of security in our work.

We should mention the handful of important interviews and corroborations that we would have liked but didn't get. Cinematographer Stanley Cortez would not speak of his work or friendship with Susan. Jess Barker, in a charming telephone call, politely refused to be interviewed about his and Susan's shared past. We also failed to receive return phone calls from either Timothy or Gregory Barker, despite repeated attempts.

But by far the majority of living people who knew Susan made themselves available. Without their help, this book could not have been written.

ROBERT LA GUARDIA
(assisted by notes from Gene Arceri)

CONTENTS

Photograph

O F THE THOUSANDS of still photographs taken of Susan Hayward during her long movie career, one particularly interested her. In it, she wasn't glamorous or even young. A harsh, three-quarter face looks out toward oblivion. A trail of cigarette smoke heads upward. The eyes are steel-cold. The overall quizzical expression seems to say, among other things, "My God! What next?" The photograph became an obsession. Wherever she went, the photograph went with her. But she was never comfortable about how it was presented or where it was. She slipped it in and out of at least six different frames. She would put it by her bed, then hang it in her bathroom, then remove it to her dressing room. It was with her in Carrollton, Georgia, during her idyllic nine-year marriage to Eaton Floyd Chalkley; with her in Fort Lauderdale while she drank her life away; in the house in Los Angeles where she struggled unendingly against the specter of death.

She said of the picture, "It's the only photo I've got that shows the real me." It was snapped during the early stages of the making of *I Want to Live!* After twenty years of movie-making, she still wanted the Oscar for Best Actress, and believed *I Want to Live!* would help her achieve it. She became absorbed in her work, wished to be distracted by nothing. But the tension of the early takes did cause a minor misunderstanding with her husband, Eaton. For a few days, they stopped having relations. That disturbed her. At the same time, her mother was hospitalized with heart trouble. Another distraction. One morning, Eaton, who had moved out of his and Susan's hotel room in a huff, came on the set. Susan was already in prison garb, working on a scene. Eaton went to the director, Robert Wise, to ask him to stop filming then walked over to Susan to tell her that her mother had died. "We have to deal with this," he said, then he left. She sat and had a cigarette. In those seconds, while she seemed only to be irritated at Eaton's interruption, a photographer, who didn't know that she had just learned of her mother's death, took that photograph.

It had great significance, for it represented a magical interplay of her own character with the events of her life. She talked about the photograph and knew, better than anyone, the terrible tale it told about her. In the quizzical "Oh, God! What next?" face was the geography of ambition and love delayed, though not wholly denied. All of her life, Susan had paid for her successes with the pain of lovelessness, only to scramble, when it was nearly too late, for the peace of love and friendship. She believed that the one person who, beyond all, should have loved her, her mother, had rejected her early in life. She believed that, in return, she could not love her mother. And so the pattern played out in most of Susan's relationships, bringing her several times to the brink of her life utterly afraid of leaving it without love. At the very end, while tumors grew in her brain, during the interminable suffering, she called out for her dead mother to come and help her.

She was a great and compelling star. In three crowded decades of work, she had made fifty-six films, ranging from the insouciance of her Paramount roles, to the elaborate sagas of her 20th Century-Fox movies, to those suffering biographies of the fifties and merely workmanlike vehicles of the sixties. If she had made no other films but *I'll Cry Tomorrow* and *I Want to Live!*, millions of people would still remember her as one of the most powerful players of the period. On the screen, she took on superb dimensions. Her movie voice, totally self-created, was low, slow and deeper than the voices of other women. Her body language, for the camera, was as carefully choreographed as any on-screen dance by Rita Hayworth: she employed, with great effect, sudden sharp movements of the arms and torso to suggest the orgasm, much as Spanish dancers do. Her eyes were as sincere as Garbo's, except that instead of hiding mysteries, they often revealed great suffering.

The Hollywood community preferred to see the Susan Hayward of the photograph. Indeed, to other players she was one of the coldest of the legendary cold stars. Robert Preston, who made three movies with her, once said to an interview request: "Anything I have to say about Susan Hayward you couldn't print." Robert Cummings found her depressing to work with. Her first studio bosses disliked her attitude so much that they deliberately kept her in second-rate movies, even though she was an obvious money-maker.

The reason for her coldness wasn't only that she was a girl from a slum who feared revealing herself in a superficial environment. In time, that reaction alone would have disappeared. There was ancient anger in her. The coldness, the withdrawal from others went deep into her being, first seen when she was a struggling child in Brooklyn. She acted to dissipate it. She saw analysts about it, received explanations, eventually found a way to transform it, but could never cure it.

Compounding the tragedy, Susan always knew who the woman in the photograph was. She could step outside it, recognize it, put her finger on the coldness, see what had brought it about. But what Susan couldn't see that can be perceived so clearly years after her death was how magnificent she really was. Through her work, her icy rigidity had metamorphosed to cinematic majesty. Her anger had become memorable sincerity. She had paid all her dues tenfold, and then some. She had made of herself, like the fabled merchant, one pearl of great worth from a tangle of shortcomings.

CHAPTER 1

Slumgirl

E LLEN MARRENNER, in labor on the top floor of a three-story red brick tenement, heard all the familiar summer noises of Flatbush from her window. The horses pulling wagons clip-clopped on the hot street below; the neighborhood kids, on vacation from school, noisily skirmished on the sidewalk; canaries, perched in their cages in front parlors, chirped along with the nerve-racking clang of the Church Avenue trolley-car bell. Normally, she would have joined the block's housewives, grandmothers and old men who congregated on the front steps and on the fire escapes to catch a breeze during the day. In the evening, she would have gone up to the roof with her husband, Walter, for any cool air that might have wafted in from the ocean. Up there, looking across the East River, they could see the skyscrapers of Manhattan and the Brooklyn Bridge.

Tiny Edythe Marrenner was born on June 30, 1917, causing a great deal of commotion in the apartment at 3507 Church Avenue. Her brother, Wally, was already five, and her sister, Florence, was seven. Wally remembers that he and Florence ran in and out of the apartment that summer, showing their friends their new baby sister. After the Labor Day holiday, when all the kids went back to school, baby Edythe seemed upset at the loss of attention.

Flatbush, which covered three and half square miles of Brooklyn's center, was only about thirty minutes from midtown Manhattan by car, train or bus, but a thousand miles from its heartbeat. It was a grand place for children, even the poor, mixed-ethnic byway the Marrenners lived in. There, city and countryside seemed to mingle. "A block from where we lived," recalls Wally, "Church Avenue turned into a dirt road and even further out there was farmland. You could walk just a little ways and come to a farmers' market." But for most grownups the Marrenners' part of Flatbush was depressing. From the start of her marriage, Ellen Marrenner had felt trapped there; she had heard the clang of the Church Avenue trolley too many times, smelled the stale odors of the Irish bars and the sweet, sticky ones of the German bakeries until she gagged.

She had married Walter Marrenner for love, not security, defying her Swedish father's wishes, and actually going against the grain of her very stock: for the Swedes were a clean, practical people, not known for their romanticism. When she met him, red-headed Walter Marrenner was a twenty-six-year-old dashing Coney Island barker. It must have been magic for young, middle-class Ellen Pearson, from a cool and conservative family, to meet the flame-topped barker among the hot dogs and roller coasters, to walk hand in hand on the boardwalk. At the time, she was working as a legal secretary and making better money than the charming Walter, which apparently didn't bother her.

She married Walter in 1909 and had her firstborn, Florence, in 1910. After a few years of trying to raise a family on Walter's small salary, Ellen realized the mistake she had made, but by then it was too late. The poverty, the sudden change from the way of life in her father's house killed the romance between her and Walter. Much of their relationship began to revolve around economics. Under pressure from her, Walter chucked his exciting barker's job and buckled down as a lineman for the Interboro Rapid Transit (IRT), where the pay was better but the world darker and messier. A perpetual anger developed between Ellen and Walter over the aspects of life that were irremediable: even Walter's better salary from the IRT couldn't rescue them from Church Avenue. She blamed him. He blamed her. After their third child, Edythe, was born, they began sleeping in separate bedrooms and never again would they sleep together.

There were deep roots to the conflict between them. Theodor Pearson, Ellen's builder father, had disliked Walter, but not merely for the obvious reasons: that he was poor and Catholic while Pearson was Baptist. Theodor Pearson knew that there was a great philosophical division between Walter's family and his own. The Marrenners were all colorful theater people, *bon vivants* who were always on the go. Walter's father was staid English, but his mother was flamboyant Irish. Katie Harrigan (her stage name) had been, in her younger days, an actress in Ireland. His sister, who took the *nom de théâtre* May Borden, had likewise become an actress and a *Ziegfeld Follies* girl. Walter's brother, Albert, performed as a stand-up comic in nightclubs with Nick Lucas. One of Walter's nephews, Eddie Langdon, played the drums at Coney Island. To Theodor, they were all poor gypsies who sang and gave a smile for their supper, not the sort of family for either his daughter or his grandchildren. Theodor was a hard-working immigrant who saw their way of life as self-indulgent.

When Edythe was only a few years old, her grandfather Theodor died a terrible death. He had burned his tongue on the wrong end of a lit cigar, the injury turned malignant, his tongue was amputated and then he died. He was only fifty. He left all of his money to his wife, Ellen (Ellen Marrenner's mother), who continued to live in the comfortable two-story brownstone on Hoyt Street in Brooklyn where she and Theodor had lived with their four children. They were all grown now. Emma was a successful lawyer with her own offices. Frankie was a piano teacher. Oscar took over his father's building business and oversaw his mother's property. They were middle-class, serious-minded young adults who would never wind up living on Church Avenue like their sister.

Ellen's mother tried to help her daughter as much as she could, slipping her money to buy extras for the household. Emma helped her sister Ellen, too. When she discovered that little Florence had a bit of dancing talent, she volunteered to pay for the girl's dancing lessons and various new clothes. Every Sunday, like clockwork, Ellen, Walter, Florence, Wally and tiny Edythe were invited to dinner at Grandmother Pearson's. Florence remembers, "They used to have a gorgeous meal for us. White tablecloth—everything. We three children would sit separately at a small table. They always had a big roast; soup, salad, cake, the whole thing. We looked forward to that." Grandmother Pearson blamed Walter for her daughter's plight; the blame was always apparent on those visits and helped worsen the lifelong dispute between Ellen and Walter. The class conflict that emerged between them and their families erupted on even the most joyous occasions.

As Florence recalls with a tinge of sarcasm, "There were never any dinners from my father's family." Instead, they offered boundless entertainment and endless laughs. Funny Al Marrenner,

Walter's brother, was always at the Church Avenue tenement-house apartment cutting up, doing stand-up routines. The Marrenners would go to New Jersey to see Walter's *Ziegfeld Follies* sister, May Borden, who was loud, pushy and wonderful. Despite herself, Ellen and her children were seduced by the greasepaint of all the performing Marrenners. She adored them, which was ironic, for she was angry at Walter for being one of them.

The starlight of Walter's family fascinated Ellen. When nine-year-old Florence (or "Florrie," or "Flo," or "Firenze," as she was called) began taking dancing lessons at Aunt Emma's expense, Ellen began to think of show business as the antidote to Flatbush. Florrie was a darling girl, with light red hair like her father's, sturdy legs, a cute smile and a nicely developing figure. After a few years, she was dancing up a storm in that Flatbush apartment and the dance studio. At first, Ellen did not give her much encouragement, but when Florence's talent and abilities became clearer, Ellen showered her with attention.

There was talk of the younger Wally, who was a slight boy with an ever present impish grin, becoming a dancer, too, because he could do a few turns around the living room like a dream. Baby Edythe didn't dance, but she appeared in a school play when she was a mere five. She had red hair like her sister's, and a lovely, snub-tipped nose which came from her father, promising that she would turn out just as pretty and no doubt as talented as Florrie.

Walter's work as a train lineman forced him to work until after midnight, pushing more responsibility on Ellen's overburdened shoulders. Florrie, when she wasn't at Erasmus High School or dancing, became the good and dutiful older sister, minding the two younger ones when Ellen was busy. She would lead her brother and sister by each hand to a nearby cemetery, where they wandered around reading tombstones, occasionally catching a funeral procession moving slowly past them. On other days, Florrie would take them to Kings County Hospital; the three children would make faces at the "crazies" on the lawn until an orderly chased them away. As Wally remembers it, all three children were quite close before Edythe grew a little older.

The name *Edythe* came from Walter's sister, Edith Marrenner. Ellen had changed the spelling. Her family nickname was "E" (and Wally's was "Wal"). E's red hair was so rich and striking that when she began in the first grade of Public School 181, the boys insulted her by calling her "Red" and "Pepper Pot" and "Carrot Top" and "Bricktop." One day, as she was walking home alone from school, a boy teased her with one of the names. She answered back and he socked her. Schoolbooks in hand, she sat down on the front steps of her building with tears in her eyes. Her father, heading out the door on his way to work, sat down beside her and she told him what had happened. He looked at his youngest and said, "Always hit back." He compared her to a rubber ball. "Remember this: the harder they hit you, the higher you'll bounce, if you're a good ball to start with. If not, you might as well give up anyway." Her thin, slight-framed father brushed back the hair from her eyes and got up.

Right after that, with her father's encouragement, six-year-old E started taking punching lessons from her brother. She learned to take care of herself among the little ruffians, slapping, punching and kicking when she had to. With the father who had given her the best advice she'd ever had, and who was always sensitive to her moods while her mother often wasn't, she developed a strong bond.

Walter Marrenner loved to build and fly kites, and perhaps, as they wandered below smoky clouds, he thought of the splendor that was denied him in life. On his days off from the IRT, he brought E and Wal to an empty lot and they would launch one of his airy creations into a passing wind.

Late one afternoon in 1923 after their father had gone off to work, Wally and some friends were flying kites by themselves on a sidewalk in front of the apartment house while a fascinated Edythe looked from the window four stories up. Wanting to join them, she rushed out to buy a paper plane in the candy store across the way. When she was returning, crossing the street, excitedly holding her new paper plane, a small, speeding car which had just turned a corner struck her and tossed her to the ground. As she lay there soaked in blood, Wally thought, "she looked just like a broken doll." He screamed her name. The driver of the car picked her up in his arms and ran up the four flights of stairs to the Marrenners', then ran right back down the stairs, straight to his bank to withdraw all of his savings. Florence adds: "My Aunt Emma, the lawyer, filed suit against that driver for my mother and father, and won a $10,000 judgment. But by then the man had put all of his money in his wife's name, so we didn't get a nickel."

Terrified, Ellen took her child to a free clinic, where the doctors—not the best—saw so much blood, suspected so much trauma, that they warned Ellen that her daughter might not live. When it was clear that she wasn't in danger, they told the Marrenners to "prepare yourselves. She has two fractured legs and a broken hip and she will be a cripple for the rest of her life. She may never walk again."

The family was frightened, but did what they could. There wasn't enough money for high-priced specialists, and Ellen, against the wishes of the clinic doctors, decided that her daughter would be better off convalescing at home. Edythe was treated only briefly at the clinic, where the doctors immobilized her in plaster casts that went above the hip. Once home, she was put in a cumbersome structure of traction lines weighted down with many pounds of sand to keep the hip from knitting badly. For six months, she was unable to do much more than look out of the bedroom window toward Manhattan, or sit by the window of her favorite room, the kitchen, facing onto the backyard.

Edythe was not completely cut off. Ladies from the church brought over a large bag of toys. She was allowed to open only one toy each day that she was bedridden, which helped the days pass more quickly. For a while, it looked as if the clinic doctors had been right. "When she got out of traction," says Wally, "we were able to take her outdoors. But she still couldn't bend one leg and she couldn't walk at all. So my folks bought her the largest wagon they could find and we used to pull her around in that." In six months, she was able to hobble around on crutches and returned to school at P.S. 181, with her mother taking her to and from the school in her wagon for more than a year.

Finally, Edythe was walking. Her left leg became a quarter of an inch shorter than the right. The shortness problem was partly corrected by a lift tacked onto her shoe heel. But because of the way her hip healed, she was burdened with a slight but permanent limp. In later years, she would blame the flaw on her mother's poor handling of the accident.

More and more of Ellen's attention, meanwhile, was centered on Florrie, who now made dancing her whole life. When she was sixteen, she quit Erasmus High School to continue full-time dancing lessons, about which her attitude became quite professional. Says Wally, "It was almost like going to work, for her." Pretty Florence also began dating. One of her first beaus was Dr. O'Connor, who had treated Edythe in their home. ("Why don't you marry him?" E asked her.) Then she began seeing brash and dashing Udo Zaenglin, a stunt pilot. She had far less time for her younger brother and sister, now that she was starting the rituals of young womanhood, but she acted as big sister when she could. She once took E to the airport, where her boyfriend, Udo, gave them both a ride in his stunt plane. The girls shrieked when he did somersaults and other tricks.

Things were often very bad for the Marrenners. Florence says, "There were times when we didn't have enough to eat. I remember once, when I was about eleven, I only had bread to eat for three days." Despite Florrie's dancing lessons, the Marrenners were still very poor. The Depression hadn't hit yet, but neither had governmental safety nets. For millions of working Americans like Walter Marrenner, poverty was an accepted way of life and there were accepted ways of coping. At Christmastime, the Marrenners did Christmas shopping at the five-and-ten and made their own cards. Edythe loved it all and felt no shame about being poor. Wally: "We would wait until Christmas Eve to get a free tree from the stands, because you knew that if they didn't sell the trees they were going to reduce them to practically nothing. When it got to a certain point in the evening, they figured they might as well give them away.

"Our parents gave us what presents they could. We would always hang up stockings. We didn't have a regular fireplace. A mantelpiece would do. As we got older, we got less and less. We used to get apples, oranges, candy and nuts. One time, I got a bottle of medicine I had to take this fish oil, Scott's Emulsion, to build myself up." (Wally had been sick for a few years with some strange intestinal problem that made him unable to walk for a while).

One Christmas, though, they got a wonderful sled. Bundled up, they went to Prospect Park, where there were some hills. But then finally there were only gift-wrapped lumps of coal. In the language of poverty, the children heard: "That's the end. No more toys for you."

Edythe was a good eater. She had learned early that one ate everything on the plate, for tomorrow's meal was never certain. Since she was the youngest, her birthdays were special. She was always given the fifty cents so that she could run down to Ebinger's bakery and choose her birthday cake.

The Marrenner children, like most of the kids in the neighborhood, had to earn their own spending money by working after school. Wal had a *Brooklyn Eagle* paper route and E, a few years after the accident, used to help deliver the newspapers. "She never tried to get out of it, even if it was cold and raining or snowing hard." When it was, Wally would sometimes stop pulling the newspaper wagon and cup his hands around his mouth to warm his numb fingers. Ten-year-old E, who often seemed much older, would grow impatient and give the soapbox wagon with solid wooden wheels a push from behind, saying: "Come on, Wal, let's get going—the sooner we'll get home." Once in a while, when E had to take over Wally's *Eagle* route alone, she would have to fight with the boys on the street: ten-year-old boys did not like ten-year-old girls who delivered papers. She held her own, sometimes even by punching first. When E and Wal weren't delivering the *Eagle*, they collected junk, mostly paper, from around the shops and heavily populated apartment buildings; they sold the paper for a penny per ten pounds.

In the summertime, brother and sister would spend some of their *Eagle* earnings by taking the BMT line to Coney Island, where they would head straight for Steeplechase Amusement Park. They would always look for friendly, middle-class adults, who often gave the unused parts of their ten-rides-for-fifty-cents tickets to excited children. But Wal and E spent most of their extra change to see movies at the Brooklyn Paramount, the Fox, the Flatbush and the Kenmore, the great palaces of the poor. They were caught up in the throes of the adolescent movie-going mania that became rampant as the country headed into the Depression. For fifty cents, they would catch a double feature at the crack of dawn, then hide in the bathrooms waiting to see another complete show and then another.

The larger movie theaters offered vaudeville shows between the films of a double feature. E got her first true whiff of show business when the stage magicians began asked the "little red-headed girl" who always sat in the first row to come up and help with the tricks. Then, after seventeen-year-old Florence began entering dance competitions at the vaudeville houses of New Jersey and Brooklyn, E and Wally won an amateur dancing contest at one of them. Afterward, Wally would take her to the DeMolay dances, big affairs sponsored by the Brooklyn Masons. She looked better than just cute in her turtle neck sweater. All the boys who had wanted to punch her for delivering papers now wanted to dance with her.

Edythe Marrenner was an especially pretty ten-year-old, with a moon-round face, the whitest Nordic skin and red hair, rare in its almost primary color intensity, which immediately drew strangers' eyes. She seemed not to be aware of her prettiness, as the more outgoing Florence appeared to be; or if Edythe was aware of her looks, she reacted oddly to them. She was aloof with other children, especially boys. The Marrenners' neighbors thought of her as a little snobbish, for she would ignore the overtures of the children around her and instead bring a couple of school friends to the apartment to do homework. Among her carefully chosen regulars were the sisters Martha and Sarah Finklestein and Ira Grossel, a nice boy whose parents owned a candy store a couple of blocks away. She would remain friends with the Finklestein sisters for decades, and with little Ira her life would later intertwine in ways unthinkable to a ten-year-old.

Edythe was pretty, but in 1927 Florence was prettier. Old photos show that at seventeen she had a striking figure, a dancer's carriage and a face so marvelous it could have won prizes. In her ballet slippers, with her devastating smile, Florrie became the unchallenged star of the family. She also became her mother's favorite, but it's by no means clear how much so. Nevertheless, the favoritism began the lifelong conflict between the two sisters.

In the last years of her life, when Edythe, a great movie star with a different name, spoke of her early relationship with her sister, it would be with an anger that seemed to be changing or exaggerating events. She accused her mother of having severely favored Florence, buying clothes and makeup for her while she, Edythe, had had to make do with hand-me-downs from her sister. She said that Florence had often been mean to her, cussing her, and had never let her wear her new clothes: sibling matters that, even if true, would hardly raise eyebrows in most families. Wally has no recollection of any such behavior. What he recalls is that he and Edythe began to feel separate from Florence because she had their mother's attention and because she was too involved in fulfilling her mother's dreams of turning into a star to mingle much with them: "She was pretty much involved in her own world."

Florence says that the favoritism was slight and that she was never mean to her baby sister, whom she always loved. She says that her mother bought her new clothes, but Edythe also received things. Aunt Emma, who had been paying for Florence's dancing lessons, bought Edythe a beautiful and expensive two-piece outfit, "and if my mother cared only for me, then why would she have dragged Edythe to school on a cart for two years, and why was she worried sick about her after the accident? I worried, too."

These matters are delicate and difficult now to resolve, but one thing that emerges is that Edythe felt second-best to Florence and harbored feelings of not being loved by her mother. It was a situation of such emotionality that Edythe's entire life would be affected by it. When Florrie was about sixteen, and Edythe about nine, they visited their Aunt May at the New Jersey shore. On the beach, Florrie did a handstand, Edythe sat a few feet away and watched with a bit of a scowl and someone took a snapshot of them. Florence today looks at the photo and says, "That was the relationship." Florence was the active, outgoing one; Edythe was "always watching and never smiled." She was dour and often withdrawn. In those days, Florence never thought much about Edythe's nature or that there might be some sort of resentment. If she was pushing Edythe into the background, Florence didn't realize it. There were no big fights. "She didn't say anything about it."

The building resentment was there but could not have been obvious because, as Martin Emslie, the older boy who lived next door, recalls, "I'd always see Florence and Edythe walking together on the street. They'd go to the stores together. They just seemed like two close sisters." They shared a bedroom and talked over one another's hopes and dreams for the future.

Why Ellen favored Florence seems no great mystery. For poor but pretty girls like the Marrenner sisters, there were only two sources of hope: great talent, which would lead to the salvation of a career, or a marriage to a man with money. Most girls wound up quitting high school early to take jobs in factories or with the telephone company, and then married other laborers. Ellen thought Florence the most likely one of her children to rise from the sea of poverty. She was determined that her daughter would not marry another Walter.

Edythe developed overwhelming feelings of jealousy and of being pushed aside. As she entered adolescence, she seemed a strange combination of opposing things: there was a tremendous drive to be as special as her sister, especially in her mother's eyes, and there was that persistent withdrawal from others. Flo and Wal saw the personalities as almost two distinct and different people. To Florence, she was mainly the girl in the photograph, the quiet watcher; to Wally, "E was always putting on an act, talking, laughing, imitating."

In the years between ten and twelve, E caught a flagrant case of stage fever. If there was a play at P.S. 181, Edythe wanted to be in it. Just to be around every production, she would volunteer to help build scenery, pull the curtains, beg or borrow material for costumes. She would volunteer to play all those hags and witches that no one else wanted. By the time she was in seventh grade, the school and the neighborhood knew she was a compulsive ham who would likely audition for any play given by any club, church or society within walking distance.

Chubby Ira Grossel loved to act, too, which drew the two of them together. When they were thirteen, they appeared at school in an operetta called *Cinderella in Flowerland*, with Edythe as the lead and Ira, at the start of production, as Prince Charming but later "recast" as the show's stage manager when his voice suddenly changed. He had melancholy eyes and a pretty smile. Florence recalls seeing Edythe in the play. Edythe had to kick a boy onstage and wound up doing it repeatedly and much too hard, then came home and chattered endlessly about the great thing she had done.

Walter Marrenner didn't care one way or the other about Florence's dancing. He was frail and hardworking and tended to live for the moment, becoming absorbed in his hobbies, making radios and kites when he wasn't at his job. He knew that his wife thought of his Catholic relatives as sometimes fun but gypsylike and beneath her family. Walter and Ellen were poles apart in what they wanted from life. While she fussed with Florence, he acted as a buffer and gravitated toward his younger daughter. He encouraged her acting projects, always wanted to hear what she was doing. There was a great deal of love between father and daughter, almost as much as between Florence and Ellen. As Florence says, there emerged "slight preferences."

But between Walter and Ellen there was increasingly less love. Around 1928, Walter was still working for the IRT, but from being a lineman he had been promoted to taking charge of the office that received trouble calls. This office, at 98th Street and Third Avenue, was filled with operators who took and relayed messages. One of the operators was a woman with whom Walter had a serious affair. Ellen found out and became deeply upset. She and he now had words. She would run to the apartment of the Emslies—the Marrenners' best friends, in the next apartment on Church Avenue—and tell sympathetic Mrs. Emslie all about her bitterness toward Walter. She would strike masochistic poses, such as offering her arm to Walter during the height of an argument, saying, "Go on! Break it! Break it!" As an outlet for her frustrations, she started smoking voluminously. But eventually Ellen became depressively resigned to her husband's infidelity.

Edythe saw her father as the saint in the family and her mother as "a cold-hearted, emasculating woman." Many years later, she would tell a friend: "I could never get over the way she treated my father." Florence, who knew about the affair, felt that she could never get over the way her *father* had treated her mother.

In 1928, Ellen must have known that she had done the right thing, for Florence, at eighteen, was offered a dancing job in the Philadelphia-based *Ned Wayburn's Gambles.* Florence toured with the dance troupe for almost a year, making a decent salary. "Your daughter," said Ellen to Walter, "is making more than you." Then Florence came home and got a job in the chorus of the Broadway show *George White's Scandals,* starring Eleanor Powell, Bert Lahr and Jack Haley. As a chorus girl, she worked herself up to $200 a week. With Florence's extra income, all the Marrenners moved to a larger apartment, at 2568 Bedford Avenue, a step up from where they had been, but not a big one.

During her stint in the chorus of the *Scandals,* hardworking twenty-one-year-old Florence had her first golden opportunity to leave poverty and the tedium of the chorus line far behind as well as help her family. She began to date a successful Broadway producer-director who proposed marriage. Although Florence worried about the difference in their backgrounds, it didn't matter to him. She brought him to Bedford Avenue to meet the Marrenners, see their terrible neighborhood and their small, shabby flat and asked him: "How can you still want to marry me?" He answered: "Because I love you." Ellen liked him, even though he was ten years older than her daughter. She thought it would be a fine marriage, after eleven years of scrimping and helping Florrie with her endless toe-dancing and ballet lessons. But when Ellen discovered that the man had been divorced and had a ten-year-old son, she decided against the match, believing that Florrie could do better. She was quite beautiful, with hair as fiery as her younger sister's. Florrie, at one with her mother, turned him down. But she never did do better; her background maintained its stranglehold. "I should have married him," she now says.

Edythe, meanwhile, left her old friends at P.S. 181, except the Finklestein sisters, and began at Girls Commercial High School, where most of the neighborhood girls took up typing and shorthand. Edythe was much more studious than most. She spent hours at the Public Library reading about young people who left drabness, like Eugene Gant of Thomas Wolfe's *Look Homeward, Angel* and *Of Time and the River* (the librarian used to call her "the Wolfe girl"). Edythe was just then beginning to feel self-conscious about the one linen dress she wore to classes during the day and the paper she had to shove into her shoes to keep the holes from ruining her socks. Wally did the same and so had Florence when she was younger.

The Marrenners were still proudly seeing Edythe in plays all over the neighborhood, including a production at the Brooklyn Masonic Lodge in which, at fifteen, she appeared as a twenty-eight-year-old woman. An English teacher at Girls Commercial, Eleanor O'Grady, helped her enter school plays and told her she was going to become a great star someday. Edythe's head was filled with glory, but there were obvious problems, such as an awkward stage presence and a high-pitched voice. Hoping for a scholarship for acting lessons, she went to an acting coach who, after a few minutes of listening to her voice, demanded that she stop. He told her that beside a squeaky voice she had an accent.

"What kind of accent?" she asked.

"A Brooklyn accent."

"But this *is* Brooklyn."

Then the acerbic gentleman, who was making strides coaching a number of local girls, told Edythe that she could never become a professional actress because she wasn't meticulous about her personal appearance. "You have a hole in your shoe," he said. That was that.

Edythe's competition with Florence, for stardom, for their mother's love, always remained unspoken between the two, but at a certain point appeared fairly obvious. Florence was tired of all the drudgery of the chorus line and was thinking of getting into acting herself. She went to professional auditions and interviews, but every time sixteen-year-old Edythe heard about the audition, she would make an appointment to attend the same one herself. Once, Florence went to read for a famous radio emcee and happened to mention it to Edythe, who immediately went to see the man, a rakish fellow who suggested they do the test in his apartment, and in the evening! After Edythe foolishly agreed and entered his lair, he locked the door and began chasing her around the apartment. Edythe escaped unharmed, but became furious at her sister. "Why are you angry at me?" said Florence. "I didn't tell you to audition for him."

In 1933, Florence, discouraged with chorus lines and thinking she had too little talent to become a dancing star, left Broadway to take an easier, low-paying job. She moved out of the crowded Bedford Avenue apartment and into her own, causing more financial strain in the family. Frail, 140-pound Walter was worn out by his IRT job, which never netted him more than $30 a week. This was the nadir of the Depression, and at Girls Commercial most of the girls of Edythe's age were quitting school to help support their poor families. Edythe wished to stay on to get her diploma. When she and Ellen would get into an argument, Ellen would remind her that they had sacrificed quite enough just to keep Edythe in school long after the other girls had quit to bring in extra money. She did not understand why Edythe was so ungrateful.

Ellen discouraged her from dating local boys, fearful that as Edythe approached late adolescence the worst might happen. Edythe complied with her mother's wishes except for, as Wally recalls, her interest in Eddie Dixon, a boy who went to the Lenox Road Baptist Church, which the Marrenners also attended. "The boy was a piano player. Edythe had a little crush on him, but it didn't last. There were other boyfriends, but her mind was on her acting." The few boys she did see were put off by her cold manner and special requirements she had learned from her mother. Once she went to a DeMolay dance with a boy who showed up without a corsage for her, and she barely talked to him at the dance.

She was not well liked at school. Years later, when all sorts of excuses would be made for her character after she became a movie queen, a myth was created that she would pass by people she knew on the street because she was so nearsighted. Her eyesight wasn't the best, but even she was aware of someone she knew, she would often ignore the person. It had to do not with eyesight but with psychological isolation. She would do the same at school, and the result was that after her grade average entitled her to join the Arista club, she was not put on the list because the other girls did the rare thing of not voting her in.

Only her acting, her continual movie-going and a painting hobby kept her in contact. In 1934, she saw *The Thin Man* and *Of Human Bondage*, loved Ronald Colman and Barbara Stanwyck, who anyone who read fan magazines knew came from a poor Brooklyn family. Later, after stardom, Stanwyck had rescued her family from the tenements: Edythe loved that. In the evening, the Marrenners would listen to "One Man's Family," a Depression saga that put emphasis not on what people had but on their family relationships.

The year that she graduated from Girls Commercial, 1935, she did a highly abstract water-color of a jellyfish (created partly by an accidental water spill), which won her $75 in an art contest. That was a lot of money, and Edythe was going to use it to start her career.

Right after graduation, Edythe took a job in a Manhattan hand-kerchief factory making cloth designs. Her best friend was Sarah

Little (the Finklestein sisters had changed their last name for the job market), whom she met every Thursday evening at the President Cafeteria on Lexington Avenue to discuss career plans. Whenever she could manage, Edythe went to Broadway auditions and tried to get herself an agent. But with movies the American pastime in the thirties, thousands of girls with far more experience than she were flocking to New York to get work. She got nowhere.

Still living at home, in early 1936 she quit her handkerchief-designing job and used her small savings to enroll in the Feagin School of Dramatic Arts at Rockefeller Center. There, she did little skits and improvisations, but was still turned down for paid theater work.

While at Feagin, she began dating one of the boys in her classes. One day, she left a note on the kitchen table which said, simply, "I'm eloping." All the Marrenners became upset. Walter said, "I have to do something about this," and Ellen rushed around looking for the boy's name and telephone number, found it and gave it to Walter. He called the boy's father, a dentist, who admitted he knew all about it because his son had asked him to wire money via Western Union. After Edythe and the boy were gone all night, the two fathers went to the Western Union office, knowing that the two would appear for the money. The boy went home with his father and Edythe went back with Walter, not at all distressed over the interference.

Walter's health was turning poor. He had symptoms of heart trouble, and it was clear the family would need more money soon. Florence couldn't help. Her $200-a-week salary was gone now that she had quit dancing and was working in a bakery shop, making only enough to support herself. Wally made only a small salary working in the mailroom of the *Reader's Digest*. Edythe was beginning to feel financial pressure.

The girls at Feagin talked about the quick cash that the prettiest of the hopefuls got by modeling for print ads. Edythe was surely not the most startling of the actresses. Her mother encouraged her to dress ultra-conservatively. She wore but a trace of make-up. Her eyebrows weren't plucked, but should have been. And yet her natural bright red hair set her apart. Red hair was in great demand for the new color magazine ads, which were not subtle and required strong color contrasts. When Walter Thornton of the Walter Thornton Agency for models saw all that white skin and flame hair come into his office on a strange hip-rolling gait, he knew, as he later said, that he had a model who would never be out of work.

Margaret Lane, one of Edythe's modeling friends in 1936, reflected on what life was like for them in and around the Thornton agency: "We had to break into modeling the hard way then. Armed with a portfolio of our pictures and a scrapbook, we'd call on photographers, artists and fashion directors—and there were about five hundred of them on our list. When we waited in reception rooms together, clutching our scrapbooks and hoping, Susan was scared, but she was wise enough to concentrate on the positive—the strong belief she had in herself. She became artist Jon Whitcomb's most beguiling cover girl when he began to draw her wistful, saucy loveliness, and that was the start of her climb as a model." Edythe, whose pearly teeth went with her red hair, did toothbrush and toothpaste ads, and posed in Luralace full-body girdles, showing pretty breasts and a nice waistline. She appeared in Noxema and pedicure ads; ads for bread, cereal and soap; photos in mail-order catalogues; ads with her as the girl-in-the-background at a picnic for color interest. There were also cigarette ads, which started her smoking, like her mother. Usually, she worked only a few days a month, but at $35 a day, her income was good, and she convinced her parents to move to a more expensive six-room apartment on 21st Street in a better part of Brooklyn.

Walter Thornton later remembered her as a good model but "a real lone wolf, a girl with no time for friends or social life." He took a liking to her looks and her aloof quality, as did prominent color photographer Ivan Dmitri. When the Vitaphone movie company contacted Thornton about participating in a short subject about models in a modeling agency, Thornton picked Edythe to appear for a few minutes in front of the movie camera. It was her first motion-picture experience. Then, in 1937, the *Saturday Evening Post* planned to run a piece by Thornton about how he and his agency marketed beauty, to be photographed by Ivan Dmitri and called "The Merchant of Venus." The photographs were to show the professional life of a Thornton model: arriving for a portrait painting, being coached by Thornton, reading her modeling notes by artist John LaGotta, being posed and painted by LaGotta. Ivan Dmitri suggested Edythe; Thornton concurred. What was remarkable about the series of photographs that appeared in the November 1, 1937, issue of the *Saturday Evening Post* (in which Edythe's last name was spelled "Marrener" by her own request) was that it showed a serious girl with an interesting face and neatly conservative attire becoming progressively more alluring and photogenic. In the last three photos, she was posed in a satin nineteenth-century gown, set off dramatically by natural red hair. The piece was bound to call attention to her.

Sadly, several weeks before the momentous publication of the *Post*, article, Walter Marrenner's heart and kidneys gave out and he collapsed at work. He was rushed to a hospital on Welfare Island, missing out on all the family commotion in the Marrenners' 21st Street apartment when agents started coming there to talk to Edythe about setting up acting auditions for her. Walter, when he was told, didn't like any of it, especially one unimaginable Hollywood invitation that suddenly came along.

Gone with the Wind had been published the year before, in 1936; David O. Selznick had already begun a nationwide search for the actress to play Scarlett O'Hara in the movie. Privately, he and everyone else in Hollywood expected that he would pick an established actress. But producers were always engaging in talent hunts; it was part of the fan-magazine publicity machine that encouraged girls to spend their last dimes at the movie houses. Indeed, the talent scouts did scour the country and come up with candidates for fame: Frances Farmer had been one of the hordes of girls invited to come to Hollywood and one of the few who were not sent back after flunking a screen test as soon as they arrived.

When director George Cukor and Irene Selznick, wife of David Selznick, happened to see the "Merchant of Venus" piece while they were in New York and offered Edythe a trip to Hollywood to screen-test for Scarlett, it was not a remarkable event. There had been hundreds of possible Scarletts and thousands of screen tests of girls from Anywhere, U.S.A. Like most of those unsavvy girls and their mothers, Edythe and Ellen Marrenner did not know that the Selznick offer was mostly hullaballoo. Only desperately sick Walter saw the trap and warned his daughter not to go:

"They'll break your heart out there." Edythe, however, believed, from the moment she heard about her screen test, that she was going to be Scarlett. She bubbled with enthusiasm and said she wanted to go on the long train trip to Hollywood. George Cukor insisted that she travel with a chaperone because she was a mere twenty years old, and Ellen, who had to stay with Walter, chose Florence to accompany Edythe. She quickly wrapped things up at the Walter Thornton agency, offering Thornton in writing, with great generosity and carelessness, ten percent of her future Hollywood income—as if the role of Scarlett were one big modeling assignment he had gotten her. Late in November, she, Florrie, Irene and David Selznick, who had just arrived in New York, and George Cukor boarded the train at Grand Central Station for the week-long journey to Hollywood. Amidst the smoke, wind and whistles as the train left were tremendous hopes.

CHAPTER 2

Starlet

FLORRIE AND EDYTHE had a lovely time on the long train trip to Hollywood. Florence recalls that Irene Selznick was particularly kind to them; Mrs. Selznick was well aware that these girls had never before been on such a trip. It was all very exciting. In less than two weeks, the girls had gone from the wintery streetcorners of New York to the semi-tropic palm trees of California. By the time they arrived in Hollywood, they had already made up their minds never to go back to their old lives.

The David O. Selznick studio supplied the Marrenner girls with a decent stipend and put them up at a nearby apartment hotel. Edythe's *Gone with the Wind* test was directed by George Cukor only days after they stepped off the train. She was given a few hours of vocal coaching to standardize Scarlett O'Hara's Southern accent, then coiffed and dressed like a Southern belle and pushed in front of the cameras to read the now famous dialogue with Ashley Wilkes (played by Alan Marshal) in the library at Twelve Oaks: "Oh, my dear, I love you ... I tell you, I love you. And I know you must care for me because ... Ashley, you *do* care?" She was quite bad: nervous, squeaky and ill-prepared. At the end of the take, she let out a long sound which was half a laugh and half a sigh of relief. Of course, not a bit of this publicity stunt was serious to anyone but Edythe, who believed that she had a good chance; with her lack of experience, her strong accent, her gawkiness, she hadn't a prayer from the start.

To get more for the money they had spent to bring Edythe and Florence to Hollywood, the Selznick people used Edythe for a few more weeks to help test other actresses and one Ashley Wilkes for the movie. She was not immediately told that she had failed her own test. The studio, meanwhile, treated the girls to a good time. Various escorts picked them up at their hotel and took them all over Los Angeles. They adored going to authentic Mexican restaurants, like El Paseo Inn, all along Olvera Street in the downtown area. Somehow they ran into Frank Fay, who had once been married to Barbara Stanwyck, and he took them around too. Everyone wanted them to return to Brooklyn with only fond memories of their few weeks in Hollywood.

About four weeks after the screen test, the Selznick studio informed Edythe that she had failed the *Gone with the Wind* test and that she and her sister should return to New York. Florence remembers that her sister was crushed at the news, but neither one of them wanted to go back. Edythe wrote to Selznick that she preferred staying in Hollywood: "I like the orange trees." But when the studio cut off their weekly stipend and rent, they were evicted and left with barely enough to eat. They cashed in their return tickets to New York, borrowed an additional $100 from Aunt Emma in Brooklyn and took an apartment in a rundown Beverly Hills court on Lasky Drive where lots of actors and writers lived. The sisters wanted to be in pictures.

George Cukor hadn't forgotten about Edythe, whom he thought pretty and with possibilities. One day, he mentioned her to his good friend Benny Medford, an independent agent in the colony who specialized in developing scriptwriters and turning pretty girls into bona fide starlets. Small, energetic, thirty-five-year-old Benny was known about town for his hardworking sincerity and for the fact that all movie moguls trusted him. While visiting one of his movie writers in the Lasky Drive court, Benny ran into Edythe. He quickly took a liking to her and, despite the fact that he had seen her Selznick screen test and thought she displayed scant talent, decided to sign her on as one of his potential starlets.

But why would any agent sign a girl who had no credits and showed little acting ability? The answer is: that was the way Hollywood worked. Benny knew all the prejudices of the moguls, the ins and outs of their power trips. Back in the days of silent films, the studio heads had imported experienced Broadway actors for movies, but found them far too stiff and theatrical, virtually untrainable for film work. The moguls wound up discovering young men and women wherever they could find them and believed that stardom was little more than an advertising feat, enhanced by makeup people, acting coaches and publicity departments. At the highest echelons of the Hollywood infrastructure, true talent was mistrusted. Aspiring actors became mere commodities that were judged by their faces and bodies, but, most importantly, their attitudes. Attitude was the key to success with the moguls.

The system was still in effect when Edythe came to Hollywood. Benny Medford thought she had the steel to cope with the system. Screen tests were secondary. Willingness was primary. "I was always a good judge of human nature. I had studied psychology in my first year at Harvard, and I knew that this girl could emerge if handled right. She had determination. I liked her spirit." He was also deeply impressed that Cukor liked her and that Selznick had gone so far as to test her for Scarlett O'Hara.

So Benny began spending much of his personal and professional time with Edythe, taking her out in the evenings to introduce her to Hollywood life, sometimes with Florence along. He would come to the Lasky Drive apartment every day to shore up Edythe's already singleminded drive to succeed, tell her which studio he was now showing her *Gone with the Wind* screen test to and to keep her spirits up. He introduced her to a group of Russian actors he knew, including Akim Tamiroff, had her read Stanislavsky's *My Life in Art*, told her she would eventually have to learn how to lower her squeaky voice and rid herself of that "Shanty Irish" Brooklyn sound. He arranged credit for her to buy her first car, through a good friend, car dealer Al Herd, and took her to dress shops. "She had no idea how to dress. I would buy her just the right green dress to go with her hair."

Word quickly got around Hollywood about Benny Medford's new protégée and the gossip itself was enough to gain him more opportunities to show Edythe's screen test at the studios, although most of the executives he showed it to hated that awkward piece of film. They didn't take much better to Edythe in person, who, even with her new green dress, couldn't hide her ingenuousness and what Benny calls her bad gait, caused by the failure of her hip to knit properly years before. But Benny kept at it doggedly, mentioning Edythe's name at all the parties he went to. He wasn't married ("I spent most of my time either arranging other people's marriages or breaking them up") and one wonders if his incessant efforts on behalf of Edythe were strictly for professional reasons.

"She was lonely and she wanted love," says Benny. "I tried to give her as much as I could, but I was never interested in her sexually. I never did that with any of my clients." The lack of love in her life, Benny felt, had made Edythe into a strange and difficult girl. He found her to be suspicious, withdrawn and fearful of contact with others. Although he never gave up, she was always hard to introduce to people. "She was a cold person. She never said thank you. When you said good night to her and she said good night, that was as final as the day is long. I arranged a date between her and a movie-studio lawyer to get her some class. That fizzled. I took her out one night with George Montgomery, whom I had started, and we went to Ciro's. I wanted to get some publicity for them. She became difficult and acted bored and I became unhappy."

Edythe and Florence loved Benny, who became beneficent and paternal to them, which they especially needed in the face of their father's increasing poor health back in Brooklyn. Benny involved them in some rather amazing experiences. At the time, he handled a number of Howard Hughes' "personal" starlets and thought it would be good if Hughes met Edythe. With multi-millionaire Hughes, who was self-involved and eccentric even in those days, there had to be a touch of harmless romance even before talk of a movie contract. Benny told Edythe about his fortune and she became excited: Depression girls like Edythe revered marriage to a wealthy man as much as or more than a fabulous career. But Edythe neglected to tell her sister any more about Hughes than his name.

One evening, Florence heard a knock at the door of the Lasky Drive apartment. "I went to the door and this man was just standing there," says Florence. "He was tall and he had on a long coat and he looked like one of those down-and-outs on Main Street. He didn't say anything, so I said, 'We don't want to buy anything,' and I shut the door. I just got back to the couch when I heard a loud knock. I went back to the door and he said, 'I'm ... Howard ...Hughes!' I didn't know who he was. I said, 'Oh, Edythe's expecting you.' So we waited for her for half an hour while he talked about Christian Science and she finally came back. She cooked a chicken dinner for him."

Edythe complained to both Florence and Benny that she didn't like Howard Hughes at all, even though she was anxious to have more dates with him and was already reconciling herself to marrying this horrible man. But, as with her screen test for *Gone with the Wind*, she couldn't see that she was a mere dot in a painting that didn't need her. Hughes would sign five or six girls at a time after dating a number of girls as *pro forma* "auditions." He had no more interest in marrying unexciting Edythe than a parrot. He didn't sign her, either. Benny soothed Edythe by saying, "He's not for you."

Florence says that at that time she and Edythe were getting along, although Benny remembers an "unfriendliness" between them which he thought was caused because Florence may have been a little bossy. He didn't really know much about their Brooklyn days. Florence admits that she may have been acting like mama, for Edythe's own good. On some nights, Edythe would come home late from a date and Florence would worry. Once, she heard her sister dallying with a boy on the street below and she threw down the keys from the apartment window. When Edythe came up, she was furious at her sister's interference.

The girls often argued about money and other matters. Once their old next-door neighbor Martin Emslie visited them in Hollywood at their mother's request, and found them bickering: Edythe would tell Florence that she didn't need her there, Florence would counter that she could be back on Broadway earning good money. Martin Emslie remembers: "I became concerned. Florence was behaving herself, but Edythe was drinking and staying out late every night. I had to talk to her about it." This, by the way, is the first one hears about Edythe drinking.

The girls would settle down for periods. Florence had become as good a cook as her mother and urged Edythe to stay home evenings. Edythe, who was dating men like Jon Whitcomb (the *Saturday Evening Post* artist) these days in Hollywood, would now often reply to a request for a dinner date, "I can't. My sister is cooking tonight."

With all the talk of screen tests and movie contracts, Florence, who had never really gotten show business out of her blood, was half hoping that Benny could get her work in the movies, too. Benny liked her red hair and her lovely skin coloring, but thought she was heavy and didn't have the attractiveness of Edythe. Florence had, after quitting dancing four years before, physically changed and gained some weight. Nevertheless, Benny, who knew

Florence had danced on Broadway, would have been willing to help her had he not sensed that Edythe would have resented it.

After a month and a half of living in Beverly Hills, the sisters moved to Hollywood proper, to another unfurnished apartment on Irving Boulevard, only a block from the Paramount studio on Melrose, making auditions easier. On March 16, 1938, the news came that their father, Walter, had died of heart and kidney failure in the Welfare Island hospital. The girls felt shock, doubly so for there was no way that they could scrape up the money to attend the funeral in Brooklyn.

Walter had only been fifty-six. The strain of trying to support his family on a pittance and perhaps the unhappiness of his married life had worked against his frailty and contributed to his early death. Edythe put all the blame on her mother, while Florence thought just the opposite: that her father, in being unfaithful to her mother, had been unkind to her. At the simple funeral in Brooklyn, Ellen Marrenner, who was there with Wally and other relatives, was stunned when suddenly the woman with whom Walter had been having a ten-year affair showed up. No one knew her name; no one wanted to know.

The girls immediately asked their mother and brother to close up the apartment and join them in California. Ellen loved the bus trip to Hollywood: she had finally gotten out of Flatbush. In Hollywood, she and Wally moved into the Irving Boulevard apartment with the girls, making things a bit cramped. The girls showed them around and eventually Ellen began taking little trips, one with Walter's sister, May Borden, to Las Vegas. May had come to Hollywood and in time many of the Marrenners and Pearsons would wind up there.

Money was very tight. The funeral had used up most of Ellen's money, and the little money Wally had saved from his job in the shipping department of the *Reader's Digest* was used to pay the rent on the family apartment. Neither Florence nor Edythe was working yet. Finally, Benny, who had never stopped singing Edythe's praises at the studios, had lunch with the Warner Brothers casting director, Max Arnow, and talked him into seeing the *Gone with the Wind* test. Arnow thought he saw something in Edythe, but it was really Benny's faith in the girl that made him offer a seven-year contract.

Edythe got the usual starlet starting salary of $150 a week, with a small raise every six months. But she wasn't a bona fide starlet yet. Hundreds of girls all over Hollywood got such salaries to enable the movie factories to see which of them was marketable. They were posed in bathing suits, used as extras, sent to elocution lessons, put in acting classes, allowed to compete with one another, but seldom used in films: all to separate out the strong attitudes from the weak ones.

Edythe followed the same pattern at Warners and, with the support of her family and Benny Medford, coped beautifully with what amounted to a less than civilized environment. Florence remembers her twenty-year-old sister saying to her more than once, "Nobody is going to stand in my way. I'm going to make it, no matter what." She was *too* determined; Florence thought she *had* to make it. Benny notes that she had wanted the role of Scarlett O'Hara badly, and when she lost that part she also lost all of her illusions, even acquired a bit of cynicism. Now, she was willing to do whatever was necessary. When Max Arnow, in her first month at Warners, changed her name from Edythe Marrenner to Susan Hayward (he liked agent Leland Hayward's last name), she was neither pleased nor irritated. She accepted it.

The Warners makeup and wardrobe departments started changing her. She was given numerous makeup tests. Her eyebrows were shaved and did not immediately grow back. She was instructed on how to dress, the correct shoes to wear. Edythe was delighted at her new glamorous appearance, as Florence recalls, but only insofar as the changes were going to bring her from point A to point B. There was also the matter of her high voice and Brooklyn accent.

Benny knew that was the hardest alteration of all to make but the most necessary. In those days, starlets had to learn to speak in a slow, deep, diaphragm-created sound. Whenever he saw her, which was almost daily, he would say to Susan: "Lower your voice." He would pick her up in his car, she would hop in and utter a greeting and Benny would snap back: "You've got to lower your voice." Her first attempts at bringing her timbre down were awkward and would even have seemed funny if one weren't aware of how hard she was trying.

To teach her the proper technique, Benny finally got George

Cukor to convince his friend Gertrude Fogler, the famous elocution coach at MGM, to take Susan on. Through the years, she taught many actors how to modify their voices for films, including Marlon Brando. Susan worked with Fogler for many months, doing scenes and readings, many of them from Shakespeare. Sounds had to come from the diaphragm, not the throat, so that the speaker could, at will, produce a startling dramatic whisper effect. Barbara Stanwyck was a master of this technique. In time, it would eliminate Edythe's persona. The key was that forevermore, on screen and off, Susan would have to speak in this new way.

The process of overhaul of Edythe Marrenner—who was, after all, just a tiny cog in the giant Hollywood wheel—was complete and staggering. After her name was changed to Susan Hayward, the family tried to continue calling her Edythe or Edie, but, as Wally explains, "It became confusing. There would be a call from the studio asking for Susan, and we'd have to think, 'Oh, they mean Edythe.' So we all started calling her Susan, too. It was just easier." And it wasn't only Edythe's name that had gotten lost. Florence understood why Susan was so desperate to lower her voice, but at times thought what was happening to her sister was strange. Susan would say, "I'm going to buy a bottle of milk," and it would now come out like a low-moaning line of dramatic dialogue. Once, Florence laughed at her and said, "Susan, stop acting." "It was just as if all the training was making her high and mighty. Whatever was happening to her was putting a distance between her and her family."

Benny was hoping that Max Arnow would take her out of the pre-starlet pattern at Warners and graduate her to movies. Arnow arranged for her to take acting lessons with a brilliant coach named Frank Beckwith, and had Beckwith report her progress. At first, Susan didn't do well with Beckwith, who put her to work on difficult material. Her greatest problem was her inability to feel real emotion in the scenes she studied. "Frank Beckwith had to beat the shit out of her," says Benny; Beckwith so lambasted her over her emotional inadequacy that she would break into tears. That was the only way he could get her to cry, for at the height of her practice scenes her tear ducts wouldn't work. Beckwith also used a great many four-letter words on Susan, who was deeply offended and would come home at night to complain bitterly to

Florence, Wally and their mother. But, without missing a beat, she also told them all how much good he was doing her.

Even before Gertrude Fogler and Frank Beckwith began working on the new Susan Hayward, Warners used her, as it did all beginners, in cheesecake publicity stills and as an extra. For the photographs, which were intended as promotion for the studio, she was dressed in two-piece bathing suits and posed with props, such as a rocket, and identified with names like Miss Fourth of July. She appeared as an extra in *The Sisters*, a lavish Bette Davis/Errol Flynn/Anita Louise 1938 vehicle about the marital problems of three sisters. (Probably, this was her first appearance for Warner Brothers, although she may have been an extra in other movies—extras weren't credited.) She played a telephone operator in one scene, showing only her back to the camera. She was trusted with a line of dialogue in her next Warners film, the Busby Berkeley drama *Comet over Broadway*. Then, in a Warners "B" film, *Girls on Probation*, she received tenth billing under Jane Bryan and Ronald Reagan as Gloria Adams, a young socialite who causes another girl to get in trouble. Susan's elocution lessons had not yet taken effect and the role was ruined by her accent. "It took a long time for Susan to get rid of it," says Florence. "I still have it."

Executives at Warners were unimpressed with Susan, who had no presence. Max Arnow was upset when Frank Beckwith told him about her poor progress in acting class: "She has no heart." She could learn dialogue, but she had no range, flexibility or warmth. Warners disposed of her quickly by putting her in a short called *Campus Cinderella*, relegating her to cheesecake photos and dropping her contract when the first six-month option period had lapsed at the end of 1938.

Benny refused to give up on her. He told the Marrenners that Susan still had a career and that he could get her another studio contract right away, but not for much more than she had been getting at Warners. He wanted Susan to hold out for $300 or $400 a week. "When you start low, you stay low," he said. Ellen Marrenner liked and trusted Benny. In her approach to him, she was never a stage-mother type; she asked questions about her daughter's career, but was always respectful. She agreed that Susan should wait, although the Marrenners knew that with only Wally working and earning very little, times would become as tough as they had been in Flatbush. No matter what, Susan's acting and elocution lessons, which were costly, had to continue. "We went without a lot of meals," says Wally of those months.

Susan was willing to find work as a model, but her mother wanted her to concentrate on acting. One wonders why Florence, who would have loved to get work at the studios, didn't find an agent and go to auditions on her own behalf. Instead, she settled for a job as a salesgirl. The answer one gleans from Florence is that her complicated relationship to her mother and sister prevented it. Her mother was now making a great fuss over Susan, and Florence was in the position that Edythe had been in as a child. Florence was now "the watching girl" in that key photograph: the tables had turned. The family energy that Florence needed to get back into the show-business world had been transferred. Was she then jealous of the family's new focus on Susan? She says no. There were no arguments, although there was clearly competition for their mother's love. Nevertheless, Florence did want Susan to succeed, but also wanted to feel better about herself.

When things were bleakest, Benny Medford came to the rescue. He helped the family with money and brought a turkey for Thanksgiving. Ellen was so grateful. When he wasn't bringing things to Susan and her family, he brought his wonderful sense of humor. Florence remembers: "He was over to the house almost every night for dinner. When things got rough, my mother said to him, 'We may not be eating anymore.' Benny joked, 'So just cook the dog.' We had a little Scotch terrier that Susan had brought home."

Early in 1939, Benny arranged a screen test for Susan at Paramount. Susan chose to do a recitation from *Alter Ego* by Arch Oboler. This was a radio piece about a girl with a Jekyll-and-Hyde problem, made into a feature film called *Bewitched* a few years later, with Phyllis Thaxter in the lead. The fifteen-minute test was done in color because of Susan's red hair, which had grown, if anything, more startling. (The test was later lost because it was done on self-destructing nitrate film.) It was directed by Henry Hathaway, who later got to know Susan well. "She was marvelous, just sensational," says Hathaway, who detected none of the awkwardness that she had shown during her Warner Brothers period, nor any accent, nor any problem with the timbre of her voice. The lessons with Fogler and Beckwith had finally taken.

When Artie Jacobson, head talent scout at Paramount, saw the test, he signed Susan for the usual seven years, without quibbling about salary. Benny got the $350 a week he was asking for her and knew that at last Susan was on her way.

During Susan's first months at Paramount Pictures, there was every indication that she would quickly rise out of the category of starlet. Director William Wellman was one of the decision makers at the studio; he immediately cast her as the sole young female in his expensive remake of the 1926 silent *Beau Geste*. This was to be Susan's first "A" picture: that is, the more prestigious lead movie on a double bill. She was to play Isobel Rivers, a wholesome girl in love with two of the three Foreign Legion brothers, played by Gary Cooper, Ray Milland and Paramount newcomer Robert Preston. It was a small role with no more than a few minutes of screen time, but Susan took it seriously, practicing her newly acquired vocal technique, reviewing the voices of such players as Ronald Colman and Barbara Stanwyck. When Susan's scenes were filmed, William Wellman, who was not much interested in those parts of the movie, was taken aback by Susan Hayward's intensity. Privately, he was only concerned with his difficulty in filming what Benny Medford called her "bulbous nose."

In August of 1939, when the film was released to good reviews, movie-goers saw a beautiful young girl who spoke in a mellifluous way. It was pure Gertrude Fogler, mixed with Colman and Stanwyck. Instead of the high voice, Susan modulated high and low, emphasizing dramatic diaphragmatic sounds. The Brooklyn accent was gone forever.

On the lot, Susan was initiated into Paramount's so-called Golden Circle, a club made up of the studio's most promising young players. It was really just another excuse for publicity, except that the angle this time was talent, not beauty. What is surprising is how many of those unknowns later became stars. The roster included Ellen Drew, Betty Field, William Holden, Evelyn Keyes, Patricia Morison and Robert Preston. The actresses each got a little gold circle pin engraved with her initials, and all the youngsters spent most of their time smiling for photographers either on the Hollywood lot or in the many cities to which they were sent to promote other people's pictures.

Patricia Morison, who was later featured in many films and

achieved stardom on Broadway in *Kiss Me, Kate*, has only fond memories of Susan at the time. She and Susan were paired off to do publicity, perhaps because they got along well, and Patricia often invited Susan to visit her home in Santa Monica to have dinner with her and her parents. Susan never invited Patricia to meet her own family, but Patricia didn't mind. She says, "The two of us had so much fun together. I can remember when we had to go on a junket to Salt Lake City for a film called *Parson of Panamint.* One day the motorcycle police were escorting our cars and I said, 'Oh, I've never been on a motorcycle,' and so they sat the two of us on the motorcycle bars and drove us out to the desert. We had a very good time together." However, Patricia did not think of Susan as happy. "She was moody." When Susan got in front of the cameras, Patricia could see the ambition come through.

John Engstead, one of Hollywood's greatest photographers, was around Susan while she was in the Golden Circle. "We did a lot of location publicity shots, which she didn't like: bathing suits and things like that." She was so small, he recalls, that he had to pin her bathing suit in the back to make it fit better. One incident with Susan stays in mind. All of the members of the Golden Circle were required to got to Hollywood parties, to be seen and meet the right people. At one party, the actors were having a good time, dancing, chatting, joking. Susan just sat by herself and watched, "a real wallflower." John asked her why she wasn't joining in and Susan replied that she didn't care, it didn't matter. "One day, I'll be bigger than all of them," she said, "and then it will be my turn."

She was still "the watching girl" in that photograph with Florence, always the onlooker, even when she seemed to be participating. Early on in her career at Paramount, Benny Medford sensed that this strange part of Susan, her standoffishness, her inability to warm up to others, would cause her serious career problems. He warned her to join in, do what the others did, be nicer. He wasn't so much interested in making her a stereotype as keeping her from hurting herself.

In 1939, Paramount put her in two unimportant "B" films: *Our Leading Citizen*, with comic Bob Burns in the lead, and *$1,000 a Touchdown*, a silliness with Martha Raye and Joe E. Brown pulling tricks on each other. Then she went on endless publicity gigs with other members of the Golden Circle, who seemed to be doing better at the studio than she was. She complained bitterly to Benny and her family about what the studio was doing to her career after *Beau Geste*.

It *was* odd, for Susan was an obvious standout among the females of her group. In her first year at Paramount, she was even more beautiful than she had been during her six months at Warners. Her face was lovely, but the focus of her looks was certainly her hair: it wasn't normal red hair; it had a depth of color, a luster and body that the inadequate color film of the time couldn't capture. She kept it full and shoulder-length. People were distracted by it. When she came to the makeup room in the morning, she would dip her head low and begin to brush it and brush it from behind the neck and up. The long ritual was chilling and mesmerizing to other actors.

Just as she had been as a child, Susan was ambivalent about the great power her hair had over others. She wanted and she didn't want it to attract attention, although she babied it as though it were the heart of a mysterious inner sanctum. Of all the famous redheads in Hollywood history, her mane was probably the most unforgettable.

Unquestionably, Susan's breathtaking looks rather than her manner were responsible for the sudden interest taken in her by powerful columnist Louella Parsons. When, late in 1939, Parsons began putting together a vaudeville touring act which would include young players from all the major studios, she ran into Susan, was taken with her and asked if she wouldn't participate. Susan jumped at the chance.

The show began its tour on November 13, 1939, in Santa Barbara, went on to the Golden Gate Theatre in San Francisco, then hit Philadelphia, Pittsburgh, Baltimore, New York, Washington, D.C., and Chicago. Called "Louella and Her Flying Stars," the act included Jane Wyman and Ronald Reagan from Warner Brothers, Joy Hodges from RKO, June Preisser from MGM and Arleen Whelan from Zanuck. The show played in movie houses between film showings, and was probably inspired by the 1937 Warner Brothers film *Hollywood Hotel*, in which Louella had played herself surrounded by aspiring Hollywood hopefuls. Susan and the others were supposed to come onstage and fall over themselves trying to cotton to Louella in order to get a mention in her column.

Offstage and on, Susan almost literally did just that. Before the tour, Benny had advised her to be friendly to Louella: "She can help you." During the tour, everything Susan did was for Louella. She was supposed to do a little skit with Ronald Reagan in which he would say something untoward to her and she would hit him on the head, enough times so that the audience would gag with hysterics. Susan would hit Ron Reagan so hard that Jane Wyman, who was then engaged to him, became incensed and complained to Louella. But Susan was really doing it for Louella's amusement, and Louella loved it.

Susan had asked Florence to join her for the New York segment of the tour; Florence had by now accompanied her on several promotional trips. She remembers seeing Susan hit Reagan and confirms that it was very hard. Florence was reminded of the time when Susan was thirteen and played the princess, kicking a boy onstage much harder than she had to and loving every moment of it.

In the New York Louella show, Susan also did a bit of extemporizing to impress the columnist. She would come out onstage and shout: "Anybody here from Brooklyn?" It was a very dull thing to do, but the audience broke into applause and Louella thought it precious. She immediately began making references in her columns to "that little redhead." In terms of the act, onstage and off, Susan had won the competition.

The tour was over around Christmastime, and Susan and Florence stayed on in New York for a week or so before returning to Hollywood. While in New York, Susan saw Walter Thornton, who reminded her that he had her signature on an agreement that gave him ten percent of her movie-making income in return for the help he had given her. She hadn't paid him a cent yet. She was furious at the suggestion. He made plans to sue for $100,000 and presumably, as later reported, just dropped the suit because he didn't want the headache. "Oh, no," says Florence. "There was a settlement. He was paid $10,000—by her studio, I think."

Something had been bothering Susan. She had been finding the Irving Boulevard apartment much too cramped for her and three others to live in. When all four of them were together again, she said: "I'd like to live alone with Mother." That disturbed Florence. It was the first of many maneuvers on Susan's part to exercise control over the family, and especially to put distance between her mother and her mother's onetime favorite, Florence. At the time, Florence didn't understand it: "She was only paying the rent. Wally and I paid for our own food. We were both working." Wally and Florence dutifully moved out. From here on, Susan became relentless in her attempt to reverse all the old patterns.

Susan, impatient to do something besides "B" pictures, was still posing and smiling with the Golden Circle youngsters. In one of those evenings on the town that she hated, she was spotted by reporter Harry Evans sitting at Mocambo with two young men. He went over to her and asked if he could do an article on her. He said he had admired her last picture. "Oh, yes," she said angrily, "my latest non-starring film. If you decide to do this article, I have some special photographs to illustrate it snapped from the neck down. You can reach me through any unimportant press agent at Paramount. And thanks for the compliment. I didn't know I looked so young and naïve." The quote ran in a Hollywood paper for every studio executive to read. A few months later, Paramount gave its usual luncheon for the exhibitors from around the country at the Ambassador Hotel, at which their major stars, like Paulette Goddard, Claudette Colbert, Marlene Dietrich, and the minor ones, like the Golden Circle youngsters, were to stand up and say a welcoming line or two. Studio head Y. Frank Freeman had flown in from New York for the event. Susan then made the most dreadful mistake of her early career. When it came her turn to speak, she got up and said: "Several of you have asked why I'm not in more Paramount pictures and that's an interesting question." She turned directly to Y. Frank Freeman and said, "Well, Mr. Freeman, do I get a break or don't I?"

Patricia Morison was there and thought it was plucky of Susan: "She was just beginning." But it was much worse than plucky. Freeman was deeply offended, and before long a general complaint got back to Benny Medford about his client's behavior. Benny told Susan to stop making waves. She was under a seven-year contract and these men, who were now beginning to find her unpleasant, could ruin her. But it was already late for warnings. Benny discovered that the studio heads had been planning to put her in an "A" picture, but now had decided to send her back to the glue factory of publicity photos and promotional tours.

* * *

Around this time, Benny Medford's association with Susan Hayward began turning into a Hollywood legend, for he did something extraordinary. With "A" pictures denied Susan at Paramount, he went to his good friend Gregory Ratoff, who was scheduled to direct the important *Adam Had Four Sons* for Harry Cohn at Columbia Pictures. Benny asked if Susan could test for the part of the bitch in the story, Hester Stoddard. "I knew she would be good in the part because I saw the bitch in her and it was an actor-proof part." Ratoff resisted. Harry Cohn wanted Ratoff to cast the future Mrs. Cohn, Joan Perry, in the part. Benny begged. He had Susan call Ratoff's wife, the Russian stage actress Eugenie Leontovich, and beg for her help. Ratoff caved in and tested Susan. The test turned out wonderful. Finally, Cohn offered a loan-out deal to Y. Frank Freeman for Susan's services. Freeman naturally agreed; the fee Paramount would receive would pay Susan's salary for a full year.

Filming of *Adam Had Four Sons* began late in 1940. The movie starred Ingrid Bergman as a shy French governess and Warner Baxter as a widower whose four growing sons Bergman must look after. Twenty-four-year-old Susan was to be third-billed as Hester, the young lady who weds one of the sons but makes a play for another of the brothers (Richard Denning) and causes all sorts of trouble. The prominence of her role and the atmosphere of excellence in this essentially drawing-room drama was all new to Susan, who relied completely on Ratoff. Since the script called for Susan's and Bergman's characters to play moral opposites, Ratoff directed Susan to be flamboyantly bitchy, make all the ladies in the movie houses hate her. He shot her scenes repeatedly, twisting her body for the camera in unusual ways, giving her odd photographic angles, having her suggest blatant genitalism with her hips.

Ratoff was quite a demanding, colorful director ("You are the steenkingest actress!" he would say to Susan with his heavy accent when he didn't like a shot) and was probably the first director ever to make her aware that odd choreographic movements could virtually create a role. But that was also a problem for Ratoff. He had gotten so carried away in his choreographic instructions that in the rushes Ingrid Bergman's dialogue delivery and stiff manner seemed dull in comparison. He called Benny and told him that Harry Cohn wanted Susan's scenes cut out to make Bergman look better. Benny didn't dare tell Susan. Ingrid Bergman, however, didn't seem to mind Susan's upstaging her and even worked to improve her on-screen rival's close-ups.

Susan's unusual performance, fortunately, was kept intact, and when *Adam Had Four Sons* was released in March of 1941 she had shed her starletdom. She had made an important transition; but it wasn't something she sensed instinctively. Benny says, "I had wanted to get that part for her so bad because I knew what it would do for her. I took her to a preview and she said to me, 'You ruined my career,' because the part was so different and she didn't like seeing herself as a bitch. I said, 'Let me tell you something. This is the steppingstone of your career. You're going to be nominated for the Academy Award—not because you were a great actress in it... because the part took care of you."

While the film was playing at the Radio City Music Hall in New York, which then, as always, was considered an award in itself, Susan was sent to New York to do promotion for the film. As she usually did when the studios sent her to New York, she asked Florence to accompany her. While the two sisters stayed at the Waldorf-Astoria hotel, something tragic happened between them, something that had been building for years. Susan had been off doing her publicity chores and had come back to the hotel room with her movie friends. She found, to her surprise, Florence, dressed in one of Susan's frocks, entertaining members of their family from their father's side, including Uncle Jack Marrenner and his girlfriend. They were the poorer, gypsy side of the family. Susan became upset and rudely demanded to know what they were doing in the hotel room. She later yelled at Florence: "How can you do this to me? How can I entertain my friends when you have company? This is supposed to be a business trip for me." The scene deteriorated into a lot of shouting, all of the old resentments finally emerging in harsh words. Florence told Susan that she shouldn't be so high and mighty and "What makes you think your friends are more wonderful than your relatives?" In the end, Susan said that she was going to fly back to Hollywood alone.

Florence was greatly injured. Her younger sister had never spoken to her like that before and she wondered where it came from: "Maybe someone connected with her said, 'Forget your family.'" Upset, Florence did not fly back to Hollywood, even though Susan had not directly asked her not to return, and instead went back to Flatbush, where she resumed her relationship with her old beau, Udo Zaenglin. She didn't feel wanted by her sister, and possibly not even by her mother, because her mother was so concerned about her relationship with Susan, the rising star and breadwinner. Florence decided to marry Udo.

Back in Hollywood, all sorts of things were happening for Susan. She was suddenly hot: everyone knew she had made a boring film moderately tolerable. Producers and studios called Benny. David O. Selznick was suddenly interested in her again. MGM wanted to know about the release date of her contract with Paramount. Independent producer Walter Wanger was eager to star her in one "A" picture after another. Meanwhile, word came from Paramount that Susan was to be loaned to Republic Pictures to play the bitch in the worst sort of "B" picture, *Sis Hopkins*, with Judy Canova and Bob Crosby. Republic was a factory that made filler films. Almost immediately afterward, in mid-1941, Paramount put Susan in another "B", a thriller called *Among the Living*, starring Albert Dekker and Frances Farmer. Farmer had been through the same sort of nightmare at Paramount that was beginning to happen to Susan. She made only one more film before her long stay at an asylum for the insane.

Benny was wringing his hands. He knew that the studio heads were trying to destroy his client by this punishment before her career had even begun. But why? That was the horror of the seven-year-contract system, which put all of the power in the hands of the studio dictators, who, more than they loved money, wanted obedience and control, especially of the minds and hearts of the girl players.

Sometimes, as with Columbia's Harry Cohn, they expressed their love of control sexually, by giving better billing to girls who offered favors. Those girls certainly deserved something for their troubles: the moguls were usually unpleasant, unattractive men. One of the Paramount players of the time, with far less talent than Susan, went much further at the studio, some say by horizontal means. When Walter Wanger first called Benny about Susan, he asked, "Can I fuck her?" In other words: "Could that be part of the deal?" It was like an innocent question about boiler plate. Wanger was certainly the least objectionable of the Hollywood executives, whom Benny knew backward and forward, and

Benny replied, without the least hint of shock or surprise, "No. I think she's a virgin." Then they went on about the possible movie deal Wanger could make for Susan if Paramount were ever to drop her.

But with many other players it was a matter of mind-and-spirit, not sexual, control. What the bosses had against Susan was that they felt she was turning into a super-temperamental bitch, and Benny had to admit that in many ways they were right about her. He would hear reports that "every hairdresser at Paramount hated her because she told them she didn't like the way they did her hair. There was a certain makeup man. She told him she didn't like the way he did her lips. A couple of cameramen didn't like her. I told her to be good to them 'because they can make you look horrible.' She was a very defiant girl and at the end of each scene she would leave the set as if it was the end of the day and it was final. She had no kind words for anyone."

A few of Susan's early directors didn't like her, either. They took their cues from the moguls and ran their sets like mini-harems, making the same overt propositions to Susan as they did to other pretty, young starlets. She always declined ungraciously, and began to get a reputation quite early in her career—an aide to one of the moguls put it this way—as a "goody-goody," the girl who wouldn't. Her inherent suspiciousness always made those awkward situations worse.

Young actresses on the climb were supposed to be fun to be around and make everybody feel good. They were not supposed to be cold-hearted money-makers like the executives. Because beneath this new façade she was still the "watching girl," a deeply withdrawn soul, it was hard for Susan to be jovial, but Benny told her she *had* to learn. So she started going over to cameramen and telling them how great the rushes looked and thanking them for certain angles she liked. Jack Marta, who photographed her in *Sis Hopkins*, recalls that the other actors "would fall all over you to get you to give them more camera shots" but Susan was more "introverted" than the others and sincere in her compliments— although she *was* complimenting now, which was certainly not easy for her. Benny tried to augment her efforts by going to her various cameramen and slipping them some money so they would be extra careful in photographing her difficult nose.

After Susan began losing important Paramount "A" roles like

the one in *Hold Back the Dawn* which went to Paulette Goddard, she asked Benny to try to break her seven-year contract with the studio. The way the system worked, the studio had the right to let a seven-year-contract lapse at the end of any six-month option period, but an actor didn't have the same privilege. Benny went to executives Henry Ginsberg and Buddy De Sylva to ask for her release, but got nowhere. He met Buddy De Sylva socially and said, "Will you do me a favor and help me get her out of the contract?" What he heard was: "I will say this, Benny. You're a sweet guy and I like you. Don't waste your time with this girl." Benny: "They were going to keep her on contract in spite of the fact that they weren't going to do anything with her. They didn't like Susan for making a fool of them when Y. Frank Freeman came out from New York." Oddly, Paramount kept giving Susan a salary increase after every option renewal, almost as a way of telling her that the punishment would be over when she grew nicer.

Little by little, Susan began to understand the jungle she was in. Other players at the studio found her cold and a little frightening, for her lack of humor and her singleminded determination suggested a threatening super-competence. Some actresses at Paramount had not failed to notice what she had done to Bergman in *Adam Had Four Sons*. Benny is sure that some of the starlets who got on better with the studio heads did their part in keeping Susan from becoming a star during these years.

Susan would never forget an incident that happened after Paramount sent her to Kentucky to judge a horserace. She was loaned a creamy beige molded-to-the-figure gown originally made for Carole Lombard. When she returned to Hollywood, a studio wardrobe woman was waiting at the station to take the gown back. She thought: So that's what they think of me.

But, despite the studio, Susan landed in a fabulous Paramount "A" film when producer Cecil B. De Mille, who worked quasi-independently at Paramount, spotted her and thought her red hair perfect for the part of the ill-fated ingenue, Drusilla, in his two-million-dollar production of *Reap the Wild Wind*. Jesse Lasky, Jr., one of its writers, helped evaluate Susan's screen test for the part, and remembers telling De Mille: "She's quite promising." Says Lasky, "Saying someone was marvelous to De Mille could have been the kiss of death for the actor. He used to say, 'Writers don't cast pictures, my boy.' But in this case he looked at the test and was very moved, very impressed."

The film was her most elaborate to date, and gave her sixth billing under John Wayne, Ray Milland, Paulette Goddard, Raymond Massey and Robert Preston in what would become a wildly successful tale of nineteenth-century schooner-salvagers in Georgia. As the pretty girl whose death inspires a major turn in the plot, Susan had to be fresh, demure and warmly enthusiastic. For the first time, the public would see her flaming hair in a Technicolor movie, not just in magazine stills. She was quite lovely and effective in the film, which is today known to many television viewers, and it gave her career a great boost.

After the De Mille epic, Paramount returned her to second fiddles and leads in fillers, none of which did her much harm or good. She was billed third, under Fred MacMurray and Paulette Goddard, in *The Forest Rangers*, made early in 1942. *The Forest Rangers*, a movie about logrollers, had Susan play a volatile back-woods girl who, after the obligatory big special-effects forest fire, loses her man, MacMurray, to rich debutante Goddard. Susan was then cast as the super-bitch in René Clair's delicious fantasy *I Married a Witch*—about a witch, Veronica Lake, who falls in love with a gubernatorial candidate, Fredric March, just before he is to marry Susan, an obnoxious society shrew. (Years later, the movie would inspire a popular television series.) Susan displayed impeccable comic timing in her nastiness and looked positively delectable; she had to be noticed by everyone in the industry, though not for her romantic possibilities. One of the rules in those years was that once an actress was successfully cast as a supporting bitch-type, that was where she forever stayed.

The same year, 1942, Susan appeared for about a minute and a half as herself in Paramount's all-star musical, *Star Spangled Rhythm*, which had everybody on the lot either singing and dancing as themselves or emoting in brainless skits. Then Susan had fourth billing in *Young and Willing*, a comedy about young adults trying to make it in show business, an older version of the Mickey Rooney gee-whiz movies. It also starred Robert Benchley and a very young William Holden, to whom Susan was attracted, possibly because, besides being handsome, he was such a gentleman. They became friends and much later on he gave her a clock that he bought in Paris with a mechanical bird that went *tweet... tweet tweet...*

Eddie Bracken, who was one of the leads in *Young and Willing*, also became Susan's friend, but only after a fascinating trial by fire. One day he and other actors were telling off-color jokes in the dressing room, and Susan, who had just entered, heard Bracken use a four-letter word. She slapped his face. "It was such a stinging blow I could feel it to this day." Before entering pictures, Bracken had been a fighter, and, reacting instinctively, he hit her back. The blow was so hard she was out for ten minutes. Bracken at first felt terrible, but soon realized, after the incident, that Susan had turned suddenly friendly. "I don't know," he says, laughing, "maybe she liked to get hit."

Around Christmas of 1942, she was loaned to Republic, Hollywood's most efficient production line, for another of their *Hit Parade* series, this one to be called *Hit Parade of 1943* (the title became *Change of Heart* when shown in later years). She played an aspiring talented songwriter. MGM's John Carroll was the singer/con man who steals one of her songs and then falls in love with her, Eve Arden was Susan's funny friend, while a slew of famous bandleaders, like Count Basie and Freddy Martin, played themselves in this excuse for lots of singing, cuteness and a good time. The film, directed by Albert S. Rogell, turned out to be a delight, with twenty-five-year-old Susan as precocious and pert as could be. It was only a Republic "B," seen by a small fraction of the number of people who had seen *Reap the Wild Wind*, but today it shows us a Susan who was not twisted into odd angles or forced into unnatural demureness or bitchiness by directors, one whose own camera instincts and talents were joyful, winsome and technically beyond reproach.

She had her first big Hollywood romance with her co-star, John Carroll, who had fine manners and a fine baritone voice. Originally from New Orleans, Carroll had been a supporting player in many MGM films and was known as a smoothy, and a bit of a con man, with women. He was the first of many Southerners whom Susan would take a shine to, and the first of several romances that began with manners and good looks and ended in disputes over money.

The gossip columns were linking Susan and John Carroll, who

quickly proposed marriage. But there is every indication that at that time Susan did not know what she felt, about either Carroll or any other man she met, partly because her mother was so much involved in her life. She was utterly ripe for a sexual relationship and needed love badly, but those typical mother-daughter concerns over marrying well were getting in the way. Benny notes that Ellen was also getting in the way by her over-protectiveness: what was uppermost in her mind was that her daughter not get pregnant out of wedlock. That fear was often communicated to Susan.

Ellen did not like Carroll's circumstances. He was ten years older than her daughter, was divorced and seemed not to have saved any of his movie salary. Caught between her mother and her feelings, Susan found a way out of the situation by calling attention to the very thing her mother wanted of a future son-in-law. After Carroll proposed marriage, he started pricing diamonds with Susan in a jewelry store, Benny Medford recalls, next to the Brown Derby. Benny understood Susan better than she knew herself and warned her: "He has no money." Finally, she and Carroll agreed that she would select her own diamond and send him the bill. She chose a whopper. Carroll objected to the price and Susan broke the engagement.

Susan was earning about $1000 a week now, but she was still obsessively concerned about money. Benny had arranged a loan-out for her to play Jack London's wife, Charmian Kittredge London, in the United Artists biography *Jack London*. Many players in those days of long studio contracts shared in a portion of the loan-out money paid to their studios by the borrowing studio. Up until now, Benny had been arranging all of Susan's loan-out deals for no other benefit to Susan but the publicity and prestige of appearing in "A" pictures, since her own lot refused to promote her to good films. By the time of *Jack London*, she was growing furious about all the money that she was earning for Paramount while receiving, for herself, only moderate salary increases. Rather than have an unhappy star, an executive of a company outside of Paramount slipped Benny $15,000 under the table to keep Susan quiet, and he says that he simply passed it along to her, for her to keep or give back as she chose. Without hesitation, she kept it. Paramount later found out about the payola and blamed Benny.

He kept after her to spend some money to advance herself in

the colony: invest, buy a home with a swimming pool, a big car. She refused to part with any of her cash. Later, she told Wally that she had said to Benny, "Well, if you keep me busy working, when will I ever be able to enjoy it? I don't need a swimming pool so all the drifters can come in while I'm working and use it." Benny also wanted Susan to be a tiny bit more generous. Once he asked her to give Gertrude Fogler a present for Christmas, since Fogler had often forgiven Susan's fees during that rough period when the Marrenners were short of funds. "Why should I do that?" Susan said. She had trouble enough saying thank you to anyone who did her a favor, let alone giving the person a present. It was, as Benny saw it, a combination of cheapness and coldness.

Susan was such a curmudgeon. Benny did finally get her to part with $500 as an investment in an ice-cream parlor which was being started by his friend Bill Walsh. "Six months later, she wanted her money back. She couldn't get her money out fast enough. The ice-cream parlor was a big success."

Every cent Susan earned went into the bank. Once in a great while, she would make a major purchase, like a mink coat, and waltz up to Wally and say, "This is from me to me." But when she did spend money, it was like a squirrel forced to give up a winter's acorn cache. She had seen a gray-and-cerise-striped Boldini hat that she adored. Not even asking the price, she said to the milliner, "Will you put that away until I have time to think about it?" Then she soul-searched for two months: should she or shouldn't she? Someone told her, "Buy it. Even if it's a hundred dollars, it's your job to look good." Susan was stunned: she had been lying awake at nights worrying it would cost twenty-five. She went back to the Beverly Hills store, closed her eyes and blurted: "The hat!" The store head told her that because she was a star, he would let her have it for nineteen dollars. After she paid the money, she was so weak she had trouble walking.

Jack London was not a success, but it was an "A" picture in which Susan, for a change, was romantically sympathetic. Then, as World War II raged, Paramount sent her back to Republic in mid-1943 for the studio's most expensive film to date, *The Fighting Seabees*, a typical war adventure that had John Wayne and Dennis O'Keefe fighting the enemy and each other over war correspondent Susan.

The Fighting Seabees did well and helped Susan's popularity among real fighting men overseas. Wally became one of them, after a brief career as a children's ice-skating instructor in Hollywood. Wally never traded on his sister's growing fame, but his Army buddies nevertheless discovered that Susan was his sister from a photo of her near his bunk, inscribed: "To Wally from his little sister Susan, also known as Edythe, Mama, movie actress, Miss Hayward and hey-red! love and kisses—Susan." They gave him no peace. Susan had to make a small career of sending autographed pictures to Wally for his friends. Says Wally, "Getting those pictures of Susan to give around kept me out of a lot of KP."

Benny arranged for her to be sent back to United Artists to appear in the classy *The Hairy Ape*, based on Eugene O'Neill's play. She played Mildred Douglas, the beautiful society girl with whom "the hairy ape," ship's stoker Hank Smith (William Bendix), falls in love. All of the original social implications were removed from the movie, which was nevertheless prestigious for Susan, who received good reviews for her convincing vampishness.

Everything was, in 1943, in a state of flux in the Marrenner family. Susan was a rising star. Florence had returned to Brooklyn in a huff to marry pilot Udo Zaenglin. Wally was in the Army. For a while, Susan had no family in Hollywood but her mother and, after a fashion, Benny. Instead of buying the house with a swimming pool that he had wanted her to, Susan moved her mother to a duplex apartment at Pico and La Cienega, then a fine neighborhood, and took a tiny flat for herself in The Townhouse, a hotel on Wilshire Boulevard in the Rampart area. Suddenly, in September of 1943, Florence showed up at Ellen's new apartment with her newborn son, Lawrence, barely two months old. Florence had given birth to him in New York in June, and two months later quarreled with her husband. She abruptly left him to return to Hollywood to be near her mother, from whom she had never really wanted to separate. Udo, Florence says, did not bother to try to get her back. She had nowhere else to go and so she moved into the apartment with her mother.

The small flat in the Wilshire Boulevard hotel was Susan's first place of her own. She decorated it with her own paintings, which Benny says were quite good, but he can't remember much about them except that they were of people. Like all the other players in Hollywood, she did her part in the war effort, mostly by going on bond-selling tours. Each week, she donned a Navy uniform and spent a few hours doing volunteer work at Navy headquarters in Long Beach.

In November 1943, she began spending evenings at the Hollywood Canteen, serving coffee and being nice to the servicemen on leave, as did dozens of other supporting players from the studios. She could never be publicly theatrical, and occasionally, when required to be spontaneous for the servicemen, she would shout her "Anybody here from Brooklyn?" line. It always worked. One night while Susan served at the Canteen, a Columbia Pictures blond supporting player named Jess Barker, six-feet tall and appealing to women, was on the Hollywood Canteen stage introducing performances by MGM people, such as singer Ginny Simms and comic Red Skelton; Harry James' band played in the background. Susan was so far from the stage that she had to stand on a stool to watch. Young Barker spotted her and later asked her to join him for coffee. Later that night, he tried to kiss her and she smacked him. It wasn't a rude kiss. She was just being cinematically "correct." She had also slapped nice John Carroll on their first date.

Jess was twenty-nine, another Southerner (from Greenville, South Carolina), more professionally experienced than Susan and in slightly better stead with his own studio than Susan was with Paramount. He had already had several screen contracts, including one with Walter Wanger, and worked on Broadway in George S. Kaufman and Moss Hart's *You Can't Take It with You* and in various stock productions. After Gregory Ratoff directed him in a screen test, Harry Cohn sighed him and began featuring him in a series of "B" fillers, such as *Good Luck, Mr. Yates, Jam Session, She's a Soldier Too* and as Rita Hayworth's boyfriend (seen in flashbacks) in the prestigious *Cover Girl*. He was not anywhere near so well known as Susan, but he had Harry Cohn behind him. While all the male stars were off in the service, bobby-soxers were beginning to notice Jess. As an actor, he was quite competent. He had a refined and impressive vocal delivery, probably enhanced by his years in the theater.

Jess was incredibly handsome, and Susan had every reason to be taken with him: she was overdue for love. She had been acting love of every type, usually the abnormal kind, but at the age of twenty-six she still didn't know what it was. She and Jess Barker, who both had their own apartments, fell into a liaison.

Susan received warning after warning. Benny warned Susan that Barker was a mistake, that his career would fall far behind hers and there would be serious trouble ahead. For years, Benny had been trying to keep Susan away from the Hollywood wolves and, time and again, had urged her to date successful men that he knew. "She was cold to them all." Ellen Marrenner disapproved of Jess Barker from the start, for, as Florence explains: "My mother was afraid that he was after all he could get." Florence, who was living with her mother, rather liked him. Jess was certainly good-looking, had fine manners, and there was nothing about him to suggest a gold-digging adventurer. What Ellen really had against him, more than likely, was that he appeared to be one of those handsome men who, like her own husband, Walter, could sweet-talk a young girl out of her intended place in life. Had Ellen never taken up with Walter Marrenner, she wouldn't have wound up missing meals in Flatbush; those eternal struggles in the family would never have begun. Ellen wanted Edythe not to marry for love but to marry well.

Some of Ellen's resentment against Barker may have been based on his reputation in Hollywood as a roustabout ladies' man. The columnists had been linking his name to numerous stars and starlets, including Marguerite Chapman, Anne Shirley, Olivia de Havilland, Gloria de Haven, Bonita Granville and Nina Foch, a promising Columbia player to whom he had been practically engaged.

Benny adamantly blames Susan's mother for what happened. "She drove Susan out of the house. She was over-protective because she was afraid that Susan was going to get pregnant." Indeed, almost on schedule, Mrs. Marrenner called Benny around April of 1944 to say: "Susan's pregnant."

Benny asked her, "Do you want me to bring her to a lock-picker?"

"Yes," said Ellen.

But Susan didn't want an abortion and also, according to Ben, didn't want to marry Jess. They were having fights and becoming testy with each other over trivial things. Susan was discovering that Jess had a temper and that she was developing one as well. Now there occurred endless family discussions over what to do.

Susan wanted her baby, but wasn't sure she wanted Jess. She told her studio. Apparently, Jess Barker or Susan's studio told Harry Cohn. The moguls wanted them to marry. Jess was worried about what the marriage would do to his bobby-soxer image. His family, says Florence, thought Susan was a gold digger.

Susan had just finished making *And Now Tomorrow*, a Paramount soap opera in which Dr. Alan Ladd falls in love with deaf socialite Loretta Young while sister Susan worries and falls in love with Loretta's fiancé, Barry Sullivan. After the studio learned about her pregnancy, she was sent on a bond tour and finally allowed to rest at home.

By early July, Susan was almost two months pregnant and a decision had to be made. Jess wanted to marry her. Susan's mother would agree to the marriage only on the condition that Susan and Jess sign a pre-nuptial financial agreement in which husband and wife would keep their own earnings in the case of a divorce. Susan told Jess, "My mother won't come to the wedding unless you sign." Jess finally did sign the agreement, probably because, as Florence suggests, his own mother thought that he would eventually become a star himself, and because, when all was said and done, as Jess Barker has said, "I really loved the woman." It's certain that Susan loved him, too, despite their arguments. More than likely, he was her first lover, and a good and patient one, too—an absolute necessity, for she would later reveal that she had had deep anxieties about lovemaking.

They were married on July 23, 1944, at St. Thomas Episcopal Church, and looked perfectly radiant. Susan had not begun to show yet, but probably chose to wear blue, not white, because she was already carrying. It was a small ceremony, with publicists Jean Pettebone and Henry Rogers as the only invited guests outside of the family. The family was just Ellen Marrenner. The bitterness that Susan had felt toward her thirty-four-year-old sister, Florence, had not abated. The growing anger between the two sisters was widening: Susan did not invite Florence to her wedding.

CHAPTER 3

Fire

THEIR BEGINNINGS couldn't have been more insecure. Susan and Jess had fought so much, had made and then unmade wedding plans so often, that Susan finally had to marry without a permanent wedding ring. Their quarreling didn't stop with "I do"; even pregnancy couldn't settle the couple down. They continued to fight about everything. Things got smashed; perfume was dumped down the sink. The height of absurdity was reached when two months after they were married, with Susan fully four months pregnant, she left Jess over his not opening a car door for her. At the time, they were both keeping the apartments they'd had before marrying while they searched for a bigger place. After the separation, she retreated to her own apartment and made calls to her lawyer to begin divorce proceedings and to Louella Parsons for a major announcement in her column (readers still had no idea she was pregnant). Susan briefly considered having her baby as a single parent, but abandoned the idea. She and Jess reconciled a few days later and went on with their marital roller-coaster ride.

Susan and Jess were either the world's most incompatible couple or the world's most dynamite lovers, depending on one's point of view. Europeans, especially the French, have always been infatuated with the fighting of honeymooners because of the presumed ecstasy the fighters achieve while making up. At some point, however, such couples stop fighting and give in to normal routines, but Susan and Jess could never do that.

Their period of adjustment seemed endless. A typical outgoing actor, Jess made friends easily. He frequented Schwab's drugstore on Sunset, where he would talk to other young actors for hours. Often, he brought friends home. Susan withdrew from people

51

and did not see her career as something to share with other actors. In those early months, she teetered between the lure of Jess's gregariousness and her tendency toward suspiciousness. Susan's personality was too deeply rooted for a smooth transition into such a marriage.

Jess frequently wondered where he stood with Susan. Evelyn Lane (now Dankner), who was executive assistant to Harry Cohn, became friends with Jess on the Columbia lot and recalls Jess, at lunch, telling her, "I'm really in love with Susan, but I'm not sure how she feels about me." He complained to Evelyn that Susan was often cold to him.

Jess began advising Susan on the management of her career and finances, and this helped cement their relationship. He was older and more experienced; Susan respected his knowledge. Up until now, Benny Medford had been Susan's sole advisor. He had set up an account for her at Bank of America and counseled her about her money. Jess put Susan in contact with a a professional business manager whom he knew, Vernon Wood, who advised her on many things, including exactly how much she could give to her mother as a tax write-off. Jess also had thoughts as to what Susan could do about her wasting Paramount contract. Until she had had to quit work because of her pregnancy, Susan had been receiving $1700 a week from the studio, but her career was going nowhere. The last straw had come when Paramount refused to hold United Artists to a loan-out deal for Susan to star in *Dark Waters* in a part eventually played by Merle Oberon—"to teach you a lesson," Buddy De Sylva told Susan. But Benny still couldn't get Susan a release from her seven-year contract.

She approached the Charles Feldman agency about representation, and that agency thought it might be able to free her for a better contract elsewhere. Susan agreed that the Feldman office should offer Benny Medford the nominal sum of $10,000 as a buy out for the remaining year of her contract with him. She was dropping Benny after years of a very close agent-actor partnership.

Few things shocked Benny Medford, not the gross ways of the moguls, not starlets involved in horizontal favors at the studios, nor bribes. But Susan's sudden betrayal did shock him. Certainly he was an old-fashioned agent who understood movie success in unsophisticated ways and who liked a small amount of control over his clients. After Susan had gotten a little experience, she sneered at a lot of his advice on how to become a more accepted member of the colony. She also didn't care for the men he wanted her to date. But no one in Hollywood had been more generous and loving toward Susan than Benny. Despite her immaturity and cold temperament, he alone helped her to become a movie personality.

In Benny's mind, the betrayal had come about because Susan didn't understand her own need for love. All her ideas about love had to do with money, work, acquisitiveness, propriety—whatever would keep her thousands of miles from her old life. She was suppressing all of her normal feelings in favor of an extreme work ethic, and, in that way she was growing closer to the thinking of the moguls.

Soon after Susan dropped Benny, the betrayal became common knowledge in Hollywood. In time, it was raised to the level of legend. A few years later, television writers would be borrowing from the Susan Hayward/Benny Medford story to write parables about ambitious writers and actors who ungraciously drop their hardworking independent agents in favor of big-time, hot-shot agencies. The legend brought Benny a kind of backward fame, the only real reward he ever received from his seven years of toil with Susan.

Ironically, the Charles Feldman agency couldn't break the Paramount contract either. Nevertheless, Susan was growing anxious to return to work. She was prone to all sorts of superstition, more so than her mother, and believed in all those old wives' tales about ways to hasten pregnancy and delivery. She ate turkey, sat in tubs of hot water, consumed cathartic-like foods. She had no idea why she was growing so huge. She said later that at the time she believed the baby was going to be "a fat, ugly girl." It wasn't.

On February 17, 1945, at St. John's Hospital in Santa Monica, Susan gave birth to fraternal, non-identical twin boys. They came into the world seven minutes apart and were pretty, but as different as imaginable. The younger infant, whom the Barkers called Timothy, after Jess's family, was blond like his father. The older child, whom Susan named Gregory after her favorite director, Gregory Ratoff, resembled Susan's family and was a redhead.

A story was given to the papers that the births were premature and there was a good deal of fuss when the Barkers wouldn't let the infants be photographed for any of the magazines. That was a slap in the faces of many powerful editors, who treated a star's giving birth with all of the attention given to a Presidential inauguration. This edict didn't help Susan's image and hurt Jess's far more fragile movie career.

After Jess married Susan, Harry Cohn, believing that the union had cost Barker his bobby-soxer appeal, terminated Jess's movie contract. Jess then went to Universal, where he was featured in films, many cuts beneath those he had appeared in for Columbia. Meanwhile, Susan and Jess needed money for their rising expenses. Toward the end of 1945, when the twins were not even a year old and when her seven-year contract with Paramount had blessedly run out, the Feldman office negotiated her first film as an independent player, RKO's *Deadline at Dawn*.

This was a handsome, cheaply made, most appealing film written by Clifford Odets and expertly directed by Harold Clurman. An excellent choice for Susan, *Deadline at Dawn* told the simple tale of a young sailor (Bill Williams) on leave in New York City who unwittingly becomes involved in a girl's murder, while a streetwise dance-hall girl (Susan) tries to help him solve the murder before he must return to his ship. Despite the recent ordeal of carrying twins, Susan looked slim and breezy and made herself easy to watch in all of her scenes. Somehow, too, the childbearing had made her suddenly fun to work with, an odd turnabout. Bill Williams recalls: "She was a heck of an actress and a lovely human being. The last shot in the picture was when I was sitting in the bus with her. Remember, she was going to go with me. We had to kiss and it wasn't right. Either I was holding her too tight or was a little too innocent about it. The kissing went on about three or four hours. I finally said, 'Gee, Susie, it's been a long time kissing you, hasn't it?' She said, 'Bill, I have to tell you something. You didn't do anything for me either.'" They parted great friends. Only months later, Bill Williams married actress Barbara Hale.

From the minute *Deadline at Dawn* premiered in Rockford, Illinois, in June of 1946, it did terrific business, even abroad. Audiences responded to Odets' literate script and the deftness with which Susan played against her character's hardness. The success of her performance couldn't have been better timed, for just then the Charles Feldman office was considering long-term studio contracts for her.

One may wonder why, after her years of frustration at Paramount, Susan didn't simply remain an independent player. But she and her agency were quite correct in seeking another seven-year studio contract. She was not yet a major star and only the studios had the equipment to build an actor into a top name. The process cost millions, and Susan did want to go to the very top.

As soon as she was free from Paramount, there had been numerous feelers. The Selznick studio, which had brought her to Hollywood, and then dropped her, wanted to sign her again at a handsome starting salary. At the same time, Walter Wanger had been talking to the Feldman office about Susan. He had been interested in her for years.

Wanger was then making his films at the Universal studio, where Jess Barker was under contract. Jess was sent a script for a Wanger-Universal Western called *Canyon Passage*. He was being considered for the third lead, and he suggested Susan for the female lead. Walter Wanger not only thought that a good idea, but promised that if she committed herself to seven years with him, he would buy properties just for her and immediately start building her into a star. The offer was genuine. Since David O. Selznick, by far the richer producer, couldn't promise Susan a similar immediate buildup, she accepted Wanger's offer. However, Jess not only didn't get his part in *Canyon Passage* but lost his contract with Universal at the end of his first six months there. He was flat out of work, while Susan was now earning $150,000 a year with Wanger.

Canyon Passage, a strangely compelling Western even for those who don't like the form, was Susan's first film with Dana Andrews. French director Jacques Tourneur constructed his movie in such a way that all of the actors' personalities became absorbed in the flow of the main action, which encompasses almost every aspect of realistic life in the old West. The story has Dana Andrews, a store-owner, escort Susan from Portland to Jackson, Oregon, to join her fiancé, played by Brian Donlevy (in the role Jess Barker wanted). Dana loves Susan, and Susan finally realizes that she doesn't love Brian. After the Indians attack, Dana and Susan ride off together. It is fascinating to see Susan in this film today because she is so natural and unstudied in it and shows none of the mannerisms that were soon to become her trademark. Her walk is not peculiar, she doesn't use her hands much and her voice is normal:

she is like a hundred other actresses, as Jacques Tourneur directed her. We have in *Canyon Passage* a rare and unforgettable view of the young Susan Hayward without those oddities of personality which would eventually elevate her to great celebrity. Underneath Hollywood's most remarkable façade, she was spirited and competent.

In her next film, Susan took control of her future. For Walter Wanger's *Smash-Up: The Story of a Woman*, the film which at last catapulted Susan to the brink of stardom, she invented highly ingenious choreographic movements. During dramatic moments in this Dorothy Parker story of an alcoholic wife, Susan imitated what could only be described as "a Latin girl having an orgasm." She takes a deep breath, heaves her bosom, crosses her arms and pulls away from something which is causing her both pain and ecstasy in the central part of her body. Female flamenco dancers perform the same gestures all the time. Clearly symbolic of the female orgasm, they produced for Susan some fairly amazing results.

What little evidence there is indicates that Susan created these sexual movements on her own. The fine director, Stuart Heisler, was concerned mostly with authenticating Susan's alcoholic behavior in the film. He had her get drunk once as real-life practice, then brought in experts, such as Mrs. Marty Mann, the director for National Committee for Education Against Alcoholism. But Susan's on camera sexuality appeared to be her own. The only director who had ever before shown her how to use movement for a sexual effect had been Gregory Ratoff during the making of *Adam Had Four Sons*.

More than likely, Susan combined Ratoff's camera instructions with flamenco dance movements she had seen in Los Angeles and developed her own interpretation of sexuality.

Smash-Up: The Story of a Woman (said to have been based on the life of Dixie Lee, who was married to Bing Crosby) was the turning point for Susan. For the first time, the audience was asked to become involved purely with the emotions she projected as a woman; she was no longer just a character in a story. All of the synthesis of her own inventions, director Stuart Heisler's insistence on authentic alcoholic sequences and the new emphasis on her own body and emotions must have been difficult for her to manage. In the evenings, Jess read lines with her and gave her support. In the daytime, Heisler tiptoed around her, nurturing her to such an extent that he would sweat and grow upset every time she did. He said, "What an ordeal that picture was. I was limp as a rag every night. Susan had so many emotional crises that she arranged a set of signals, like a lifted finger or a nod of the head, to let me know that she was in the proper mood to start a scene."

Under orders from Walter Wanger, Heisler and others behind the cameras gave Susan the full star treatment, favoring her over the other actors in the movie in camera angles, lighting and staging. No movie-goer could fail to see that in *Smash-Up* she was intended to be the big personality. But as the movie's obvious star, she did little to make the less favored actors feel comfortable. After takes, she would turn abruptly away from her colleagues and run to her dressing room. Lee Bowman, who played Susan's successful singer husband, felt so damaged by her behavior that he later refused to speak of the film or her. Marsha Hunt, who played the woman that Susan, in her alcoholism, suspects of trying to steal her husband (she and Susan had a wonderful hair-pulling on-camera fight in a powder room), remembers: "Sadly, she had absolutely nothing to do with me. I never understood why. I finally realized it was nothing personal. I couldn't have offended her. This was a person so private and so closely involved with her job at hand that all relationships with others are non-existent. After the scene [in which she attacks Miss Hunt in the powder room], she went back to her dressing room. She would turn on her heel and walk away. I don't think I ever worked with anyone more private, more excluding. Maybe she felt it might break the spell."

It wasn't quite so complicated. Whether Susan was working on a difficult scene or an easy one, she was totally self-involved. She was pathologically withdrawn and had always been so. Time and again, actors who worked with Susan would either rationalize the way Marsha Hunt did (that Susan hated to break her concentration) or else merely feel angry and perplexed like Bowman. Susan did not have good eyesight, but it was a myth that Susan's disinterest in others had mostly to do with poor vision.

A few people saw a different side of Susan. They were usually men, not actors, not remotely in competition and in positions that would enhance her image. One of them was Stanley Cortez, the brilliant cinematographer who made her look breathtaking in

Smash-Up and whom she would repeatedly ask to work with in future films. They apparently got along famously. Another of her rare early professional friendships was with Graham Kislingbury, the chief publicist for Walter Wanger, who met Susan around the time of the release of *Canyon Passage* in August of 1946. He found Susan "a lovely gal, down to earth, feet on the ground, a hard worker" and sometimes even affectionate with him. He vividly remembers that she hugged him after not seeing him for a year.

Susan liked Graham and did all the publicity he asked her to do, even though she hated going out on public-relations dates and waving for still cameras. It reminded her of all the nonsense she had gone through at Paramount. She told Graham, while they were driving up to Sacramento for a party with the Lieutenant Governor and other politicians, "I think I'm getting too old for this sort of thing." He almost laughed; she was twenty-seven. Nevertheless, she was genuine with him, and after they got to know one another she paid a visit to him in the rickety old writers' building at one end of the studio. "Every time you went up the stairs the building shook. Susan came up and I said, 'Isn't this awful?' She said, 'It's all right. Someday you'll have a good office. You got to have faith. It sure carried *me* a long way.'" He never forgot the sentiment, nor how wonderful she was to him in those days.

Her main source of gossip-column publicity for years was Louella Parsons, who was second only to Benny Medford as an influence on Susan's rise to stardom. When something happened, whether dire or lovely, Susan got on the hotline to Louella, who invariably championed the case of "that little redhead" and kept her name alive on a daily basis. Louella's main rival, Hedda Hopper, was hotly jealous of the relationship and sniped at Susan whenever she could. Graham recalls that after Susan and Jess were evicted with the twins from their rented Beverly Hills house (it had to do with a technical violation; the owner wanted the house back), he received a blustering call from Hedda.

"Are you Graham Kislingbury? This is *Hedda Hopper*! Look, you, I understand that Jess Barker and Susan Hayward have split up. He's looking for an apartment."

Graham said, "I don't know anything like that at all."

"Where's Susan?"

"I don't know where she is right now."

"What kind of press agent are you?" she exploded. "Don't you know where Susan Hayward is? You're one hell of a press agent! Look, you—you find out where she is and you call me right back, you understand?"

Bang went the telephone. When Susan heard about the call, she told Graham, "If she calls again, just hang up on her." He loved it.

Graham's first impression of Susan and Jess was that they were a happy young couple. With time on his hands, Jess was glad to help his wife with every aspect of her career, as well as giving lots of smiles and chit-chat to reporters and photographers on Susan's behalf. He went to that Sacramento party with Susan and Graham and endured the gag of having policemen rush up to him, handcuff him and arrest him for impersonating Susan Hayward's husband. They told him, while dragging him out, "This beautiful girl couldn't be married to a guy like you," while Susan mock-shouted, "You bring back my husband! Bring him back!" Susan so hated these silly publicity things that often Jess would attend out-of-town ones for her. Graham always found Jess to be gracious, responsive and well-mannered. He didn't know about the couple's troubles.

He did think that they were living a little strangely. Toward the end of 1946, Susan borrowed money from Walter Wanger and bought a house in the Sherman Oaks section of the San Fernando Valley, on Longridge Avenue. Graham, visiting the Barkers there, found that they hadn't any furniture in the living room, which was used mostly for storage of clothes. The living room stayed that way for many months and was never put into proper shape for entertaining. Susan used to tell Graham that they couldn't afford furniture. But she was earning $3000 a week!

Wally sensed that there was a strain between Susan and Jess but couldn't get her to talk about it. He admonished her, "Susan, don't keep it all to yourself. It's not good for you." She snapped at Wally, "Just leave me alone." ("She was always like that," says Wally. "She would never confide in the people closest to her.")

She was bottling up a difficult situation. Eventually, Graham did find out that something was indeed wrong. She told him, "I'm having a rough time with Jess. I wouldn't care if he got a job in a department store as a clerk. He lies around all day and criticizes me constantly. He's very down. He hasn't been able to get work and won't do anything else. What the heck, if I couldn't make it in this business, I would do something else."

After his Universal contract was terminated, Jess could only find a handful of low-paying freelance acting jobs, and even they came to a halt. Jess was an above-average actor who at one time had had a career ahead of him. The problem seemed to be that Susan's rising star was burning Jess's out. He had lost his image as a handsome lone wolf and now was seen as a man who was basking in his wife's fame. Producers wouldn't offer him small parts for fear of offending a man whose wife was earning six figures a year. Perhaps, also, he was losing some of his motivation, with his home life ringing with Susan's career success. Susan may well have been putting Jess into the same position in which she had put Florence, so subtly changing the environment that he had no chance of achieving.

Jess was a wonderful father to the twins, making up for the scant time that Susan's one-movie-after-another schedule allowed her to spend with them. He did the grocery shopping, kept the household going in the daytime and when Susan was shooting on location. The enforced role-reversal wasn't easy for him. He was an upbeat man who now suffered occasional lows as one film assignment after another slipped through his fingers. He would become depressed, sometimes sleep late in the morning. Wally, home from the Army two years already, would sometimes drive over to his sister's house in the daytime to see the boys. He recalls arriving one day after the noon hour and seeing Jess coming down from his bedroom, quite upset about sleeping so late. That day, Wally made lunch for the boys.

Susan and Jess's early love bickering simply proceeded now on a different level. There was great bitterness. Susan would come home from the studio exhausted and tense, find him basking in the pool or otherwise relaxing and lose her temper. He would then lose his. The twins suffered. Florence remembers hearing that the boys on several occasions had packed their bags and wanted to run away.

In early November of 1947, Susan went through the motions of filing for a divorce, but changed her mind around Thanksgiving and settled for counseling as the possible solution for her problems with Jess.

Susan was also having troubles with the Marrenners. An edginess had been developing between Susan and her mother for some time. Money became an issue. Florence and her small son, Larry, had left Ellen Marrenner's duplex apartment at Pico and La Cienega when Wally came home from the Army in 1945. A fine son, Wally moved in with his mother and helped support her from his earnings as a page at the Santa Anita racetrack. Susan was also contributing to her mother's support, but, as Florence tells it, Susan's contributions were arranged so that they would become tax write-offs and not really leave Susan with less money. Ellen was annoyed and felt she needed more. "When my mother asked Susan for more money to live on," says Florence, "Susan said, 'Well, why don't you apply for Welfare?' So my mother did, but when she told the welfare workers that she was Susan Hayward's mother, they laughed at her and told her to go home." Another time, says Florence, after it was obvious that Susan was becoming wealthy, Ellen told Susan that her one dream was to have a house of her own. Wouldn't Susan buy her a small house? "You could own it. I would just live in it." Susan replied that if she did buy a second house and let her mother live in it, she would lose rentals.

Ellen told Florence everything. She was a little frightened of her daughter and of the very success which Ellen had wanted for her. That success now seemed to be turning Susan against her. She was not often invited to her daughter's home and resented being kept from the twins. Susan would come to the apartment to see her, usually, and never stayed long. Ellen saw more of Susan's friends or professional associates. The thought occurred to her, and to Florence, more than once that her younger daughter was ashamed of her family and feared they would hold her back. Susan still had harsh feelings toward her mother over the way she felt her father had been treated. Susan also later said that her mother was jealous of her success, manipulative and too interested in money. In addition, there was the strong belief that her mother had never loved her.

An equal tragedy was the deteriorating relationship between Susan and Florence. After she returned from Brooklyn with her baby, Florence couldn't seem to make up with Susan, no matter how hard she tried. Some anger from some long-ago place seemed to be festering. The closer Susan got to stardom, the angrier she became toward her sister and the less she bothered to hide it. Florence almost never got to see Susan, and when she did, there was terrible tension between them. Larry Zaenglin, Florence's son, says that when he was small he could almost feel that tension, which clearly came from his mother as well as from Susan. On those occasions when Susan would invite the family to her house, along with aunts and uncles who were living in Los Angeles, she would deliberately exclude her older sister. She couldn't have hurt Florence more. Florence would go to her and ask: "Why are you doing this?" "I'd only get a long, cold stare. She wouldn't explain."

At the time, Florence did not realize how deep was the conflict between them, and Ellen was fearful of interceding. With her own relationship with her famous daughter now precarious, Ellen felt she had to walk carefully. Florence simply couldn't bear it. Even on those few occasions when she did see her sister, Susan was curt with her. Florence never had enough money and would say to Susan (rather injudiciously): "Larry needs clothes. Could I have some of the old clothes that the twins don't need anymore?" Susan snapped that she certainly couldn't.

So bothered by all this did Florence become that she took little Larry and moved to Tucson, Arizona, hoping to start a new life away from famous sister and fawning relatives. A long-standing pattern would begin. After two years of working in Tucson, Florence wanted to be near her mother again and returned with Larry to Hollywood. She worked and saved some money. After some months, she was upset all over again by the problem with Susan, by the Barkers' dinners to which she was never invited, and moved with Larry first to Tampa and then Jackson, Florida. She thought she and Larry could make a new life in the warm climates. And again she returned to Hollywood. Then she went to Clearwater, Florida. There was also a journey to New Orleans. Hers was the strangest odyssey of repulsion and attraction, of freedom-seeking and family enslavement. Certainly, Ellen knew what was bothering her older daughter, but felt there was nothing she could do. Perhaps Ellen also felt that Susan was happier when Florence was away and not asking for a share in their mother's love.

Little by little, Florence felt she was being destroyed. People who knew she was Susan Hayward's sister would ask her: "Well, why haven't you seen her? What's going on between you?" It was all those questions, Florence says, that made her feel guilty rather than merely angry. She was victimized and debilitated by that guilt, caused by something she couldn't understand and to this day still cannot. Susan would only say, behind Florence's back, that her older sister did not wish her well and was only interested in her money. Florence, of course, denies that vehemently.

The reviews of *Smash-Up* were extraordinarily good, except for the *New York Times*, whose Bosley Crowther had taken a persistent dislike to Susan's acting. He said: "Susan Hayward performs the boozy heroine with a solemn fastidiousness which turns most of her scenes and drunken fumbling and heebies into key burlesque." *Life*, however, gave her a four-page spread and the *New York Herald Tribune*'s Howard Barnes extolled typically: "Susan Hayward plays the afflicted heroine with considerable power." In February of 1948 she received her first Academy Award nomination for Best Actress for *Smash-Up*. She was headed straight to the top.

She knew it and pushed harder than ever. She pressured Walter Wanger to buy book properties as starring vehicles for her. Wanger kept reminding her that he couldn't afford to buy options on everything she saw. But he didn't lose a dime on her. He put her in one picture after another, without a break, in hectic location-shooting schedules which would have caused a less determined actress to come apart. He made some quick money by loaning her to Howard Hughes' studio, RKO-Radio, early in 1947, for *They Won't Believe Me*. The audience distinctly didn't like saintly Robert Young as an evil manipulator who causes his wife's death, nor Susan as the paramour who meets an untimely end. Now Wanger went for broke on building Susan, deliberately extending her range in costume dramas.

The Lost Moment, made at Universal studio in the middle of 1947, was based on Henry James' *The Aspern Papers*, and co-starred Robert Cummings as the young nineteenth-century publisher who travels to Venice in search of a famous poet's lost love letters. Agnes Moorehead played an ancient woman who had once been the poet's intended, and Susan was her beautiful but deranged niece. The film was a thoroughly unpleasant experience for Susan and apparently for everyone else involved. Susan couldn't bear the director, Martin Gabel, who was new to Hollywood and not used to film actresses. Normally, Susan was very cooperative on a set, but when Gabel asked her to repeat a line for the twelfth time, after she had told him she was losing patience, she hurled a lamp at him. For Robert Cummings, however, it was Susan who was the problem. "She was distant, non-talkative, no sense of humor. Most of us kept our dressing-room doors open. It was the friendly thing to do. We'd visit each other. Not her. After a scene, she'd go to her dressing room and shut the door, shut out the world. It was embarrassing as hell to be playing a scene with someone like that. You'd be playing a scene. There were old friends on the set, laughing and talking. Suddenly, there she was, and the mood was changed. Everything got silent."

It was the same complaint about Susan that many other actors made. Even Walter Wanger, with whom Susan got on well and who had become her mentor, sometimes felt a little of the chill that others felt. She would never call him "Walter," always "Mr. Wanger," despite his pleas. When anyone complained to him about her coldness, Wanger always said, "That's just Susan." (However, she knew that he was physically attracted to her, and in this case her formality was probably a way of telling him "No." It's doubtful whether Wanger ever understood it that way.)

No let-up. Early in 1948, at about the time she received her Academy Award nomination for *Smash-Up*, she rushed into *Tap Roots*, Walter Wanger's spectacular Technicolor attempt to show that Susan Hayward could have played Scarlett O'Hara after all. She went on location in Asheville, North Carolina, to play fiery Mississippi plantation belle Morna Dabney, who, during the Civil War, helps her family rebel against the Confederacy and, in the process, falls in love with a dashing newspaper publisher and rebel, played by Van Heflin.

Everyone worked hard to pull off this *Gone with the Wind* imitation, Susan the hardest. Wanger put her in Southern-belle togs that were very heavy and had her hair done in elaborate coifs similar to Vivien Leigh's. Susan would have to get up at the crack of dawn to have her hair washed and set, go to makeup, then travel fifty or sixty miles to the day's location; after spending the day in a corset, she would return to her hotel at six or seven at night. Her physical stamina was amazing.

She didn't go to any parties. She saw Jess during the last week of shooting, but had no other outlet in the evening except an occasional dinner with publicist Graham Kislingbury. She would call her friend two or three times a week and the two of them would hunt around for new restaurants in the area. Over dinner, she would talk about her problems with Jess and the film. One time, heading for a restaurant they had heard about in the mountains, they grabbed a cab, and soon began to notice that the driver was ogling her in the rearview mirror. Finally, he turned and said, "You're Susan Hayward." He whirled the cab around, sailed down a side street and started speeding. It was heart-stopping. Graham shouted, "Where are you going?" The driver didn't answer. Susan yelled, "What are you trying to do?" He stopped at last in front of a house, grabbed the car keys and ran inside. At that moment, Graham understood.

"You know what he's going to do?" Graham said to Susan. "He's going to bring his whole family out to meet you."

"You're kidding," she said, a second before, indeed, the whole family emerged.

"You're our favorite star," said the driver. One by one, the others came over to meet Susan, who tactfully smiled and wrote autographs. Susan and Graham, happy to be alive, declined the driver's offer to take them back, and instead called a studio limousine.

Still no rest. Immediately after *Tap Roots*, she went into an interesting film called *The Saxon Charm*. In it, she was basically a plot help, even though she received second billing. Her name was big enough now to justify big billing for what was essentially a supporting role. The true star of the film was Robert Montgomery, who played a perverse genius of the theatrical world.

The three movies which had followed *Smash-Up* had not been of much help to this young woman in a hurry. In 1948, Walter Wanger accepted an offer from a "B" studio, Eagle-Lion Films, to finance his "A" pictures. He moved his production facilities from Universal to Eagle-Lion and, in June, sent Susan, Robert Preston, Pedro Armendariz, director Stuart Heisler and a substantial crew to Ada, Oklahoma, to make *Tulsa*. The movie was perfect for Susan at this point in her career; it was one of those lovely genre films about a beautiful young firebrand who rides horses, gets sassy, provokes male passions, has courage, makes dreadful mistakes and in the end wins man and homestead: a kind of *Gone with the Wind* of the Oklahoma oilfields. Susan was

Cherokee Lansing (her dad dies in the script, just like Scarlett's), who has valuable oil leases, and Bob Preston was the handsome geologist who loves her and helps her make millions.

The location work was exceptionally difficult. Howard W. Koch, the assistant director (now a prominent producer), notes that the weather was hot and unpredictable. One minute, it would be thundering and pouring rain, requiring that equipment be packed onto trucks, and the next, the sun would burst through and they would have to unload the cameras. Nobody could sleep. The hotel rooms were like moist ovens, and everyone would be up half the night walking outdoors and eating watermelon. Whatever the discomforts, there could be no shooting delays. The budget was a tight one million dollars.

Susan was not merely her usual trouper self in putting up with these conditions, she was splendid. She had good instincts for a script that had magic in it for her and she *knew* that in this film something was afoot. That alone may have put her in a rare mood: she was friendly, talkative, even outgoing, a bit of Cherokee Lansing herself. Still, Howard Koch noted that there was no rapport between Susan and Robert Preston, and this was their last film together.

Chiggers were eating everyone alive in the heat. Susan had to wear a girdle under her slit-skirt Western costume, and those frenzied little things were killing her. As the chief makeup man on *Tulsa*, Del Armstrong, recalls, "Susan called the whole crew together and warned them not to be put off if they caught her scratching her private parts. The men loved her for that." Suddenly, they were all joking about chiggers. They called Harry Ray, a funny man who was actually doing Susan's makeup, "Chigger bait," saying he was giving them to everybody. Susan was in on the fun.

Susan was becoming "hot." A mature sexuality was beginning to set in. From *Tulsa* on, one hears in one interview after another the strong response she caused in the men she worked with, despite the "no" signals she usually sent out. Howard Koch said he was secretly attracted to her; all the men were. Everything about Susan was beginning to heat up. Her breasts, after childbirth, had become full and luscious. Her face was losing that too-innocent quality of very young carrot tops. her body had a new fullness.

Even her peculiar walk was seen as disturbingly sexual. In *Tulsa*, on and off screen, it was all beginning to show.

Her takes in the movies were blissfully painless for everyone. She was completely facile in front of the camera and needed no lengthy preparation. Koch recalls her walking onstage and, without delays or discussions, expertly getting into her scenes with Preston or Pedro Armendariz. "She didn't have to work herself up. She just did it. She was a marvelous girl and my idea of a movie star."

Jess came to the location for *Tulsa*, and all the men behind the scenes must have been jealous of him. Shooting was completed on August 13. When the film was released a few months later (to mixed reviews), the public loved it and loved Susan as Cherokee. She was the best thing the short-lived Eagle-Lion Films ever had.

CHAPTER 4

Ice

WALTER WANGER made good money on Susan and then he blew it. He put his assets into a multimillion-dollar film, *Joan of Arc*, written by Maxwell Anderson and starring Ingrid Bergman, who, unfortunately for Wanger, left her husband for Roberto Rossellini just as the movie was released. The scandal murdered the film at the box office. He was forced to sell the remaining two and half years of Susan's contract to Darryl F. Zanuck, head of Twentieth Century-Fox and controller of one of the largest studio purses in Hollywood.

Zanuck had plans for Susan, but wanted her for a full seven years. He was willing to renegotiate her original Wanger deal, offering her a starting salary of $200,000 a year, guaranteed raises and all sorts of actor power. But Howard Hughes also wanted her for RKO, waving more money than Zanuck. She finally turned down Hughes' offer because, as she told him, "You don't make pictures and I want to work," and was even toying with walking away from Zanuck's offer in favor of freelancing. She knew that the moguls were users and she had already been burned.

Susan resolved the matter in her own way. She paid a visit to the astrologer of the movie stars, Carroll Righter, a tall, trim, imposing, much-admired gentleman from a distinguished Philadelphia family. Susan had been receiving forecasts for years and, says Righter, was a "total believer." It was one of those amazing contradictions about Susan: her enormous cynicism and lack of trust, pitted against a rather childlike belief in the supernatural. Like her mother, she was fearful of walking under ladders and the like (although Righter's charts were of a superior category). He advised her to sign with a major studio or else suffer a career decline if she remained independent. He told her the best day and exact time to sign her Fox contract. One night, she went to sleep and was jangled awake by the alarm clock, which read 3:23 A.M. She signed the next seven years of her life away and fell back to sleep.

Her agreement with Twentieth Century-Fox was a good one. The studio could not cut her hair unless she agreed. She could quit filming at six o'clock on the dot. She had her choice of hairdressers, makeup people, cameramen. It was basically the contract of a top star, even though she was not yet one.

Susan's first movie at Fox was *House of Strangers*, the much-admired chronicle of a battling Italian-American family, directed by Joseph L. Mankiewicz. He encouraged Susan and Richard Conte, who played the vengeful brother, to act out a sexual fight for supremacy. Susan, as Conte's paramour, allowed the ice in her to surface, and used it against Conte and his brothers in the movie. Amidst Mankiewicz's shadowy effects and brilliant direction, Susan was superb. The movie gained a large following in Europe and is often hailed by students of film.

That iciness which she used in *House of Strangers*, and which often turned to rage, was part of the Susan Hayward *persona* she had been carefully elaborating. What was wonderful about it was that almost every woman could see this same coldness in herself and could revel in the cure which Susan's characters always offered for the condition, the humanizing warmth of others. Yet the movie which did finally push Susan into the stardom for which she had worked, day and night, for ten years was, interestingly, one that reversed her usual image.

In *My Foolish Heart*, which she had made for Samuel Goldwyn (on loan-out to RKO-Radio) in 1949, audiences saw a subdued and good-natured creature even when the character, at the start of the movie, was supposed to be a shrew. *My Foolish Heart* became her greatest triumph to date. Much of the credit for Susan's success, however, should go to the director, Mark Robson, whose decision to inject constant humor into a tragic story of wartime lovers kept *My Foolish Heart* from becoming a saccharine woman's film. He directed Susan to underplay her part and smile, and under Robson's masterful hand Susan was kept fresh and believable, far removed from her usual larger-than-life firebrand character.

The story was tender. College girl Eloise Winters meets would-be wolf Walt Dreiser (Dana Andrews) and falls in love with him. The war breaks out and Walt must leave for duty in the Air Force. Not willing to trap him into marriage, she can't bring herself to tell him that she is pregnant. When word comes that he has been killed, she lets herself trick her old boyfriend, Lew (Kent Smith), into marrying her. The two live miserably until Lew finally leaves her and Eloise comes to her senses. She is left at the end with her daughter, the living reminder of her love for Walt.

The heart of the movie was the easy on-screen relationship between Susan and Dana Andrews. Things had loosened up enough by 1950 so that the audience could accept the idea of a young girl's having pre-marital relations with a man with whom she falls in love, especially when she engages in a good deal of charming soul-searching beforehand. What woman in the audience in 1950 would object to a man who admits he's the world's least successful wolf, yet still hopes for a physical relationship with the girl he loves? But after Walt and Eloise do make love, years of tragedy ensue, ultimately causing a drastic personality change in Eloise.

To understand the furor that *My Foolish Heart* caused, one would have to have lived through the post-war period of its release, when men and women wanted more permissive movies but did not wish underlying morals to be upset. Early in 1950, in time for the Academy Award nominations, *My Foolish Heart* played in the Radio City Music Hall and countless first-run theaters across the country. It was the perfect film for dating men and women to see together. The haunting theme song ("Take care, my foolish heart"), written by Victor Young and Ned Washington, ran unobtrusively throughout the movie, and the movie's theme song became as important as the movie itself. Countless couples still recall the song, Dana and one of the most unforgettable Susan roles ever played.

Even though she received second billing after Dana Andrews, no one could have failed to see that this was her movie. She appeared in all but two of the scenes; her emotions, rather than Andrews', were at the movie's center. The critics were deeply impressed. Said *Newsweek*, "This is very much Susan Hayward's picture, and she makes the most of her first chance at an honest, demanding characterization by realizing it with an admirable sincerity and understanding." Fan-magazine polls, right after *My Foolish Heart*, began to show a surge in Susan's popularity among movie-goers, especially among women. In February, she received her second Academy Award nomination for Best Actress, then, in March, lost to Olivia de Havilland for *The Heiress*.

Everyone knew that Susan had reached the top. What Susan now wanted was to find more scripts as good as *My Foolish Heart* and to root herself. There were still all those old fears about losing it all. The next three years would bring one fight after another with Darryl F. Zanuck about story material.

Much has been written about the old Hollywood studio system and the enslavement of even the highest-paid actors. Susan, like most major stars, had all sorts of contractual rights, but not script approval. Zanuck was no different from the other moguls, walking a fine line between finding scripts that would keep his big stars at the top and using those very stars as mere "guarantees" to keep questionable films from losing money. When, after her great success in *My Foolish Heart*, Zanuck scheduled her for a contrived screwball comedy called *Stella* (the audience was supposed to laugh about a corpse that no one could get rid of), Susan flatly refused to do it. By the rules of her contract, she was put on suspension without salary, without the right to work anywhere else. But Susan wasn't being foolish. Stars who wished to remain stars had to risk suspension occasionally as part of the on-going war with the moguls. After a few weeks, Zanuck gave in, slightly, and threw an above-average Western at her.

Rawhide had Susan and Tyrone Power being held hostage by bandits after their stagecoach is held up, and falling in love during the ordeal of trying to escape a situation that will mean certain death. It was nicely directed by the very accomplished Henry Hathaway, who helped impart the film's many moments of unusual suspense. It was Susan's and Hathaway's first feature film together (he had directed her *Alter Ego* screen test at Paramount more than ten years before) and the beginning, as Mr. Hathaway himself notes, of a long and abrasive professional relationship. However, on *Rawhide* there was minimal trouble. The mutual clashes and temperament would come on later films.

Zanuck was determined to use his high-priced star to buoy his losers. When, in the first half of 1951, Jeanne Crain became pregnant and could not appear in *I'd Climb the Highest Mountain*, Zanuck

replaced her with Susan. She was fine as the mild wife of a back-
woods minister, but a hundred actresses with lesser names could
have done just as well, and in the end the Hayward name (opposite
William Lundigan's) didn't help the poor box office. *I'd Climb the
Highest Mountain* was Susan's first movie with Henry King, who
would soon become one of her favorite directors.

The movie was made in Dawsonville, Georgia, near Atlanta.
One afternoon, movie history was almost changed when Susan
wandered off, began taking snapshots of Amicolola Falls, a 729-
foot drop, and lost her footing. Fox chauffeur Will Gray caught
her seconds before she would have fallen to her death.

During the production, cast and crew began eating at Aunt
Fanny's cabin, a restaurant owned by a fat, funny, outgoing, wonderful man names Harvey Hester. Everyone liked him, including
Susan and Henry King, who wound up casting him as one of the
locals in the film, Susan took to going into the restaurant by herself just to talk to Harvey. The two struck up a friendship which
would last for years. Harvey Hester would afterward show up in
Hollywood and introduce Susan to *his* friends in that town. It
turned out he knew everyone. Harvey's friendliness would play
a crucial part in Susan's later life.

Shooting on *I'd Climb the Highest Mountain* was completed by
the summer of 1950—none too soon, for Susan hated all that
gingham and gentility, although she had to admit she loved
Georgia. At last, Zanuck decided to pander to Susan's new top-
star status and chose a property especially for her, *I Can Get It for
You Wholesale*, based on the 1937 Jerome Weidman novel about
unscrupulous people in the New York garment industry. To star
Susan in the film, Zanuck had the male character in the book,
Harry Bogen, changed to Harriet Boyd, a kind of Seventh Avenue
female Sammy Glick, possessing a dollar sign where her heart
should have been. In the story, she was willing to trade in her
love for her business partner, played by Dan Dailey, for a piece
of the action offered by a dress tycoon, George Sanders. The role
was certainly much more Susan than that of the minister's wife
and helped advance the image that she wanted for herself. (Even
the phony ending helped it: Harriet's ice suddenly melts and she
chooses love over money.) The heart of the movie, however, was
not so much the work done by the actors, but the location shooting
in New York's garment center.

It was on the streets of New York that Susan had a chance to feel the true impact of her new stardom. With her merciless three-pictures-a-year schedule and her secluded family life, she had had little contact with the public which was watching her in darkened theaters. One night the director, Michael Gordon, was shooting Susan and Dan Dailey in the back seat of a car, outside Bonwit Teller. As Susan's makeup man, Tom Tuttle, recalls, the crowd around the car was so thick and aggressively interested in Susan that Dailey was afraid to open the car door and Susan was petrified. "The fans just crowded around quietly, but it got deeper and deeper and scary." The mob around the car tied up traffic for hours. Director Gordon finally came over to the two stars and said, "You'd better sign some autographs." They did and were eventually able to leave the car.

But there were many less fearful ways in which Susan could sense her new status. During that two-year work-jammed period between *Tulsa* and the April 5, 1951, release of *I Can Get It for You Wholesale*, which did well at the box office, her name kept cropping up in the big-circulation magazines. *Esquire* ran a full-page color photo of her. She was beginning to receive all those domestic and overseas awards which really mean "star." On August 10, 1951, she was invited to press her hands and feet into the wet cement outside of Grauman's Chinese Theater. That was Hollywood's quaint but unassailable sign. But the best sign was: her pictures were grossing.

What was Susan like now that she had become a true star? The ice frosted over. The efficiency peaked. The manner grew fearsome at times. Fox hairdresser Helen Turpin, who later became Susan's friend, recalls that when she first began doing Susan's hair, Susan thought nothing of just grabbing the comb and mirror out of her hand and working on her own hair. Every bit as independent as the star, Helen Turpin said, "Whenever you're ready to be taken care of, I'll be down in the sound truck." Susan had a habit of devastating someone with a gush of temper one moment, and the next, finishing the person off with a dead stare. Helen endured a few of these flare-ups and finally had to sit down with her and say, "Susan, now if you want me to work with you, you're going to have to treat me like a human being. You can't treat me as if I weren't." Around the innards of Twentieth Century-Fox, there were many warnings about the iceberg that could explode if wrongly approached. Ben Nye, head of the makeup department at the studio, had heard the caveats and remembers being a little afraid of Susan. Once, on *I Can Get It for You Wholesale*, producer Sol Siegel wanted him to get Susan to change something about her makeup. Instead of going to her directly, Ben Nye wrote her a letter. She approached him about it.

"Did you write this?" she shot.

"Yes, they wanted me to have you—"

Not waiting for Nye's explanation, she cut in: "Don't you ever do that again!" Her anger was quite hurtful but absolutely effective. He confronted her face to face from then on.

The temper seemed to be under exquisite control, and was always mollified by the ice which formed immediately after the storm. There was a kind of even, rational, Hammurabic justice about Susan's highs and lows during this period at Fox. By her manner, everyone around her knew she was a star, but the information was not communicated grotesquely. People like Ben Nye, Helen Turpin, Tom Tuttle, who did her makeup for years, eventually began to respect that fire and ice as part of her extraordinary actress's equipment.

Even Zanuck had to respect it. During lunch breaks, she was often invited to eat in his private dining room, but there were times, as Tom Tuttle remembers, when she would refuse, sending back relayed messages such as "Please tell Mr. Zanuck that I'm working on the set and I don't have time for lunch."

Many of the Susan storms at Twentieth Century-Fox had to do with her unflappable involvement with her hair. Occasionally, a film would come along that required shorter hair. Susan would always refuse the shortening, pointing to the relevant clause in her contract, and thousands of words were written in memos about persuading Susan to have her hair cut. Susan was rigid about how her hair had to be done. She wanted it full (Helen started using rollers), combed back in certain ways. It was around this period that the redness began to disappear, leaving her an ordinary brunette. She began to dye it secretly. Only those closest to her knew she was doing it.

The combination of her star power and her increasing sexuality affected everyone. She was like an iridescent jewel: destructive to the touch but demanding to be touched. Yet, at the heart of the jewel there seemed to be great unhappiness. During breaks in the shooting of *Rawhide*, Susan would not socialize with the director, Henry Hathaway, or her co-stars. Sometimes, her sons joined her on location at Lone Pine, California, and she would simply wander off with them to look for arrowheads. Hathaway didn't appreciate that: "It sort of bothered her to be friendly." At Lone Pine, he, his assistant director, Buck Hall, and others on the film used to go to a certain café and sit together. Susan would deliberately go to a different café with her maid or hairdresser. But one night Buck Hall, a makeup man and three others were in their usual café, chatting at a table, when Susan did come in, quite alone. She sat by herself at the bar, smoking, getting a little tight on three or four drinks, while her co-worker males glanced at her. She was quite a knockout in that isolated bar. Buck Hall notes, "We all remarked about it at the same time. That is the only time in my life that I saw a woman that good-looking at a bar and the seats on both sides of her were empty. She just wasn't the kind of woman you approached."

There was a growing sense of danger about Susan in her stardom: not bitchery, but a kind of don't-you-dare-touch-me quality which even extended to her on-camera work. Says Buck Hall, "Everett Sloane was originally the heavy in *Rawhide*. He was right off Broadway and he was playing a cowboy from the days of William S. Hart. She had to run out of the house, where the bad guys were holding her hostage, and Everett Sloane had to take off after her and tackle her. Boy, did she hit the ground pretty hard! She didn't say one word. She got up, stood there, looked at him: glared, ice, just glared like ice, not saying a word. The next thing we knew, Jack Elam was in the part."

But to a handful of her fellow workers she could be as devoted as she was short-tempered with others. She would repeatedly ask to work with the same people: makeup man Tom Tuttle, hairdressers Emmy Eckhardt and Helen Turpin, cameraman Stanley Cortez. These people knew her for years and held great affection for her. She confided in them and trusted them without reservation. Tom Tuttle, who received a bit of the famous frost when he first worked with her, wound up becoming a guest in her home.

During this period of her early years at Twentieth Century-Fox, there were often whispers about the problems between Susan and Jess, although no one knew for sure what was going on. Jess would dutifully show up at all of her locations and the two would look happy together. Susan would give interviews to the magazines saying that they were compatible and thoroughly contented with their home life with the boys. The problem of Jess's not working was, according to those interviews, not serious in terms of their marriage.

It was, however, indeed serious and may have been one reason why Susan was driving herself and didn't seek vacations. Her mother, who continued to dislike Jess, kept after Susan to do something about his not working, which also may be why Susan saw Ellen less and less. Susan apparently dreamed of having more children, but with things unresolved with Jess, she appeared to put off plans to become pregnant again. (One day, Florence was at her mother's apartment when Susan was there. Susan spotted a footstool and suddenly said that she wanted to have it. "Oh, I would love to have a little girl," said Susan. "I can just imagine her sitting on that stool.")

She couldn't or wouldn't help Jess. She certainly must have seen that he was slowly being worn down by his position as "Mr. Hayward," by her tight-fisted control over their lives. This was, interestingly, the same sort of control that she maintained with her mother.

But in Susan's thick walls of ice there were cracks toward those closest to her. She was not especially generous to Jess, yet at Christmastime she would leave a nice check for him under the tree. In fact, during all the holidays of the early fifties she seemed to ease up toward everyone. She would suddenly feel sisterly and invite Florence and Larry, now about nine, to holiday dinners, along with the rest of the family. As Larry recalls, this happened no more than three times, but each time Susan was quite generous to him. One Christmas, she gave him two checks, one for $100 and one for $50, along with toys.

What sticks in his mind today is the almost palpable tension between his mother and his aunt during those rare get-togethers, and his aunt's terrible temper. Once, when his grandmother was in the hospital, he and his mother ran into Susan there. "She had been drinking and she brought half a mocha cream cake. I remember she said, 'Larry, do you want this half a mocha cake?' In those days, I was such a mama's boy. I said, 'Is it okay, Mama?'

Susan's eyes flashed and she said, 'If you got to ask your mother's approval, I'm not going to give it to you.' I would say my aunt was mostly reserved, but there was temperament." Larry didn't see her much because of his mother's exclusion from her sister's life, and after a certain point, to young Larry, Susan Hayward was only a figure high up on a screen.

Her non-stop work schedule, her problems with Jess and her new stardom caused further problems with her mother. Florence can't remember exactly when a certain upsetting episode concerning Susan and her mother occurred, but knows it was in the early fifties. "One Sunday, my mother came to the door of Susan's house. Susan had forgotten that she had invited her several weeks before for dinner. She had people in the house, maybe some of her movie friends, and wouldn't let my mother in. 'You can't come in,' said Susan. 'I don't want you mixing with my friends.' My mother was offended and never came to Susan's house again."

The entire makeup of Susan's private life was tenuous, except for her strong relationship with Timothy and Gregory. Even people who had grudges against Susan for the way she handled her power, like Benny Medford, have to admit that she loved those boys and tried to be the best mother she could. She loved talking about them and about that special thing which made the boys seem almost miracles to her: their nearly opposite natures. They had shared the same womb, but took their main characteristics, physical and emotional, from different parents. Blond Timothy had his father's outgoing actor's nature. When a stranger greeted him, out would go his hand for a handshake with no hesitation. Gregory was more like Susan. He was shy and difficult with strangers, but could eventually be won over. She loved watching them, interacting with them, although, like most movie stars, she did not have a great deal of time for motherhood.

Zanuck had decided to make Susan the main attraction in *David and Bathsheba*, which went into production late in 1950. With Susan's films at Fox now beginning to outgross those of the studio's perennial dancing favorite, Betty Grable, Susan was natural insurance for an expensive biblical spectacle. The script was aimed at the talents of Gregory Peck, who, as David, the just king of Israel, must cope with scandal, opprobrium and even the wrath of God when he commits bigamy with Bathsheba, the wife of one of his soldiers. Susan, as Bathsheba, was gorgeously photographed by Leon Shamroy, under Henry King's direction, but had essentially little to do except simper at David's pain and God's anger, although she did so in magnificent clothes and jewels.

Except for a handful of desert exteriors shot in Nogales, Arizona, *David and Bathsheba* was filmed mostly at Century City on the Fox lot. It was convenient for Zanuck, who loved to check out, personally, every set and costume; but the lack of imaginative locations tended to keep the film confined and talky. A good many of Hollywood's spectacles during this period had the same flaw.

Susan had at last decided to give herself a rest and take Jess and the boys to Europe. Before they all left, however, Zanuck came to a decision about which of his actresses was to play the choice role of Jane Froman in a musical biography of the famous handicapped singer's life, *The Jane Froman Story*. The Barkers had to cancel their trip.

Jane Froman had been a popular singer of the forties who, on her way to entertain American troops abroad, suffered injuries in a plane crash. Her leg was nearly amputated at the knee and required dozens of painful operations through the years, while, on crutches, she bravely went on with her singing career. Lamar Trotti's script and production were strictly Hollywood biopic, with Jane's personal life boiled down to a simplistic love triangle between Jane, her unsuccessful husband, Don Ross (David Wayne), and John Burn (Rory Calhoun), the pilot who saves her life. But the dynamite that Trotti used to elevate his conventional scenario was the extraordinary voice of the living Froman. Before filming began, she recorded some thirty songs for Susan to mime in the film.

Susan at last allowed Fox to cut her hair for the Froman role. It's fascinating to see how the usually icy Susan, while working on a handful of films, like *Tulsa* and *With a Song in My Heart* (the new title for *The Jane Froman Story*), would suddenly warm up on her sets. Perhaps the change had something to do with the upbeat nature of the films. For instance, Herman Boden, one of the dancers in *With a Song in My Heart*, recalls that when Susan first came into the rehearsal hall for the big title-song production number, "We loved her warmth and her naturalness, and she looked at everybody in the chorus and wanted them to like her." She had already received private dance coaching before meeting with the choreographer and dancers, and was tense about having to dance while miming (actually singing along with) Froman's recordings in front of Jane Froman herself, who was always watching from her wheelchair. Susan would keep asking the two dancers, "Is this right?" or "Am I holding myself correctly?" They liked her, but thought her serious: "It wasn't like working with Betty Grable, who would break up constantly and was just fun."

(Susan's twins came to the set and sat near Froman during rehearsals for the big number. They had never seen their mother do anything quite like it, and went home in a near-trance, scream- ing for hours, "With a song in my heart, heaven opens its *port- holes* [portals] to me.")

Everyone else on *With a Song in My Heart* found Susan just as earnest and likable, not just her old work-machine self. Rory Calhoun, who had already taken to Susan during *I'd Climb the Highest Mountain*, remembered, "We were always very friendly. She couldn't have been nicer. I have often said on talk shows, when they asked me who my favorite leading lady was, that she was number one, along with Marilyn Monroe, Gene Tierney and Betty Grable [Fox players]." She was *"the* most professional lady I had ever worked with." Her minute-by-minute dedication was incredible. She would listen to Jane Froman records at home and in her dressing room, where Rory Calhoun remembers seeing her mouth them while watching herself in the mirror. Jane Froman, who was on the set with her husband, John (whom Calhoun was playing), found herself riveted on the intensity of Susan's efforts to become her in every detail. When Jane was recording her songs for the film and suddenly looked up, there was huge star Susan studying her movements.

Susan, on this and every other movie she worked on, was a director's dream of a competent performer, coming into scenes knowing every word. Ben Chapman, who was the assistant director on a couple of Susan's movies during this period, says he doesn't recall Susan even once asking for a line in rehearsals. During the long and basically boring process of movie-making, with the in- terminable waiting for the director and crew to set up shots, she was always a consummate professional, never complaining or growing irritable. Leonard Doss, the Technicolor consultant on *With a Song in My Heart* and most of Susan's color movies at Fox, remembers her as the soul of patience, absolutely prompt for her fittings and color coordinations. She was always in tune with the needs of the technical people whose job it was to transform her to the screen, and during fittings she shot out one-word opinions that were invariably correct: "Higher!" or "Lower!" Whatever reservations the workers at Fox had about her, there was consensus about her unyielding dedication and expertise.

With a Song in My Heart, wrapped up in August of 1951, was released early in 1952, just before the televised Academy Awards. It would become the film most closely associated with the first and more glamorous half of Susan's long career; it represented the summation of all of her technical skills. To wring tears, she did her orgasmic Latin girl, broke up on cue, suffered in her inimitable way. (The audience got throat lumps when she cried out to Thelma Ritter, as her best friend, "Oh, Clancy, they're going to yank off my leg. What am I going to do?") She used karate chops and other sudden movements in her mimed song-and-dance numbers. She was technical perfection.

She received her third Academy Award nomination, losing this time to Shirley Booth for *Come Back, Little Sheba*. During 1952, *With a Song in My Heart* turned into a huge grosser, one of the three most popular films of the year, and pushed Susan higher than she has ever been before. Fox was flooded with her fan mail. The fan-magazine awards (from *Photoplay*, *Motion Picture*, *Box Office*, others) cascaded. The Foreign Press gave Susan and John Wayne their 1952 award as the most popular stars in the world. The American Beauticians Congress voted her "the most beautiful redhead in the world" and the National Florists Association crowned her their queen.

Just before *With a Song in My Heart* was released, Zanuck squeezed her into *The Snows of Kilimanjaro*, based on a Hemingway short story about a writer dying in Africa and mulling over his past loves. Gregory Peck, a polite, outgoing actor, played the Hemingway character, Ava Gardner had the main female role as his earlier lover, seen in flashback, and Susan played the wife in the present who nurses him through. Susan received second billing because her name sold movie tickets, but the film was Peck's and Gardner's. As the wife, Susan played "technical" sincerity, doing her usual tricks with her eyes and outstretched arms, and only made Ava Gardner (with whom she shared no scenes) look better. It was not a good movie for her, nor was her next. While all of America was worshiping her in *With a Song in My Heart*, Zanuck was thinking about his coffers and shipped Susan off to RKO-Radio in return for big money from Howard Hughes. Hughes' pet film, *The Lusty Men*, directed by Nicholas Ray, was an interesting real-life-type movie about rodeo riders and their oppressed wives, but did nothing for her. She certainly must have known that the months she spent working on it would be wasted ones, for, while she was competent in it, her performance lacked drive. In the released print, there are times when her eyes go dead and she seems bored.

Toward the end of the year, Zanuck found something decent for her, *The President's Lady*, a biography of Rachel Jackson, based on Irving Stone's novel. She was appealing as Andrew Jackson's scandal-ridden wife, although she and Charlton Heston received mixed notices. Part of the problem may have been Zanuck's decision to make the film in black and white when the story clearly deserved treatment as a spectacle. Nevertheless, it made money. All of Susan's movies did.

It was an ongoing struggle. Even at the height of her popularity, Zanuck made her do four or five movie "jobs" for every *With a Song in My Heart* that he gave her. She had to fight for her good scripts, along with all the other ladies at Fox. It was the continuing injustice of the seven-year-contract system.

Darryl Zanuck had already begun production, late in 1953, on a jungle fantasy-adventure called *White Witch Doctor*. He had decided to spend some $600,000 sending a crew to Africa to film all the jungle backdrops and bring back "real things" from the Bakuba tribe there: beadwork, money skins, religious relics and anything else that looked exotic. He hadn't yet assigned the stars because he preferred to shoot them on the Fox lot and have "Africa" emblazoned on screens behind them; that way, he could personally keep an eye on every aspect of the production: camera, lights, hair and costumes. It was the same mistake other moguls were making in Hollywood's losing war against television.

The script had to do with a nurse on her way to heal African natives, her mercenary guide who falls in love with her, and a few gun-toting villains who cause the natives' spears to fly. Susan and Robert Mitchum got the assignments. She usually followed orders, but when she found out that Robert Mitchum, with whom she had worked (at arms' length) in *The Lusty Men*, hated the script as much as she, she went with Mitchum to Zanuck's office and flatly refused to work on *White Witch Doctor* unless a new script was ordered. Zanuck begged them both to begin work, since he would have to pay their substantial salaries for the months it would take to have a new script written and he already had $600,000 invested. They said no. Nervous Zanuck then called in reliable Henry Hathaway to ask his opinion of the script. "Jesus, Darryl," he said, "I don't blame them. It's a lousy script." Hathaway suggested that he (Hathaway) could revamp it quickly. Zanuck said he would think about it.

What happened next is revealing. Within an hour, Hathaway received a call from Zanuck, who said, "Henry, if you can do anything at all with the script, I'll give you a couple of writers. I can't lose a million if I make the picture. There is no way to lose it with those two people in it." (His thinking was thus: He had already spent more than half of the film's budget on exteriors. Even with the world's worst script, enough people would pay to see Susan and Mitchum for him to be better off making the picture than not.) With Hathaway now in charge of the writers and also assigned as the new director, Susan and Mitchum agreed to work. The rewriting was done in two weeks. For all the fuss, however, the actors never had to leave Twentieth Century-Fox's back lot while they suposely endured the heat and the tsetse flies.

Henry Hathaway and Susan were never friendly and would grow increasingly irritable with one another as they worked on more films together. It was an antipathy that was under the surface, only occasionally whiplashing into an occurrence that anyone else would see. Hathaway was basically a man's director and always the center of his own working world, which tended to be an outdoors, physical one. He had great expertise and control of that world. Susan was never comfortable in anyone else's universe and so, during every Hathaway film, she would withdraw even more than was her habit on sets. Sometimes, he would try to break the ice with her and joke, but, as he says, "she would stay where she was and wouldn't crack a smile, then turn around and walk away and never say anything." Anyone close to Hathaway she would shun. Normally, she was more human with lower-on-the-ladder males, such as assistant directors. But the A.D. on *White Witch Doctor*, Gerd Oswald, reports that he couldn't get near her, even though his sister and Susan had once been quite friendly. "She knew that I was close to Henry Hathaway, so immediately there was a block formed there," says Oswald. "Also, my extremely close friendship with Mitchum: I spent all of my time in his dressing room, which was right next to hers, so it was a natural animosity."

Hathaway grew to dislike Susan intensely. "She always had that stoic, coldly appraising look, as if to say, 'Prove it.' She was a belligerent bitch. She was a little twisted, twisted in her walk. It was a thing that was in her nature, in her head. She always walked a little sideways, stood a little sideways." What made Susan avoid him? "I think this was a deliberate thing, her never wanting to become involved with anybody in the business. Instead of making friendships, she would walk away from everything and keep it on a lower level: with makeup people and hairdressers. She would go to dinner with them, but never the top echelon, where she thought she might be hurt."

Because of Hathaway's personal feelings about Susan, his assessment of her abilities are all the more interesting. "She was competent and had enormous belief in herself. Lord knows, she was never insecure about her acting. She was capable of any kind of emotion and doing it well. She never had to be prodded into doing anything. I would talk to her about what I thought should be done and that was it." He recalls that she was "camera wise"— would always note where the camera was and, without being instructed, tilt her face toward it. (She favored the left side.) She also loved to stand with her hands on her hips during scenes; it was part of her Latin-girl routine. "A little awkward, I thought," Hathaway says.

Even Susan's tremendous physical stamina couldn't sustain her through her eleven back-to-back films at Fox and RKO without some sort of artificial propping. She had begun using sleeping pills to counteract her physical exhaustion, which, combined with the moderate drinking she and Jess did at home, acted to put a sharp edge on her nervous system. In the winter of 1953, she did finally convince Zanuck to give her her long-postponed vacation.

She left the boys at home and took Jess to Paris, where they began a two-month motoring trip through France and Spain, talking to reporters here and there to keep Zanuck happy.

To Susan, the jaunt was meant as much for rest and recreation as for a clarification of her deteriorating marriage. The situation of Jess's lack of income and her burgeoning one had not changed, nor had her ambivalent feelings toward maintaining all the control. She had been seriously thinking about divorce for several years now. Actually, she had never really abandoned her earliest impulse to end it all if the going with him got too rough.

What made the two-month vacation all too real was the fact that *she* was taking Jess, paying expenses away from home as she did at Longridge Avenue. One can imagine her feelings when Jess remarked to the press such things as "She spends money like molasses."

In April of 1953, they were back to Hollywood, where she began work on *Demetrius and the Gladiators,* Fox's quick follow-up to *The Robe,* the first picture to use the new CinemaScope process. Once again, she was being used as glamorous window dressing, despite her hard-earned laurels. *The Robe,* based on the Lloyd C. Douglas novel, had been about the conversation of a Roman soldier (Richard Burton) through the powers of the red robe that Christ wore before his crucifixion. After the soldier willingly becomes a martyr, his Christian friend, the former slave Demetrius (Victor Mature), retrieves and hides the magic robe. So begins the sequel, *Demetrius and the Gladiators,* which cast Susan in her old bitch role as Messalina, a temptress and adulteress who takes possession of Demetrius. The film, a top grosser, was a blatant misuse of Susan's time and talents.

All during the filming, she brooded over her marriage, saying little to Victor Mature or anyone else.

A few months earlier, Susan had hired Cleo Miller, a tall, handsome black woman, as a live-in housekeeper. Cleo was a most sympathetic person, the same age as Susan, and she became one of Susan's chief confidantes. They would meet in the kitchen to exchange girl-talk; in the bedroom to sit on the bed and read Susan's dream-analysis books. For Susan, the friendship became a welcome respite from the tensions of her work and her marriage. She would tell Cleo secret things, such as her feelings about her

Left: The "watching girl" photo. Edythe, at nine or ten, watches impassively her sister dominates the foreground (just as she did the family's entions) with her physical skills. *(Courtesy of Florence Marrenner Dietrich)*

Right: At sixteen, Florence was the family star. *(Courtesy of Florence Marrenner Dietrich)*

ve: The three Marrenner children, about 1920, one block from the Church nue tenement. Wally, far left, was seven; Edythe was three; Florrie, ind hedge, was ten. *(Courtesy of Florence Marrenner Dietrich)*

Edythe and Florence a few years later,
about 1928. *(Doug McClelland collection)*

Edythe, age eighteen, with Walter Thornton, who gave her a modeling job
in 1936. (The model at center is unidentified.) *(Courtesy of Wally Marrenner)*

"A favorite early still, taken in 1938 shortly after Edythe Marrenner became Susan Hayward." *(Courtesy of Wally Marrenner)*

Above: Susan spent much of her mere six months at Warner Bros. posing for photos like these three. No one at the studio thought she could act. *(Courtesy of Wally Marrenner)*

Opposite: They would eventually be on top of the world but they didn't know it then. Susan and Ronald Reagan did this publicity still for Warner Bros. in 1938. *(Courtesy of Wally Marrenner)*

Top: Susan's first film for Paramount was the 1939 "A" picture *Beau Geste*. She only had a handful of lines, but they were opposite Robert Preston, Gary Cooper and Ray Milland. *(Doug McClelland collection)*

Above: After *Beau Geste*, Susan's relegation to "B" films like the 1939 *Our Leading Citizen* (here with Bob Burns and Al Williams) filled her with bitterness toward the studio executives. *(Gene Arceri collection)*

op: Paramount put Susan into a group of promising new players called
he Golden Circle. From left, top row: Louise Campbell, Betty Field,
oseph Allen, Ellen Drew, Judith Barrett; center row: Robert Preston,
atricia Morison, Susan, William Henry; sitting: Joyce Matthews, Janice
ogan, William Holden, Evelyn Keyes. *(Doug McClelland collection)*

bove: Her big break was a 1941 loan-out to Columbia for *Adam Had Four Sons*,
pposite Warner Baxter and Ingrid Bergman. *(Doug McClelland collection)*

The beautiful bitch in *I Married a Witch*, 1942. *(Gene Arceri collection)*

Reap the Wild Wind, 1942, with Ray Milland, Paulette Goddard and John Wayne, was Susan's biggest part to date in her own studio. *(Doug McClelland collection)*

own body. She hated her legs, she said, thought she looked plain without makeup, and told Cleo that the two things she was truly proud of were her hair and—as Susan put it—her "boobs": "Oh, I know I've got big boobs, Cleo, and I'm glad." Then the two would laugh.

After Cleo began working at Longridge Avenue, Susan convinced Cleo's husband to come from San Francisco to live in the house, and soon afterward invited Cleo's seventeen-year-old daughter, Willie Jean, to join them as well. Susan encouraged Cleo to invite relatives from Texas to visit, and treated them with great respect. Cleo had been warned by friends that Susan Hayward acted like a monster to employees, and found her generosity overwhelming. "She was a doll," says Cleo.

Susan won her absolute loyalty. Cleo saw, day after day, her employer arise at four or five in the morning, leave the house in a studio limousine, come home exhausted from the studio quite late, usually missing supper; and she saw that Jess did not wake until noon, since he had a habit of staying up all night reading papers; and Cleo would feel sorry for the unfairness of Susan's domestic life. She wonders if Jess didn't also find the situation strange because she recalls him once saying to her, "If anybody had said to me in Georgia, sitting under my father's pecan trees, that I would be sitting on my fanny today, I would never have believed it."

She does not remember many arguments between Susan and Jess—apparently that was all done by now—but on those rare occasions when Susan's mother came to the house, there would be rows over Jess. Ellen Marrenner would tell her daughter that her husband was a bum and that there had to be something "wrong with that man." She had picked up on Jess's lyrical walk, quite charming though meaningless in itself, and used that as *prima facie* evidence that Jess wasn't normal. That was nonsense, of course, but Susan was forced to deny such accusations repeatedly. They had their effect on her.

Demetrius and the Gladiators was completed the first week of July 1953, leaving Susan particularly moody and irritable. There had been much activity in the Sherman Oaks house. For years, Susan had been inviting her old friend from Brooklyn, Martha Little, to come to Los Angeles every Christmas to stay at the house and create hand-made decorations for the tree. Susan was shocked to discover that young Martha was now dying of cancer, and insisted that Martha move in and receive care from physicians at Susan's expense.

During her long stay at the house, Martha would sit in the kitchen and say, "Cleo, this is the last time I'll be with you." Cleo would reply, "No, Martha, honey," and put her arms around her and they would hug and kiss.

On the evening of July 16, 1953, Martha was sickly and had gone to bed early. So had the twins. Susan and Jess sat alone reading in their living room. Cleo was off that evening, while her sister replaced her, but she later heard from Susan about the first argument that Jess and Susan had that night: "He started up. He asked her for $3000 to invest in Dallas, Texas, oil shares. She said no, she wouldn't let him have the money. She said, 'Get yourself a job.' He said, 'I am an actor. What do you want me to be, a department-store clerk or a filling-station attendant?' She said, 'Whatever...if it's an honest living. But I'm not going to let you have the money.'"

What began so routinely turned gradually into a shriek. It grew late. He was fully dressed and she was naked under a terry-cloth bathrobe, for she slept in the raw. The Barkers continued talking, and Jess confided a childhood incident involving his mother. Suddenly, Susan made an unpleasant remark about her and snapped, "Possibly that's what's wrong with you. I think you're queer." Then she went into a tirade against him that included a demand for a divorce. He refused. "Why?" she asked. She would later report that he replied: "Because you're a good meal ticket." Her tirade continued. He struck her. She struck back, biting him hard on the left arm. The night was turning surreal: in no time there was smacking, shoving, socking. Their anger gushed from the living room to the garden area, where Susan ran, screaming: "Don't kill me! Please, somebody...help me! Don't kill me!" The neighbors were awakened, but nobody interfered. He dragged her back to their bedroom, gave her a spanking and warned her to cool off. She rushed out into the night, screaming again, and Jess picked her up, brought her to the pool and threw her in, her terry-cloth bathrobe still clinging. Susan would later say that he held her head underwater and that she now feared for her life. She emerged naked from the pool and went peaceably back to her bedroom, while Jess went out to the driveway to calm down. Next, he saw her come out of the house and into the driveway, fully dressed, a scarf over her head and the dog in her arms. She began walking down the street in the dark. Jess forced her back to the front door, where, suddenly, Martha Little appeared, shouting, "Stop it! Stop it!" Jess asked Martha to put Susan to bed, but, unstoppable, Susan ran inside and began dialing the police. It wasn't necessary. A few seconds later, they arrived at the door. Jess only said one apologetic word to them: "Domestic."

Susan and Jess, who never had less than two drinks every evening, must have been quite tight that night, although neither one of them would admit it. There was something oddly sexual about all the violence, which did not appear to be anything like wife-beating but rather an extreme form of a kind of sexual confrontation. She was relentlessly catlike, while his response was an elaborate pattern.

The events of that energetic evening ended with Susan's calling a cab and taking Martha Little to her mother's for the night. The next morning, her eye blackened, bruises here and there, she came back to the house with her brother and Vernon Wood, her business manager, and asked Jess to leave, which he did without a fuss, going to a motel in Encino. A few days later, he came back to the house to see the boys, flowers in hand for Susan. She thought they were quite lovely, but had already begun meetings with a divorce lawyer.

For the next few months, Jess and Susan maintained an informal separation, although he badly wanted a reconciliation, as did the twins, who couldn't understand why their father was living in a motel. She finally agreed to consider resuming the marriage if both she and Jess began seeing a psychiatrist who would advise them on how to live together. Meanwhile, Jess visited the boys frequently.

By the end of summer, Susan had decided on a divorce, but hadn't yet told Jess. She took the twins to Hawaii for ten days. When they returned, Jess came over on Labor Day to take the twins to see their mother in *White Witch Doctor*. Father and sons returned to the house around six. Susan, who was entertaining a married couple, Mr. and Mrs. Dorsen, politely asked Jess to join them for a drink beside the pool. Once there, Jess said he wanted a word with Susan, and the Dorsens walked off. He wanted to talk about getting back together. Susan said she had decided on a divorce, a Nevada quickie, and would offer him a substantial settlement, saying, "How does it feel to know you're going to receive a hundred thousand dollars at the end of the week?" He remarked in amazement, "Is that all?" But he didn't want a settlement; he wanted her back. Then she became uncomfortable and asked him to leave, while he insisted on working things out there. She walked away from him, lit a cigarette, came to his side again, looked at the end of her cigarette and said, "I ought to push this right in your eye." Once again, she invoked that violent sexual chemistry and Jess appropriately responded, "You haven't got the guts." She pushed the cigarette toward his face and he blocked the jab with his hand and arm, apparently hitting her inadvertently, for the next instant she began yelling that she had been struck. The Dorsens rushed back to the pool area and suggested that Jess have a drink and leave, but before Jess could be handed a whiskey, Susan grabbed it and threw it in Jess's face. "You hit me! You hit me!" Susan kept yelling, while Jess followed her as she moved, shouting, so his boys could overhear, "I didn't hit you! Tell the truth! I'll not leave this house until you tell the truth!" But he did leave. Susan's divorce action was filed the following day.

With her divorce decision now irrevocable, Susan faced a personal chasm of unknown dimensions. Her daytime nervousness and sleeplessness at night only became worse. Her mother was helping her look after the boys, who were not happy and often grew perplexed as the war between their parents deepened. Susan had few friends to prop her. There was Ned Marin, her agent with the Charles Feldman Agency, who became a regular escort to all those functions that Jess normally would have taken her to. There was also Howard Hughes, whom Susan had known personally for years (not counting her dates with him while she was still at Warners).

She was one of a handful of his favorite actresses, and through his close ties with Darryl Zanuck, he was always anxious to borrow her for RKO. For some nine months, just after the breakup with Jess, the two of them dated regularly. She introduced him to the boys as "Mr. Magic" and Hughes flew Susan, either alone or with the twins, all over Arizona and New Mexico in his planes. He often came to the house, dozens of yellow roses for Susan in his arms, and Susan animatedly catered to his whims. Cleo, who baked apple pies for him (he would eat a whole one at a sitting), recalls him as looking "tall, wrinkly, reddish, like a tramp, never a dime in his pocket." Susan would tell Cleo stories about how Howard would take her to restaurants and not have enough money with him to pay the bill. Cleo thought him nice, even though Hughes, a Southerner, treated her and her family standoffishly. Florence says that Susan, at this time, told her mother that she and Hughes were growing serious and "I may become the next Mrs. Howard Hughes," but Cleo is sure it was just friendship. Susan told her there was no physical attraction and Cleo could see that Howard was shy and sexless around Susan. The relationship apparently came to an abrupt end when Susan, uninvited, looked up Hughes in Florida and found him involved with another movie star. Susan returned to Hollywood and told Ellen Marrenner the relationship was over.

And there was Ira Grossel, who had once been the chubby Flatbush Jewish boy with a flare for acting and a crush on pretty Edythe Marrenner. He had come to Hollywood in the mid-forties and everything about him had changed. He was now swarthily good-looking, spoke in measured masculine tones and was known only by the name of Jeff Chandler, a star of "B" Westerns. Once in a great while, some old friend, like Wally Marrenner, would stun him by calling out, "Hey, Ira!" around the studios. It was not amazing that, with her world caving in, Susan would welcome calls from Ira/"Jeff," nor that Ira, his own marriage to an actress having gone awry, would seek out a relationship with his child-hood girlfriend. They saw one another on and off immediately after Susan's separation, eventually becoming an item in the columns.

Early in November, Susan and Jess had to meet at the Children's Court of Reconciliation for some obligatory talk about reconciliation. (They only succeeded in causing a public dispute between the judge and a social worker over which one was to be photographed with the famous movie couple.) Jess intended to contest the divorce, which was scheduled for trial early the following year. Susan feared the publicity would be dreadful for the boys, not to mention her career. She had to concentrate on her new project, *Garden of Evil*, a Western which was to be filmed late in November in various out-of-the-way locations in Mexico. She intented to take the twins. Jess struck the first real blow in the developing divorce battle when his lawyer filed a motion to prevent her from taking the boys to the locations. Certain he was just using the boys to get at her, she retaliated by having her lawyers file a motion barring Jess from staying with the twins at the house. Her mother would look after them while she was away.

Garden of Evil would be her third film with Henry Hathaway, not the most soothing director for the nervous shape she was in. Their mutual antagonism would reach new levels during the months to follow. She also resented the movie, which was a lackluster kind of *Treasure of the Sierra Madre*, about four men and a woman on a search for gold within ancient Mexican ruins, and the human evil that destroys all but Gary Cooper and Susan, who literally ride off into the sunset at the end. Despite the derivative plot, Zanuck knew that his stars, who included Richard Widmark and Cameron Mitchell, together with the new wide-screen CinemaScope process and a dozen exotic Mexican locations, would ensure success.

Susan's extreme nervousness showed on camera and fairly ruined her performance. She was like a Susan Hayward robot. Henry Hathaway thought she wasn't doing her best because she was angry at having to do the film. She was just at loose ends.

The nervousness translated into an unusually independent stance toward Hathaway and the others. The first part of December, the traveling company settled at Parícutin Mountain, a volcano in picturesque terrain. Cameron Mitchell, who developed a crush on Susan, remembers an incident between Susan and Hathaway during that part of the shooting: "Henry Hathaway is a very nice man, but on the set he can be difficult. He couldn't drink coffee in the morning and he resented other people drinking it. So we were in this very primitive place and Hank, the generator man, would make this marvelous coffee with his generator. Susan was drinking the coffee with her long, beautiful hair and in that feminine way of hers. Hathaway would never yell at her. He yelled at Stan Hough, our assistant director, using profanity: 'Stan, I told you we won't have any damn coffee-drinking on this set. Anyone drinks coffee, they got to get off my set and when they finish they can come back and go to work.'" What probably made the remark even more cutting to Susan was that young, good-looking Stan Hough (who would later become a producer and the husband of Jean Peters) had become Susan's only real confidant during shooting and her main defense against the strong-minded Hathaway. "So Susan," says Cameron Mitchell, "very quietly took her cup of coffee and went to Mexico City for a week. Every time they called her, she said she wasn't finished with her coffee yet."

With Henry Hathaway, she could be feisty and belligerent, but professional and reasonable as well. She was not being herself at all the morning that Hathaway spotted her dressed and ready in her dressing room and sent Stan Hough over to bring her back for an early take. Hathaway says, "Stan came back and said, 'I don't want to tell you all this, but she looked at her watch and said, "Well, is it nine o'clock?"'" So I went over to her dressing room and said, 'We're ready to work and I see you're ready.' She said, 'Is it nine o'clock?' I said, 'No.' She said, 'My contract says I work at nine.' And I said, 'Your contract also says you work from nine until six. And I want to tell you something, lady. I am going to work you every fucking night until six o'clock. You've been getting off at four-thirty and five. How do you like that? I am going to work you all day and save your close-ups for after five at night. And one minute to six I'm going to let you go.' She said, 'You can't take a joke, can you? I was only kidding.'" Hathaway says that he cursed her and walked away. She immediately came over to him and said, "I'm ready to work."

She was obviously greatly distracted, but alert enough at Parícutin Mountain to save the life of a small Indian boy. While the cameras were setting up, he slipped and was about to fall many feet on the mountain when Susan spotted him and grabbed him. She paid the tab on her own rescue from a high fall years before in Georgia while she was making *I'd Climb the Highest Mountain.*

Just before Christmas, Susan learned that, because she and the others were in Mexico on complicated work permits, none of the actors and crew could join their families at home for Christmas.

Susan had to be with the twins this year. There had been too much disruption of their family life. Somehow, through a series of connections, she alone in the company received permission to leave and return. Over the holidays, she learned that Jess had defied the court's order and come into the house to be with his sons, and she became furious. Jess was equally furious. He had learned that his mother-in-law had told his sons, "I could kill your father." The war threatened to become a prolonged one and was wearing everyone down.

When she got back to the Mexican location, she was especially high-strung. Tinges of that sexual violence which had first appeared in her relations with Jess began surfacing again.

The *Garden of Evil* company thought it was loathsomely selfish of Susan to have used tricks to go home for Christmas when everyone else wanted to leave but couldn't. They "excommunicated" her from normal human exchanges for the entire week of her return. Cameron Mitchell, attracted to her, couldn't bear her exclusion and her great unhappiness, which at the time he believed to be from a bad affair with Jeff Chandler. (That relationship was never corroborated.) Meanwhile, the company received an invitation to attend a Mexican New Year's Eve party at the Cuernavaca estate of Bruno Pagliai, Hathaway's friend, who later married Merle Oberon. There was champagne, caviar and appetizers. Hathaway says, "She came in with the assistant director, Stan Hough, looked at the table and said, 'When do we eat?' Bruno said, 'We are going to eat later.' In Mexico, they don't eat until ten o'clock. 'Look,' she said, 'I eat at seven-thirty, and if this is all you got to eat, goodbye.' She was just goddamn mean. She came back later and said she had already eaten." Much later, she, Hathaway and some others went to a café which, Cameron Mitchell says, must have held about nine hundred Mexicans. She sat between Cameron and the script girl, Rose Steinberg. Susan had already had a few brandies when Mitchell, who she knew was interested in her, leaned over to whisper "Happy New Year" in her ear. With her long fingernails, she clawed one side of his face, making a sound like a cat. Blood gushed from the nail wounds. Everyone was startled. Rose Steinberg remembers looking at his face and crying out, "My God, he's going to have to work!" Hathaway had to halt shooting for two days until the scabs were small enough to be covered with makeup. Mitchell can still show the scars.

The cat-like hurtful behavior which had only recently appeared in Susan was indeed odd. Another man also claimed to have received scars from her nails. At the time that she began exhibiting this violent sexuality, she had also begun seeing a therapist for what she would later describe as frigidity. Her violence may have begun as part of the divorce war, but also appeared to be her cure for a deeply ingrained problem.

The therapist, the new violence seemed to be but parts of some larger mysterious process of emerging. She was violating all of her old taboos, experimenting with change. For one, her conversation could now be peppered with four-letter words. The days when a four-letter word so shocked her that she felt compelled to slap the utterer had vanished. For another, and far more profoundly, she was violating old sexual taboos. She attempted a handful of affairs even while seeing the therapist, her very first excursions away from her marriage bed. They were new and upsetting to her. She told Cleo about her discoveries, and now there was a good deal of guilt, too.

During her years with Jess, Susan would drink heavily for periods, especially between films (she liked to switch from hard liquor to wine just before beginning a picture to keep her weight down). The drinking, however, was always within reason. But the disruptions in her old monogamous pattern of living caused her to drink differently. Late at night, she would drink herself into a stupor. Cleo observed, "She didn't like to go out that much. She'd just get her bottle and have a good time. She'd drink until she couldn't drink any more and then she'd go to bed. You'd find her on the couch, you'd find her on the floor. She'd say, 'I'm cold, Cleo. Wrap me up. I'm cold...cold.' But she was naked as anything come into the world—lying on the couch in the nude." Cleo would worry that the boys, asleep upstairs, might see their mother that way and she would hurry to cover Susan.

At the party of radio man Bill Ballance, whom she dated, she passed out on the floor, quite snokered.

Nothing had ever been easy for Susan, but the divorce trial, which began as soon as she returned from Mexico, was sheer pain.

Jess had rejected the $100,000 settlement, saying he wanted it in a lump sum as community property, not, as she was offering it, as alimony-type payments spread out over ten years. Testimony started in mid-February of 1954. The newspapers loved it. Susan gave her version of the violent July quarrel that had started the divorce action, pursuing in great, righteous detail the beating, the chase into the garden and around the pool, the dunking and the "bruises...mostly on my fanny." Then she narrated the Labor Day violence. She told of her frustration over Jess's refusal to work, his alleged laziness, the boys' confusion over why their father lay around the house all day while other fathers went to work. Later, Jess testified, rebutting her accusations of violence, portraying himself as a husband who had good reason to be indignant toward a nasty wife. He had merely slapped Susan for calling him "queer" and had later given her a spanking and a dunking when she refused to stop screaming. When asked why he refused to get steady work, he replied, "Mrs. Barker knew I was an actor when she married me." A maid who lived next door also testified, telling the court that she had seen a man chasing a naked woman around a pool while the woman kept screaming for her life. It all made hot copy for weeks.

The numerous testimonies were jammed with distracting details. The attorneys actually had an accountant testify about the Barkers' respective incomes, stating that in 1951 Jess earned $318.75 while Susan made $163,692. But the most revealing moments were when Susan told the courtroom that she no longer loved Jess and, in his turn, Jess told the same courtroom, while looking straight at Susan, that he was still in love with her.

Over the next four months, the court would make a series of decisions in the case. Susan was immediately awarded custody of the twins, with Jess receiving once-a-week visitation rights. In June, the divorce was granted, and in August the court ruled against Jess's community-property claim, awarding him nothing more than a Ford station wagon and some cash for his attorneys' fees. The pre-nuptial agreement he and Susan had signed eliminated him from a community-property award. Jess had lost everything, except, perhaps, his youth, his good looks and the love of his sons.

Time would tell that Jess's decision to endure a trial had not only robbed him of a comfortable settlement but would further devastate his career. In the months and years to follow, he would work only sporadically as an actor, in the wake of all those ugly revelations of his and Susan's domestic life. Perhaps Jess had believed that only through openly declaring his love for Susan in court could he win her back.

A kind of nobility about Jess would always be overlooked. What no one bothered to notice during the trial was that, for all of his supposed failure as a provider, he had never been unfaithful to his wife. He had also been absolutely loyal to Susan in keeping to himself her pre-marital pregnancy and various other details of her life that would have harmed her career. To this day, he refuses to discuss Susan in any disparaging way. He remains the gentleman that she had first loved.

Susan categorically refused to appear in *The Conqueror*, Howard Hughes' six-million-dollar epic about the rise of Genghis Khan, the thirteenth-century Mongol warrior who conquered half of Asia. She was to play Bortai, the Tartar princess with whom John Wayne, as the emerging Khan, would fall in love while Susan did half-naked sword dances, got captured in caravans, kicked a black panther and rode all over the Utah desert being "fiery." The script she read was juvenile, but Hughes insisted on her, offering to pay Zanuck dearly. Susan agreed only when Zanuck threatened suspension.

She was angry over the coercion and at first difficult to work with. Bob Sidney, the choreographer on *The Conqueror*, recalls visiting her house on Longridge Avenue with the costume designer, Michael Woulfe, for her to look at Woulfe's early designs. She came to the door herself and Woulfe introduced himself. Susan looked at Bob Sidney and asked who he was. He explained.

"Why are you here? Who needs you?" she snapped to Bob.

A clever, agile man, he was not the sort to be put down easily. He did a little routine at the door to the words, "Well, I was told that people are very hospitable here, and if I come to your house, you have got to be polite, don't you?"

She loved it and broke out laughing: "Oh, come on in."

Michael Woulfe carted in his costume sketches and showed them to Susan. He had already known the sort of clothes she liked—not frilly things, but spare, clinging constructions that would show off her excellent hips but underplay her legs, which she found hatefully thin. Susan looked at each sketch and blurted, in a rising litany, "Hate it! Hate *it*! Hate IT! Don't like anything! No!"

Michael Woulfe, who had worked hard on Susan's behalf, became upset. Bob went back to the director, Dick Powell, and told him what she had done to Woulfe, saying, "She's a monster!" Powell became hysterical and went to Susan himself, telling her that she was needlessly endangering a man's job. (That wasn't true. Howard Hughes greatly admired Woulfe's work.) When she heard that, she approved the clothing designs.

Susan grew fond of Bob Sidney, who, in his animation, was every bit a match for Susan's acidity. Early in their work on *The Conqueror*, Bob reminded her that he had met her years before at Dick Wyman's house while she had been married to Jess Barker. Susan said, to Bob's recollection, "You must have made no impression. I don't remember you."

Bob countered the meanness. "You're sweet. The only reason I remembered you was because you had all this dyed red hair."

He knew he was playing with fire. Susan went wild and screamed, *"It wasn't dyed! Then!* You're going too far." Then she smiled and said, "If I ever hit you, you'll know it." Bob had taken the risk and won her over.

She and Bob laughed over the idiotic script, which had all the characters talking in backward English so that the audience would be impressed with the historical nature of the film. John Wayne had to say lines like "Go now from my sight, brother of mine." With his eyes slanted and a Fu Manchu mustache pasted on, he looked and sounded ridiculous, which he knew. Throughout the film, Susan had to be devilishly angry at Wayne, who says the line to her, "You are byootiful in yer wrath." His fans would never recover from the shock.

Despite her recalcitrance, Susan was utterly professional during the filming, which was done partially at Hughes' studio and partially in the Utah desert. There had been a fire on the RKO set at the very moment Susan was rehearsing. Actresses were screaming and scurrying. Bob Sidney said she thought nothing of it and kept on performing like Nero. She was afraid of nothing. In the hot July desert, she rode and jumped horses herself, with no stand-in. There was a scene in which John Wayne had to pull Susan brutally from her caravan and subdue her. She chose to do the scene herself, even though her body was particularly sensitive at the time. Dick Powell called for numerous takes. In agony after each, Susan would go to Bob Sidney and say, "He's hurting me, the son of a bitch." Her arms were black and blue, but she refused to say a word to Wayne.

(She would not have complained to him, for, in fact, she had a crush on Duke, who was manly, courteous and outgoing with her. Cleo recalls Susan, at the St. George, Utah location, spending much of her free time with Wayne and Pilar Weldy, the woman he would marry, and sensed the jealousy that Susan felt. One night, Susan's building anger over the divorce situation, and her complicated relationship with Wayne and Pilar, whom she liked, caused her to act out a steamy little drama during a party Wayne gave at his rented house. She pulled off her shoes, gave Pilar one and mock-challenged her: "Let's fight." Later, a soused Susan made Wayne take her back to her own house a few blocks away, kicking him continuously in the rear end as they walked. Once there, she asked Duke and Willie Jean, Cleo's daughter, to go for a ride, and while driving she pulled off her $3000 diamond ring—she had bought it herself as a kind of second wedding ring—and tossed it into the pitch-black desert, quite as if she were throwing Jess away! The ring was never recovered.)

From the start of production, Susan had said she would not learn to do the sword dance required in the script, but would appear in two close-ups in the dance scene to give the appearance that she was dancing. When time came to film the close-ups, Susan came on the set wearing nothing but a bra-halter with spangles and a diaphanous skirt which merely suggested her legs.

Bob had hired a dancer to do the sword dance in long shots, along with two other girls who were to be part of the dance. In veils and spangles, Susan was evil from the moment she saw the three of them. After a bit of icy politeness to the girls, she asked to see the dances performed.

The girl danced for Susan and was, as Bob says, exciting and strong, with a manner similar to Susan's, even down to the odd walk. Susan became frantic and abruptly asked for an explanation of her close-ups in relation to the dance she had just seen. Bob reminded her that she had washed her hands of the dance. So why couldn't she do it now? she said, kicking off her shoes. She forced him to rehearse her that very minute, and for weeks afterward Susan drove Bob mad with relentless daily sessions to learn the routine and build up her legs. *She* suddenly became the taskmaster. Bob admired her willpower, but, exhausted, he would stop a long rehearsal with "Susan, I'm bored with this. Enough!"

When the day finally came to shoot the sword-dance long shots, Susan and the girl dancer both showed up on the stage in costume. Susan had told Bob that he could use his own judgment about who was to do the long shots, but once they were on the stage Susan never even allowed the girl to get lined up with the camera, saying, "I'm doing it." Susan did the entire dance scene herself and was fabulous.

That summer, the winds blew hard through the Utah desert, whipping up the sand around the actors and crew of *The Conqueror*, blowing tiny particles into their faces. No one on the movie set knew of the potential hazard in those desert windstorms. In May, just before the production began, the United States government had set off an atomic bomb in the Nevada desert, above ground, near the movie location. Susan, Dick Powell, Agnes Moorehead, Pedro Armendariz, John Wayne, art director Carroll Clark all felt the desert wind in their faces.

At the completion of *The Conqueror* in September, Susan was immediately to begin *Untamed*, her best movie script at Fox in more than a year. Meanwhile, her domestic life continued to be strained. She resented Jess's using the courts to keep her from taking the boys with her to movie locations, which meant she had to tell Zanuck she would prefer not to travel. That presented a problem, for more and more films were being shot away from Hollywood. She was so angry at Jess for the interference that she barely spoke to him when he came to the house on Wednesdays to see the boys.

Untamed would later be referred to as a kind of South African *Gone with the Wind*, about spunky Irish Katie O'Neill, who journeys to South Africa with a husband she marries for convenience, builds a life, remeets the Boer leader (Tyrone Power) who had fathered her baby, loses her husband, is fought over by the Boer and another South African (Richard Egan) and finally settles down with the Boer. Zanuck accommodated Susan's complicated divorce situation by sending a filming crew to South Africa, as he had for *White Witch Doctor*, to capture background footage of the South African countryside, thousands of attacking Zulu warriors and various prowling snakes and lions, then projecting all the African footage on rear screens while in front of them Susan, Ty Power and Richard Egan emoted comfortably on a Twentieth Century-Fox soundstage. Susan especially liked two people on this movie— Richard Egan and assistant director Stan Hough, with whom she was again working.

While *The Conqueror* would not be released for another year and a half, *Untamed* was finished September 30 and released early in 1955. The reviews were mixed, but on the positive side. Before that release, however, Zanuck had already assigned her to one of those clinkers that could only partially be salvaged by an exotic location and big-name stars. For *Soldier of Fortune*, he assigned Susan and Clark Gable, who had just signed one of the best deals in Hollywood with Zanuck after twenty years as an MGM contract player. Gable's deal called for him to make two pictures a year, receiving ten percent of gross receipts and $400,000 in salary.

Much of *Soldier of Fortune* was supposed to take place in Hong Kong, where Susan's photographer husband (Gene Barry) is being held by the Red Chinese while Susan and soldier of fortune Gable (in love with her, of course) look for the husband. Zanuck insisted that Susan and Gable go to Hong Kong to shoot the picture. Susan, once again, had to file a court motion for permission to take the boys, and again Jess's attorneys objected, telling the court that Hong Kong was too dangerous for the twins. When she then told Zanuck that under no circumstances could she journey to Hong Kong without the twins, Zanuck did a rather unbelievable thing. He revised the script, sent Gable, director Edward Dmytryk and everyone else in the cast except Susan to Hong Kong for the exterior scenes, and later shot Susan in her scenes with Gable and the others on the Fox soundstages, using rear-screen projection in the few necessary outdoor shots of her. He thought Susan's name now such a box-office draw that he was willing to compromise the scope of his movie.

Sixteen years before, Susan had thought she had a good chance of working with the King in the greatest motion picture ever made.

On *Soldier of Fortune*, she did work well with him, during the handful of weeks that had been reserved for her studio scenes, although on screen they seemed bored with each other and the whole setting.

This was just one in a series of terrible films in which Zanuck paraded her. It must have been clear to Susan that he was burning her up through over-exposure in poor movies, and that without better ones her name would lose its appeal. Zanuck was already building up Marilyn Monroe as Twentieth's new movie queen. Susan's situation at Twentieth had parallels to her years at Paramount, except that now the problem was exploitation rather than the lack of it.

Susan had been a Hollywood contract player now for sixteen years, the normal period of time for a star to rise and fade. She told Stan Hough, while they worked together, that she just didn't trust her stardom. He says, "There were times when she really didn't think she was going to make it, even though she had become a big star. It was for her, like, 'Okay, that was yesterday. We'll have to do it again tomorrow.'"

CHAPTER 5

Crisis

T HE COMPLEX PATTERNS of Susan's internal workings were approaching resolutions, but much too quickly and dangerously. Part of her was still fighting the great divorce-and-custody battles with Jess, with that newly tapped violence now turning inward and against her; and part of her was still competing against every other actress in Hollywood, forcing her into increasingly difficult career maneuvers and further exhaustion.

After reading singer Lillian Roth's best-selling autobiography, *I'll Cry Tomorrow*, Susan, along with a dozen other top actresses, campaigned for the part of the singer who fought her way out of an alcoholic maze. Taking no chances on bungling middlemen, Susan went directly to MGM studio head Dore Schary and asked for the role, while at the same time contacting Roth herself. June Allyson, whom Schary had briefly considered for the part, had no chance against Susan, who rightly pointed out to him that her troubled-women pictures, like *Smash-Up* and *With a Song in My Heart*, had made millions for studios. Susan wasn't personally loved by the moguls, but they respected her money-making ability. With Susan also the choice of Lillian Roth, Schary agreed to lend Spencer Tracy to Fox (for *Broken Lance*) in return for Susan, then gave her free reign in putting together her own film.

Her choice for director was Daniel Mann, who had directed Shirley Booth in *Come Back, Little Sheba* and had just finished *The Rose Tattoo* with Anna Magnani. Mann, who was not Hollywood-wise and had never met a really studio-bred movie star like Susan before, remembers that at their first meeting Susan showed up wearing a plain suit, blouse and gloves and light makeup, and, from behind a shy, businesslike exterior, was clearly sizing him up as they talked about the months of work ahead of them. What Susan saw was a serious man with dark hair, blue eyes and an athletic build; but it wasn't until their first day of shooting, at the El Capitan Theatre at Hollywood and Vine, early in 1955, that Susan was able to get a true look at her director.

The theater had been remodeled to look like the "This Is Your Life" television show that Lillian Roth had appeared on to tell her harrowing alcoholic story to forty million television viewers. Mann had wanted a complex shot, with Susan, as Lillian, walking slowly and deliberately down the aisle toward Ralph Edwards onstage right after Edwards announces, "This is your life . . . Lillian Roth!" while the movie camera follows her and picks up the reactions of the studio audience. An elaborate ramp was built over the tops of seats for the full length of the theater so that the camera could move with Susan. During the first runthrough, Mann noticed that all he could see in the camera lens was Susan's head and shoulders, and not the faces of the audience. Mann turned to his assistant director and the MGM chiefs standing by and told them that he couldn't go on with the shot until the ramps were rebuilt. When reminded that the theater had been contracted for and was loaded with lighting equipment, and that hundreds of extras had to be paid, Mann said that the shot without the audience's faces didn't make any sense and he was going home. "I have a nice backyard and I'll just sit there."

Susan, who had been standing by, was deeply impressed by this kind of dedication. On all her previous films, Susan had never been less than competent and fully involved. Yet, typical of movie stars who had come up the studio ladder, Susan had to put compromise and self-preservation before art. She had always imposed technical tricks between herself and her roles. One of the results was that she was able to keep a lid on that Pandora's box of self-awareness which waited deep in her nature.

Now, for reasons having as much to do with her new director as with the great upheavals happening within and without her—the decision to free herself from a ten-year marriage, the emotional disruptions of sexual experiments, conflicts with her mother, the recent deaths of Martha Little and her agent Ned Marin, the very fact that she was at that critical mid-thirties juncture, and for a galaxy of other reasons that she never properly understood—she chanced the perils of a complete commitment to a role. It would become the biggest and most dangerous gamble of her life.

Mann, who had guided less self-protective actresses through the living hells of emotional roles, recalls feeling fear for Susan at the outset. Her early preparations involved the usual: a trip to Las Vegas to watch Roth perform, then to see the singer herself, several sessions at Alcoholics Anonymous, a visit to seriously ill alcoholics in the local jail to study their delirium tremens and other mannerisms. Method acting schools would have approved. But after filming began, Susan, who had always been detached between scenes and after her filming day, started going into long trances, at times becoming quite unreachable. She brooded all the time and had fists of severe nervousness. She suffered prolonged depressions. Her emotions were no longer coming from some surface place, but from her early years and from deep within the basic problems of her life.

Mann encouraged her in this reliving-rather-than-acting nightmare and was getting wonderful results in the rushes. In one shattering scene, Susan played the drunken Roth sitting at a bar, reciting a childhood job-seeking speech—"I'm Lillian Roth. I'm eight years old. I do imitations and dramatic parts"—and then, when her fellow winos recognize her as the famous singer and laugh at her, she begins laughing, too, while tears pour down her cheeks. Mann found the scene "one of the great moments of my career," but Susan, within her perpetual self-induced nerve-racking trance, couldn't step back to see the achievement. She was in character a good part of the day. Her torment became exquisite.

Before important takes, Mann and she would huddle. "She would become very upset and begin crying and making other sounds, like animal noises, while I was talking to her. She would generate this terrible, painful emotion from deep inside herself, this searing conflict, and would begin to cry and finally shout, 'All right!' Now I'd watch her start to walk onto the set. Then she would grab hold of me and I would push her back, and we'd shoot the scene. At the end of the day, I would really be involved with the most amazing kind of nervous energy. Her pain was the source of it. Somehow, she would generate it and use it in the scene. On some days, she would start crying at nine o'clock in the morning and keep it going all day."

Mann would plead with her: "Susan, this is a rehearsal, darling. Don't, don't."

"No, Danny, it's all right," she would say as she persisted in remaining in the emotional wringer.

Word got out quickly that Susan was doing Academy Award work; the MGM studio was suddenly abuzz with entertainment reporters who smelled big copy ahead. But the cost to Susan, who had never before so let down her defense mechanisms for a role, was enormous. Several weeks into filming, she was well past exhaustion. Her doctor gave her sleeping pills to help her end the day with some semblance of calm. She was drinking bourbon.

From behind the war zone of her creatively induced fits and depressions and her long bouts with the script of *I'll Cry Tomorrow*, she was still upset over Jess's legal threats to her custody of the twins as well as her confusion over what she still felt for him. Jess had just finished a western, *Kentucky Rifle* and, now that he was back at work once again, wanted to talk about a reconciliation. Susan agreed and he flew from New Orleans, where he had been promoting his new film, to meet with her and her lawyer. It turned into a near-Donnybrook. The two were almost at each other's throats, Susan shouting that she was furious that he had been petty enough to keep her from bringing the twins to Hong Kong, and Jess shouting that she was just using the boys to get back at him. The pattern of violence was too well established to end so easily.

But Susan still loved him and directed all the anger she felt toward him, when he wasn't around, toward herself. After the meeting at the Ambassador Hotel, she became especially moody. Cleo saw: "She was depressed—terribly, terribly unhappy." On the evening of April 25, she put the twins to bed and asked Willie Jean, Cleo's seventeen-year-old daughter, to go to the liquor store and "get me a big bottle of gin." Willie Jean, underage though she was, bought the gin, and Susan mixed it half-and-half with grapefruit juice in a glass. About nine p.m., Cleo and Willie Jean told Susan they were going to bed, and Susan said she would study her script. "You gonna like this one?" asked Cleo. "I'd better like it!" said Susan; "it's the third one they've written for me." All seemed well. Susan began drinking and working on her bed.

Although Susan never explained all the whys of what happened next, most of it is clear. She was studying the scene in which Lillian assures her mother (played by Jo Van Fleet) that, no matter how bad her drinking becomes, her mother will always be taken care of. Susan underlined the dialogue. At some point, either before or after she fixated on that passage, she used the grapefruit juice and gin to down several handfuls of sleeping pills which had been prescribed for her by her physician. Hours later, a stuporous Susan called her own mother and repeated the words from the script: "Don't worry, Mother, you're taken care of."

Ellen was doubly alarmed. The hour was quite late and her daughter sounded drugged. She told Susan to hang on and immediately went into Wally's room and woke him up. Wally vividly recalls: "My mother said, 'Susan's on the phone. She's talking kind of funny. Something is going on out there. I'll keep her talking. You get out there right away.'" Wally dressed, dashed to his car and in fifteen minutes was at Susan's house in the valley. "When I arrived, the police had just arrived, but the ambulance wasn't there yet, and Susan was lying on the floor near the couch."

Minutes before, a squad car had screeched to a halt on Longridge Avenue and two police officers had run across the patio and pounded on the door. Finding it locked, they broke through the kitchen door and found Susan unconscious in the living room. The time was just 3 a.m.

Meanwhile, Cleo, who was sleeping with her husband in their room at the back of the house, out of earshot, was jarred awake by a "horrible" knocking and crashing downstairs. "When I woke up, I heard all this rumbling going on. I jumped out of bed, threw a robe on and ran through the kitchen. The police had broken through the den door and there was Susan lying on the floor, nothing on but a terry-cloth robe. The detective said, 'Why didn't you answer the door?'" Cleo tried to explain, then rushed to Susan in the big living room. "There she was, one leg stretched out on the floor, and the other ... rocking. She was looking up at the ceiling and rocking, and I waved by hands over her eyes and said, 'Miss Hayward, Miss Hayward. This is Cleo, baby! This is Cleo!' She just kept smiling and looking up at the ceiling. She was going very fast."

The detectives found three empty pill-bottles in the bathroom.

Wally was frightened. "They just stood there. 'What are you going to do,' I cried out, 'just let her lie here until the ambulance gets here? Why don't you put her in your car?' That might have been against the law. But anyway, the police put her in their car. They picked her up, one grabbing her under the arms, the other by the legs, with me holding her under the middle."

Reporters and photographers arrived at the house just as Susan, expressionless, in pajamas, was being carried down the steps, strobes and flashbulbs suddenly lighting the street. The reporters yelled questions at Wally and the two detectives, Wilkerson and Brondell. Wally was only able to tell them that he was Susan Hayward's brother, which they didn't believe. Moments later, Wally followed the squad car to Ventura Boulevard, where they passed the tardy ambulance coming to get Susan, and then on to North Hollywood Receiving Hospital. In the emergency room, a team of doctors and nursed pumped her stomach. The doctors told Wally that they weren't sure if his sister would live. She was put on the critical list.

During the crisis, Ellen Marrenner had called Florence and the two had gone to Susan's house. Wally came back and told them that Susan might not make it. The three sat fearfully around the kitchen table. The twins, who had by now awakened and were worried, heard from their grandmother, "Mommie has a stomachache and is going to be fine," and were sent back to bed. Nine-year-old Timmy, though, knew that it was far worse and crept downstairs to listen by the door. He was crushed when he heard his grandmother discussing the possibility that his mother might not survive and what they should all do if the worst happened.

Later that morning, Susan was transferred, under an assumed name, to Cedars of Lebanon Hospital, still in coma. She was fed intravenously while drugs were given to correct shock. She remained on the critical list until, twenty-four hours later, she finally awakened. By the morning of April 27, her recovery was certain.

That same morning, a photo of the nearly dead Susan being carried from her home made the front pages with headlines bannering her suicide attempt. An endless stream of "Why did Susan do it?" articles appeared. Most of the pieces assumed that the strain of the divorce from Jess had brought on the overdose. Mystery lovers (including Howard Hughes, whom Susan hadn't seen since her divorce) were dragged into the conjectures. Jess himself, believing that he was the cause of the tragedy, broke down in front of a reporter and cried, "I love her!" over and over. He flew once again from New Orleans and tried unsuccessfully to see Susan at Cedars of Lebanon.

"She was kind of miserable," says Wally. "They stationed a guard at her door so you couldn't get in to see her. She said she didn't want anybody to see her. After two days, my mother and myself were allowed in. She looked kind of sheepish because my mother was ready to ball her out, but I told my mother, 'Now, don't say anything to her. If she wants to tell us anything, let her do it.'" All she told them was that she was reading the script and had forgotten how many pills she had taken. Other than a thank-you to God that she was still alive, she never said more about why she had taken those pills.

The filming of *I'll Cry Tomorrow* had come to a halt. When Daniel Mann first heard about the overdose, he was stunned. He had had such a close relationship with her and had no idea this would happen. After Susan came home from the hospital on April 29, she went into seclusion at the Longridge Avenue house and wouldn't see any of the clamoring MGM executives—only Danny Mann. "The studio sent a limousine to take me to the Sherman Oaks house. When I arrived, there were reporters outside. I rang the bell and the door was opened about four inches wide by the housekeeper. I announced who I was and she said, 'Yes, come in.' It was all very hokus-pokus, like a bad mystery. She ushered me into the living room and I sat down. 'Miss Hayward will be down shortly,' she said. The last I had seen of her was the picture in the newspapers as she was being carried out inert. Now I heard footsteps on the staircase behind me and I turned around. There was Susan coming down the stairs, her hair all beautifully coiffured, and wearing an organdy dress and looking absolutely marvelous."

Susan said, "Hello, Danny," and he came back with, "Susan, you look so alive!" (Mann calls the remark "the *faux pas* of my life.")

"Oh!" she laughed.

"Oh, no, no, no, excuse me," he said. "I didn't mean to be facetious. But you look wonderful, marvelous."

She laughed again and he embraced her.

A few days later, Susan returned to work at the MGM studio. The first scene to be filmed was a big production number built

around the son "Sing, You Sinners," in which Susan was to perform on a multi-level set with a platoon of dancers. Veteran costume designer Helen Rose recalls that Susan, before the suicide
attempt, had been "very lonely and very unfriendly." I knew she
was going through some big personal problems. I remember when
she came back that day she was in a black mood and when I was
alone with her in her dressing room I told her off: 'Susan, when
are you going to wake up and stop feeling sorry for yourself?'
Her response was a sharply withdrawn silence, but from that time
on she began to perk up."

Susan sat in her dressing room, waiting to be called for her
big number. When the knock on the door finally came, she looked
into her mirror, checking her hair and makeup and the low-cut,
sleeveless, beaded gown that Helen Rose had designed to display
her beautiful shoulders and arms. She emerged looking quite
radiant, though serious. Only days before, Susan had been com-
atose, full of drugs, full of syringes and needles and on a critical
list. Her flawless appearance drew all eyes to her as she made her
way, stepping over wires and in between lights and cameras, climb-
ing a ladder to the top of a two-floor set. When James Wong
Howe had the light he wanted, the musical number began.

Her dancing was superb, but what made her performance seem
all the more impressive to everyone was that she was mouthing
the words to her own singing. After months of coaching and
testing by MGM musical director Johnny Green and the movie's
musical director, Charles Henderson, Susan was doing her own
singing for the first time in a film. Her voice was deep and lovely.
Her face glowed happily. Yet, as Helen Rose recalls, moments
after the scene was over, Susan ran back to her dressing room
and that sad look came back to her eyes.

Although Susan's brush with death was constantly on everyone's mind, it was actually brought up to her only once. After
several months of overwrought scenes in which Susan was obviously acting out not only Lillian Roth's pain but her own, Mann
was ready to shoot Lillian Roth's suicide attempt from the window
ledge of a hotel room. He surmised that Susan would bring her
own recent experience to the scene, which had to be shockingly
real. He sent everyone else away and sat down with her. He told
her: "We're going to do the suicide scene and you know all about

it. I can't tell you about suicide. Whatever that pain is you can't live with anymore, that's an area of yours alone. I'll leave that to you. We're not going to pretend to deal with the actual experience, your life's worth, to live or not to live, what is going through your mind. The way we're going to dramatize it is not to try to understand or discuss it; but what I want you to do is to look *now* and hear *now* and see *now* all the things you are never going to be able to see, hear and touch again. This is your last time."

He was taking a great risk in discussing her own suicide attempt so soon. Susan grew suddenly silent. Moments later, James Wong Howe lit the hotel set and Susan went into the scene, her acting so real that onlookers became frightened. She looked at the walls, the objects in the room, as if for the last time and also with a desire for these lifeless objects to stop her from taking her own life. Susan, as Lillian, finally got to the high window ledge, looked down at the traffic far below, sat on the sill, was filled with horror, fainted and by a stroke of good fortune, instead of falling out, fell in.

Movie audiences were later filled with dread when they saw this and other scenes of such gripping realism. They experienced a wholly new Susan Hayward. She was no longer the deep-voiced heroine with those lusty, quick movements, really just choreographic tricks, but a mature performer who could keep moviegoers on the raw edge of their emotions. Susan had already been a major star, but with *I'll Cry Tomorrow* she entered into that small pantheon of players who will never be forgotten. And Susan herself was personally changed by her ordeal in making the film, which became a kind of psychodrama for her. Danny Mann says, "I really believed that Susan got back on her feet from the experience of playing the role of Lillian Roth. That was the road back, so to speak, from personal problems: her mother, her marriage. She could have gone one way or another, like the suicide scene. I was with her and walked this path with all its pitfalls."

The filming of *I'll Cry Tomorrow* was wrapped up on the afternoon of August 19, 1955, with pick-up shots of a sequence in which Susan, her hair matted down, her face tear-streaked and her clothes filthy with grime from the streets and wino bars, wrecks her mother's living room. Susan knew that she had done the best work of her career, felt exhilarated and, with a growing canniness about her own needs, decided for the first time since she arrived in Hollywood to take time off to improve her confused personal life.

She had already begun an affair with an actor named Don Barry (better known in Hollywood as "Red" Barry because of his red hair), a Southerner who had a small part in *I'll Cry Tomorrow*. What she didn't know, because she was still learning how to cope with life away from the set and the marriage bed, was that Barry was already engaged to someone else.

Susan's four-month fling ended in a real-life vignette that was funny enough to be filmed as a modern-day screwball comedy, except that the actress would have to have more of a sense of humor about herself than Susan. Susan had spent the night of November 3 with Don Barry at his North Hollywood home. While they were sitting around in pajamas the next morning, drinking coffee, a young starlet called Jill Jarmyn suddenly walked in, was stunned to find another woman, so attired, in her fiancé's bedroom and voiced her understandable objections. Susan, humiliated, picked up a clothes brush and hit Jarmyn on the noggin. "If you'll get out of my way, I'll leave," said the young woman, while a thoroughly embarrassed Red Barry kept pleading, "Susan, will you let her by?" Susan calmed down momentarily, then hit the girl again, then calmed down again, had some coffee while Barry tried to get his harem in order, and came at Jarmyn once more, this time with a lit cigarette. She threw Jarmyn down, ripped the buttons off her blouse, bit her thumb, bruised her arm and socked her square in the jaw.

The starlet somehow linked up with Jess Barker's attorneys, who threatened to press charges against Susan on Jarmyn's behalf and would obviously use the incident as further weaponry in Jess's battle either to reconcile with Susan or to gain custody of the twins. A photo of the battered girl ran in all the papers. The big problem for Susan was her name once again in the headlines, connected with further unsavory behavior: there had been the salacious revelations of the divorce trial, the suicide attempt and now an assault-and-battery and a frank admission by Susan of lewd conduct. She told the papers, "I could say I was in the dining room at the time, but I wasn't. I was in the bedroom in my pajamas."

Twentieth Century-Fox joined Susan's lawyers in asking Jill

Jarmyn to drop all charges for fear of more bad press, and three days later the starlet did just that. The whole episode was utterly in character for Susan. To anyone who knew of her sudden violent temper, her eagerness to claw, burn, splatter, kick, dowse or sock whoever crossed her, the scenario was stupefyingly familiar. Her family was not exactly shocked. Florence's eyes light up at the mention of the incident, and Wally smiles. Ellen, who automatically disapproved of any loose behavior, nevertheless probably understood her daughter's actions better than anyone else.

After Red Barry, Susan ran around Hollywood for several months with the monied and the powerful, looking for the antithesis to impoverished Jess. They included a Brazilian millionaire named Jorge Guinele, another millionaire called Bob Neal, wealthy businessman Hal Hayes and publisher Gordon White. Susan was looking hard for the right man, even turning down good parts so as not to distract her search. In December of 1955, a month before the scheduled general release of *I'll Cry Tomorrow*, she attended a cocktail party thrown by Vincent X. Flaherty, a columnist for the *Los Angeles Examiner*. She was the date of corpulent, outgoing "Uncle" Harvey Hester, whom she had met while making *I'd Climb the Highest Mountain* in Georgia and in whose Aunt Fanny's restaurant she had repeatedly been a guest.

Uncle Harvey had really come to the party to meet a friend of Flaherty's from Georgia. Susan couldn't help spotting the stranger beside the tinseled Christmas tree because he was so tall and good-looking. The two smiled at once another from across the room. Minutes later, their host, Vincent Flaherty, brought the gentleman over to meet her.

"Merry Christmas, Miss Hayward," he said politely.

"Is that Dixie I hear?"

It was and Susan found herself involved in small talk with the genteel Southerner who was, as even some of Susan's male friends would later describe him, "a real hunk." His name was Eaton Floyd Chalkley, Jr., and he was a lawyer who had his fingers in a number of commercial ventures, including a General Mortors dealership in Carrollton, Georgia, where he had just moved. He had come to the party primarily to meet Harvey Hester, since their mutual friend Vincent Flaherty thought that Uncle Harvey could help Eaton get settled in Georgia.

While Susan and the Southerner talked, a number of their

friends took notice of them. Helen Rackin, Marty Rackin's wife, remembered that Susan particularly brightened; Flaherty, who was playing Cupid, watched them throughout. The Southerner had brought his own attractive date to the party, but seemed not much interested in the woman, now off socializing. Later, when the party broke up, Flaherty suggested that the few remaining guests go to Mocambo for Sunday-night dinner.

At Mocambo, Susan sat out most of the evening, since Uncle Harvey didn't dance. The two talked about the Brooklyn Dodgers, one of her favorite subjects, although most of the time her eyes were on the Southerner, who was dancing with his date. Eventually, Vincent Flaherty, trying to get things going, suggested to Eaton he should ask Susan to dance.

"Why should she want to dance with me?" said the shy Southerner.

"Just ask her."

Meanwhile, the matchmaking writer went to Susan and told her that Eaton wanted to dance with her, then made things easier by whisking the Southerner's date off to the dance floor. The moment the two were alone at the table, Susan said: "Well, shall we?"

It was quite a conspiracy. After the evening was over, Vincent Flaherty called a boyhood friend of his and Eaton's, Thomas Brew, now a priest, and told him all about Eaton's evening with the movie star. But no one seriously thought it would go much further. Eaton Chalkley was a conservative gentleman and a devout Catholic. Susan had been the subject of countless headlines in the scandal sheets. Soon after the party, he flew back to Carrollton.

Susan had been trying hard to cope with herself. She was not faring well with the life she had been living ever since the break-up with Jess, despite her on-going psychoanalysis. The tensions, the nervousness, the drinking, the sleepless nights were still there. Her doctor took her off the sleeping pills which had almost cost her her life and put her on Miltown, making her more unresponsive to people than usual. Someone would speak to her and her answer was often a long silence.

She had moved from the house in Sherman Oaks where she and Jess had spent most of their wedded life and bought one just two houses away, at 3801 Longridge Avenue. She had discarded all of her old furniture and knickknacks and moved into the new house with nary a place to put her ashtrays. She was worth several million dollars, but, for some reason, couldn't bring herself to spend money decorating the new house.

But she wasn't about to give in to its emptiness: the boys were now in boarding school, returning home only on weekends and vacations. When she discovered that Cleo's brother had fathered a child out of wedlock, she offered to help Cleo adopt the baby. Susan would pay all the legal expenses, all the food and medical costs. Finally, Cleo agreed and Pamela was adopted. Susan became a second mother to the child, fussing and cooing, buying cases of baby food, baby bottles, a little bed, bassinet, shoes and an expensive English carriage. Susan was in second heaven. Cleo always knew Susan was happy when she could crack jokes. She once took Cleo and tiny Pamela to Babytown in Studio City to buy clothing for her new charge. Cleo says, "Susan went over to the cashier to pay for it all. So the girl said, 'Oh, Miss Hayward, I didn't know you had a new baby.' Susan said, 'Oh, didn't you know, honey? I had it by Sammy Davis, Jr.'"

Flaherty's friend from Carrollton soon returned to Hollywood and began casually calling Susan. Her reaction to Eaton, though, wasn't at all casual. She was positively taken with his manners, his looks and, underneath his shyness, his strong libido. Above all, he was Southern, a representative of a way of life she had always wanted for herself. Says Helen Rackin, "Susie, being in this kind of atmosphere, the movie industry...well, let's face it: these are not Southern gentlemen. He was like a breath of fresh air to her, the kind of man she had wanted all of her life."

Susan began changing her life to impress the forty-eight-year-old gentleman. She had already hired publicist Stanley Musgrove to campaign to get her an Academy Award for Best Actress for *I'll Cry Tomorrow*, a practice followed by most Oscar nominees and their studios. Susan phoned him and said she needed help. She said she wanted to give a party, but didn't know how. "I've never given one before. This place needs all kinds of fixing up. And who is the right caterer?"

He recommended Clara Blore, the wife of the character actor Eric Blore, to do the catering. Clara went over to the house, says Musgrove, took a look around and "nearly fainted." There was nothing to work with. She told him, "Do you realize the only glasses in that house are Kraft cheese jars?" The twins liked process spreads. "It was true. Everything had to be brought in. Furniture had to be rented. She only wanted to make an impression on Eaton, to show him she could entertain and do things in style, so that when she got to his home in Carrollton she would be able to do it."

Susan, whose taste had always been poor to nonexistent, left everything to Clara Blore, who did miraculous work, transforming Susan's empty house into an elegant setting for a gathering, with a myriad of little touches, including gardenias placed in little urns in all the powder rooms. But the big problem was that, besides Eaton, Susan had no one to invite. Her list of friends wouldn't have filled a matchbook cover. In the end, she invited a handful of Hollywood people—no name stars, but her then-agent, Hugh French, and others she considered the intelligentsia: educated people, like doctors, dentists, psychiatrists and friends of theirs.

She hadn't the foggiest how her concoction of people would interact, for none of them knew each other. The night of the party for Eaton, the house was jammed with guests and there was an understandable strain among them. Then, as Stan Musgrove tells it, "suddenly everybody seemed to get drunk and the whole party took off. They turned out to be the worst-behaved bunch I've ever seen in my life. They got smashed and jumped in the pool with their clothes on. It had her crazy. She was about to pass out... until she saw that Eaton loved it."

I'll Cry Tomorrow, which was released in January just in time for the Academy Awards, surpassed all of MGM's expectations. Critics wrote paeans to the movie and especially to Susan's performance. *Look* ran a long, heavily illustrated article promising heartaches and involvements for movie-goers. *Cosmopolitan* had Susan on its cover, *Redbook* picked the film as the best of the month and *Life* devoted pages to Susan and the film. Foreign film magazines were equally preoccupied. Susan easily received her fourth nomination as Best Actress and she believed that this time she would win.

At the Pantages Theatre, on the night of the awards, March 21, 1956, Susan sat between her eleven-year-old sons. She had invited Eaton, who was sitting at a discreet distance. Competition for Best Actress that year had been stiff. Susan was up against Katharine Hepburn (*Summertime*), Anna Magnani (*The Rose*

Tattoo), Jennifer Jones (*Love Is a Many-Splendored Thing*) and Eleanor Parker (*Interrupted Melody*). The tension built. Timothy and Gregory heard their mother lose to Anna Magnani.

It was a terrible blow for Susan, who believed in and needed awards and knew, just as did the whole colony and most movie patrons, that she had given the best performance. People today still recall that terrible injustice of that evening. No one had any doubt that Susan had lost the Oscar because of Hollywood's feelings about her. She had caused so many wounds, frostbitten so many actors' egos, that the general dislike of her had turned into a virtual polical voting blok. There were other reasons for her loss—namely, the scandalous headlines of the previous year—but had Susan been Elizabeth Taylor, for example, these wouldn't have mattered.

She had made plans for an elaborate party after the ceremonies and decided to go on with it. Once again, Clara Blore took care of the amenities. Susan's good friend Louella Parsons came. Everyone thought Susan quite courageous that evening. Instead of pouting about her fate, she behaved as if she had indeed won, hugging Louella, moving about, talking to everyone. Stan Musgrove believed that her mind was now on a much bigger prize than the Oscar: Eaton, who stayed with her until quite late that night.

Susan came up to Musgrove, gave him a big kiss and told him how sorry she was that he wouldn't be getting the $5000 bonus she had promised him if she won the Oscar. He was taken aback by her light-hearted lucidity after her Oscar loss and her apparent disconnectedness during the previous few months. More than that, a hugging, kissing Susan seemed rather strange. The next thing he knew, she might even begin to joke and laugh. In fact, actress Mary McCarty, whom Musgrove had brought to the party, went over to Susan and said, mock seriously: "Let's all go over to Joe's Little Italy and have some spaghetti." Everyone around them screamed with laughter at the sly reference to Magnani. Susan just froze.

One evening shortly after the Oscar party, Mary McCarty was having dinner with a friend at the Villa Nova, a popular Italian restaurant on the Sunset Strip. Susan, who loved Italian food, showed up with Eaton and they all met briefly. Mary McCarty thanked Susan for the party the other night and attempted another joke: "You know, you should have won that Oscar, Susan, but you were drunk too much. You could tell in every scene that you had been drinking." As McCarty later told Musgrove, "The look that Susan gave me—I just prayed that the floor would open up and dump me into hell." Musgrove explains it this way: "I never heard Susan laugh. She was humorless. Even Garbo had humor. Susan was the only one I've been around [who was like that] and I've been around plenty. Some roared with laughter. I mean Ava Gardner, Myrna Loy, Mae West. Susan, nothing. That's why I think she was a little more cracked than the rest of them."

Not long after the Academy Awards (she finally did have herself a good cry with Cleo that night), Eaton Chalkley went back to Carrollton. As close as they had been in Hollywood, much psychological as well as physical distance separated them. He had been no more than momentarily taken with Susan's Hollywood scene. Then, too, his friends back in Georgia tried to discourage him from seeing her again. Susan, well aware of the problems, began, early in 1956, what could only be described as the heroic effort of her life, an intense campaign of courting. There were numerous calls to Carrollton. Time and again, she brought Eaton back to Hollywood, either by calling him directly or using his friends as go-betweens. Each of his visits entailed great propriety, for Eaton was a gentleman: he always stayed at the Beverly Wilshire; she always dined with him in out-of-the-way spots. It was several months before the colony flaks even knew who he was.

She did date others when Eaton wasn't around. She put the twins in a Palos Verde boarding school and flew to various European cities to collect important awards for her performance in *I'll Cry Tomorrow*: to the Cannes Film Festival in April, meeting reporters in a tight pink sweater and a lovely smile (and, on the way back, shouting so loudly at the quarantine official who took away her new toy Yorkshire terrier that she held up the plane and made headlines), to the Cork Film Festival in May, to the Mar del Plata in South America. With only a few months left on her old Twentieth Century-Fox contract, she was still turning down roles, including *Hilda Crane* (for which Fox put her on temporary suspension, a meaningless punishment since her contract would be up in August) and *The Three Faces of Eve*. The latter was a juicy part, but she was still too busy building a personal life.

In August, after the Fox contract had ended, Susan became

an independent for the first time in her career. Almost immediately, she negotiated an enviable one-million-dollar-a-movie deal with Fox for six movies, each to be approved by her. She had become the highest-paid actress in Hollywood. Later, Elizabeth Taylor would be touted as the first movie star to receive one million dollars for a film (*Cleopatra*), since Hayward's fees were to be spread over a twenty-year period. But Susan was actually receiving more than Elizabeth because of the tax savings.

Susan did make a movie, around the time of her new Fox contract, for producer Marty Rackin. Warners' *Top Secret Affair* (earlier titled *Melville Goodwin, U.S.A.*), a comedy, had been intended for Humphrey Bogart and Lauren Bacall, but after Bogie became gravely ill with cancer Susan and Kirk Douglas were approached. Susan agreed.

Everyone around her recalls that Susan, as the involvement with Eaton Chalkley grew, was losing some of her ultra-seriousness and becoming lighter and happier. "Eaton was flying in regularly to see her," says Helen Rackin, who spent a good deal of time with Eaton and Susan. "When Eaton came back, Susan was divinely happy and she looked marvelous. you could see that she was very much in love with him." As a mature actress, she had never done comedy, but she made *Top Secret Affair* because of Eaton and her new feelings about herself.

Top Secret Affair took two months to film, and during the course of it Eaton stayed at the Beverly Wilshire and regularly sent Susan dozens of yellow roses. She adored them and kept them in her dressing room. One day, at lunch with Helen Rackin and Kirk Douglas, Susan began to hint at the plans she was making for herself and her boys. Talking about how she hoped her sons wouldn't go into show business, she made a point of saying that she wanted to give them a life away from Hollywood.

Top Secret Affair, which she thought would be sophisticated comedy, turned out to be one of her worst efforts. The film had Susan as a magazine publisher trying to ruin the reputation of an uptight general (Kirk Douglas) and ultimately falling in love with him. Apart from the problem of a strange and unfunny script, the movie often had Susan mugging at the camera rather than reacting normally. Susan had comic instincts, but this was not the vehicle for them. It would not be the last time that Marty Rackin would head a project which would waste her time and her energies. But he was breezy with her, called her "Hooligan" because of her feistiness, and she trusted him. The picture came out at Christmastime and did poor business.

Susan gave a Christmas party. She flew in her old New York friend Sarah Little, who still worked for *House Beautiful* and had the same decorating talents as her deceased sister Martha, to help transform the house. By now, almost a year after her last party, Susan had acquired some taste of her own for Eaton. "It was incredible, the transformation, from the silver and the linen to the crystal," says Stan Musgrove. Susan had actually purchased furniture, opting for simplicity rather than lavishness, even to decorating the Christmas tree with ribbons and bows instead of tinsel and balls. The homey effects were wonderful and had to impress Eaton.

As the campaign to win him progressed, she made many adjustments to prepare for a new life. The fact that the boys were in a boarding school, called Chapman, made the relationship with Eaton easier, and she began discarding propriety and living openly with Eaton at the house during his three- and four-day visits to Hollywood.

It wasn't all happiness during this time; there were severe disappointments. She had learned months earlier, through an investigator she hired, that Eaton's talk about his various business ventures—including a car dealership, a law firm and a motel in Carrollton—had less substance than she had believed. He had businesses, all right, but not appreciable assets. Then she discovered something far worse about Eaton. Cleo recounts that one day while Eaton was at the house, Susan was in a celebrating mood and offered Eaton champagne, then turned to Cleo's husband and told him to go to the bar and pour himself a beer. As soon as Cleo and her husband left the room, Eaton grew furious, telling Susan that he didn't like her servants because "they are Negroes and I don't believe in Negroes speaking until they are spoken to." Soon after, Susan and Eaton went on a trip to Big Bear Mountain and the subject seemed to haunt them, Susan defending her close relationship with her housekeeper, while Eaton, a quintessential Southerner, referred to blacks disparagingly, calling them "damn fools." Stunned that Eaton seemed no more advanced than other Southerners, Susan left Eaton at Big Bear and rushed back to

Longridge Avenue to tell Cleo about the upsetting episode. She said, "Cleo, I'm done with him."

But, by now, Susan was too much in love with Eaton to worry long about such matters, and in no time the two were reconciled. They began making serious plans. After the New Year, Susan flew to Carrollton to join Eaton in a kind of dress rehearsal of their future life there. She saw Eaton's large house and met his friends, driving around the small, quiet town. She returned to Hollywood and asked Cleo if she wouldn't come with her to Georgia. Cleo refused. A few weeks later, on the evening of February 9, 1957, Marty and Helen Rackin were expecting Susan for dinner to help them celebrate their new house in Benedict Canyon. Actor Edmund O'Brien, who had once been at school with Susan, was to be her dinner partner. Susan never arrived. The Rackins decided to hold up dinner and wait for her. But after they called her house and hours passed, they finally sat down. A knock suddenly came at the door. It was a telegram from Susan: SORRY COULDN'T MAKE DINNER STOP MARRIED EATON CHALKLEY STOP. There was no further problem with small talk that night.

The forty-eight-year-old Chalkley married the thirty-nine-year-old Susan in a secret ceremony in Phoenix, Arizona, conducted by a justice of the peace. Vincent Flaherty was best man. Phone calls were quickly made to Fathers Brew and Farrell, Eaton's best friends. Ellen and Wally Marrenner had to learn about the marriage on the radio the next morning.

"When I read in the papers they had flown to Phoenix and got married," says Stan Musgrove, "I just wanted to yell and cheer: *'She got him!'*"

The crisis was over.

CHAPTER 6

Love

THE GOOD-LOOKING and well-mannered Southerner, the love of Edythe Marrenner's life, was not the carefree Rhett Butler he appeared on the surface. He was also not, of course, the millionaire tower-of-strength that reporters of Susan's day portrayed.

Eaton Floyd Chalkley, Jr., was born in Virginia in 1909 to devout Episcopalian parents. But if a life could begin on a street-corner in late adolescence, Eaton was really born at Sixth and B in the capital—according to his lifelong best friend, Father Thomas Brew. Eaton's parents had moved with him and his brother and sister to Washington, D.C., where he went to Eastern High School. He turned into a splendid seventeen-year-old: good at school, dapper, outgoing. People naturally liked him. In the late afternoons, he fell in with a crowd of clean-cut, older teenage boys who hung out on the corner of Sixth and B Streets, in and around one of those wonderful all-purpose drugstores of the era. It was owned by a kindly gentleman named Doc Geiger. The police and the neighbors hated the noisy boys, but Doc Geiger and his wife encouraged them to gather in the store, for the sheer pleasure of their company, for their endless conversations on politics and sports and because, as Doc Geiger would always say, they were "my boys."

Eaton and three other exceptionally bright boys at Doc Geiger's formed a baseball team, calling themselves the Renrocs ("corner" spelled backward), and grew close as brothers. One was Tom Farrell, who was studying for the priesthood. So impressed with Tom Farrell was Doc Geiger, a fallen-away Catholic himself, that he swore to everyone that the day Tom was ordained he would go to confession and make his peace with the Lord. Thomas Brew, the leader of the four, had just accepted an athletic scholarship to Georgetown University. Vincent Flaherty was the oldest and a bad stutterer. Eaton Chalkley, at seventeen, was the tallest of the four and so handsome and robust, with such a remarkable self-assurance for one so young, that Thomas Brew's mother once blurted: "Why don't you all look more like Eaton?"

The four boys formed friendships that were the most important relationships of their lives and deeply influenced one another. For Eaton, the most searing influence was the Catholicism of the other three; in fact, all the other boys at Doc Geiger's were Catholic. As the four boys' friendship deepened, the backdrop of their mutual memories was almost exclusively Catholic. After the ordination of Tom Farrell, attended by the entire Renroc team, Eaton and the others were moved when Doc Geiger, keeping to his word, followed young Father Tom to the apartment above the drugstore and made his confession for the first time in decades.

Eaton's Episcopal upbringing had been rock-solid. He and his parents continued to attend St. Mary's Episcopal Church, where Eaton had once been an altar boy and sung in the choir. But after Eaton and Thomas Brew both began attending Mount St. Mary's, a Catholic college, Eaton started going to all the devotions in the college chapel. At first, he went because there wasn't an Episcopal church nearby. Then he passed on to another stage of interest and soon became the first in the morning to say the rosary behind the chapel. He virtually became a practicing Catholic. Later, he told Thomas that he wanted to become a real Catholic, he loved the religion so; maybe even a priest someday, just like Tom Farrell.

Around the time of Eaton's graduation from Mount St. Mary's, the Federal Bureau of Investigation began to expand from a rather insignificant branch of the government to what it was later to become under the guidance of native Washingtonian J. Edgar Hoover. He gave special consideration to young men living in his own city who wanted to work for him. In June of 1934, Eaton began as a clerk for the Bureau, making $1200 a year, not a bad starting salary in the Depression. Ambitious, Eaton wanted to advance to Special Agent and began attending law classes in the evenings, working his way up at the FBI as he accumulated credits. Eventually, Eaton and Thomas Brew decided to enter law school together and took the same classes. Their friendship remained steadfast. The other two of the Renroc team had gone to different cities. (Vincent Flaherty already had a job at the *Los Angeles Examiner* as a sports columnist; Father Tom Farrell went to Baltimore to head a parish.)

During his early years with the FBI, Eaton began seeing a quiet Catholic girl named Dorothy Rowland, and in 1936 they were married at St. Patrick's Church in Washington—but in the rectory, because of their mixed faiths. Thomas Brew was Eaton's best man. Eight months after the wedding, Eaton and Thomas received their law degrees from George Washington Law School. Thomas, for years, had been confiding to his best friend his desire to be not a lawyer, which he was becoming only for the sake of his family, but a priest. And so, four months later, Brew entered the Jesuit Novitiate to begin his studies for the priesthood and Eaton was driven all the more toward Catholicism. In the early 1940s, Eaton formally converted, his marriage to Dorothy Rowland finally receiving the blessing of the Church.

Eaton, with law degree in hand, was promoted to Special Agent and sent to Indianapolis on his first assignment. "It was there," says Father Brew, "where the cracks first started to appear with Dorothy. She wanted to go home, to live near her mother. In Indianapolis, their first boy, Joseph, was born. He was named after the director of the choir of St. Mark's Church. Eaton was very loyal. From Indianapolis, the next stop was Seattle, and things got worse. I can't remember the exact year that Eaton left the FBI to take a job with General Motors in Detroit. He was an investigator with the legal department. It had to do with the dealers not properly operating, complaints, anti-trust charges and all that. He went out after the facts."

In time, Eaton returned to the Washington, D.C., office and bought a house with Dorothy in Falls Church, Virginia. "I can still see it, a Colonial on top of a hill. Dorothy was back home, but she was now disturbed because Eaton was never home. He had to be away, as he explained." Eaton often confessed his frustrations to Brew. By now, Eaton and Dorothy had two more children, daughters. The situation could not have been easy for Dorothy or for the three children either. "It was around 1951 or 1952 that the marriage fell apart. I tired to see if there was any possibility of a reconciliation. Finally, the boy went with Eaton and the two girls with the mother. I found myself in the middle of things."

The divorce had been disastrous for Eaton, not just because it separated him from his daughters but because in the eyes of the Church, and indeed in his own, he was still married to his wife. Like so many other converts to a religion, Eaton was much more zealous in his commitment to his adopted faith than many born Catholics, and he therefore began to reconcile himself to living without a wife indefinitely. More than that, the divorce left him feeling that he had failed his church and his family.

By the time of the divorce, Eaton's health was not of the best. While an agent he had been shot several times, and during a stay in Chicago he had developed bleeding ulcers, so severe that he required blood transfusions. Those transfusions had been tainted and in turn led to an outbreak of serum hepatitis, an extremely dangerous form of the virus. He appeared to recover.

He continued to work for General Motors, traveling to every state of the union in his investigative work. On one of his trips, he discovered Carrollton, Georgia, fifty miles outside of Atlanta, population ten thousand, a fertile farm area on the Little Tallapposa River. He bought a farm of three hundred red Georgian acres a few miles from the center of town and began making plans to practice law through his business contacts around the country. Meanwhile, he met a man in town who owned a General Motors dealership which sold Chevrolets, Oldsmobiles and Cadillacs. The man took a liking to Eaton and offered to sell him the business on terms that no businessman could refuse. Eaton bought it and began to build a business-law practice, with the Sunkist orange-juice company as one of his early clients.

He tried, in Carrollton, to undo his past by living an exemplary Catholic bachelor's life and devoting himself to local religious affairs. "He was the first Catholic to go in business in that area," says Father Brew, "and he was regarded with wonder, suspicion and prejudice. But his charm and friendliness worked for him and all of that disappeared. He joined the Rotary International and other organizations and suggested that they have a Catholic priest come in to say grace once in a while. Either through fear or timidity, Catholics down there gave up going to church and now they came out of the woodwork. The Catholic church there had formerly been an Episcopalian church; it wasn't very large. Slowly, it began to grow, with Eaton leading the way."

The few practicing Catholics in Carrollton attended a tiny,

backwater church presided over by Father Charles Duke, an energetic missionary who had come to the area in 1950 and was stationed in Marietta. After Eaton bought his Carrollton farm in 1952, he began attending the little church and soon became fast friends with Father Duke. Some people still think of Eaton as having been Charlie Duke's patron, for the two were seen together a lot and Duke often stayed at Eaton's Sunset Boulevard farmhouse. Eaton loved the company of priests; ever since college, they had been his closest friends. Eaton shared Charlie's missionary ambitions to get Carrollton a better structure to house the Catholic church and began convincing a number of the town's wealthier Catholics to make contributions. After one of Eaton's friends donated $10,000 to the Catholic Extension Society in Chicago, Father Duke persuaded the diocese to purchase the seldom used St. Marcus Episcopal Church, which now became Carrollton's Our Lady of Perpetual Help. It was still designated a missionary church, headed by Father Duke, with the administration of the parish itself located in Cedartown. Eaton was upset by this, for in practical terms it meant that he could only attend mass in Carrollton on Sundays and on the other days of the week had to go forty miles to Cedartown for daily mass. Eaton also felt that Carrollton's Catholics were not being properly served, yet he also knew that it would be expensive to establish Carrollton as the center of a new parish. Now, with Duke and Eaton getting to know more and more of the town's Catholics, who were beginning to attend our Lady of Perpetual Help, they were certain they would eventually establish a new parish and have daily masses. Eaton and his friend Charlie became a wonderful team.

Eaton was growing closer to his priest friends, for, in a way, he was in the same boat as they: he could not marry again while his marriage to Dorothy was still recognized by the Church, and, as a good Catholic, he lived a fairly celibate life. During 1956, however, after Eaton met Susan, he was under a good deal of emotional stress. He loved her, knew she loved him, but was haunted by the impossibility of a remarriage to any woman. Papal dispensations for Catholics to remarry (usually by annulling the first marriage) took years. In many cases, the permission never came. If Eaton were to marry without Church permission, he knew that technically he would be committing adultery and therefore, as a fallen-away Catholic, could not receive the sacraments, including communion at mass. To a man like Eaton, who believed wholeheartedly in his adopted religion, such a situation would be unbearable. After Eaton had become involved with Susan, his friends in the Church advised him repeatedly not to flout the rules, as much for his own peace of mind as for the sake of his soul. Eaton often discussed the problem with Father Brew. Susan, he said, was pressuring him to marry her, would not wait much longer or accept any less. Brew, a sophisticated priest, understood that his friend was a man of strong physical drives who had fallen in love with a woman who adored him and that a reconciliation with Dorothy was hopeless, but he could offer little encouragement.

Eaton remained in great turmoil, even after he decided he had to marry Susan. The day before the civil ceremony, he wrote his friend Thomas Brew a touching letter saying that he did comprehend the guilt he was taking upon himself by what he was doing, and that the last thing he wanted was to lose the sacraments and the comfort of his Catholic faith, but he needed to be married to Susan. Perhaps, as time went on, the Church would give its permission. The letter was filled with regrets.

Eaton was especially agitated about Father Duke, whom he never could bring himself to tell about his decision to marry, or, as it would have been seen by some, to "commit adultery." According to another priest, Father Richard Morrow, Charlie Duke only learned of the marriage just before the wedding, and felt greatly hurt. He would not attend the wedding reception in Carrollton. The friendship between the two men ceased. Eaton told other friends that he couldn't honestly blame Charlie and accepted the end of the friendship as his own punishment. At the same time, he was very much in love.

Following the civil ceremony in Phoenix, the honeymoon in New Orleans and the wedding reception for Eaton's friends in Carrollton, Susan and Eaton began occupying his rich and red three hundred acres. They settled in the seventy-five-year-old red-painted farmhouse that Eaton had been living in, at 202 Sunset Boulevard, one of a handful of older wooden houses that sat on the farm, just off the Maple Street crossing of Club Drive. For a while, the two kept to themselves and a few close friends of Eaton's.

Eventually, Susan emerged and circulated in and about the

town. Everyone was curious about the movie star that Eaton had married, but, as Susan soon learned, their interest was politely innocuous. From the first, no one ever accosted her with "Aren't you Susan Hayward?" or some such; as she walked around Carrollton's few main streets, people would glance at her with startled recognition but not a word.

She became instantly comfortable in her new environment, which was, and still is, one of those tiny rural places in America that seem almost to have emerged from a time capsule. It remained little changed from its heyday in the forties, despite the growing pains of encroaching cities. It had Norman Rockwell peace and simplicity. Houses lining its streets were allowed, like people, to grow old without being replaced or remodeled. Yet the town was always neat as a pin. Susan grew to love it almost as much as Eaton.

A gregarious soul, he knew just about everyone in Carrollton, but thought it wise to introduce his famous wife to his friends and acquaintances only gradually. The Chalkleys gave little teas and dinner parties, for which Susan dressed plainly and comfortably and behaved quite modestly.

In an instant her legendary coldness was nowhere to be felt. If she did not become, in those first days in Carrollton, adorably gracious, she was at least forthright and friendly to all of the neighbors who came to call. Eaton's Carrollton friends—among them: Ebb Duncan, Jack Treadgill, Dr. Patrick, Mrs. Hollingsworth, Edith Foster, Charles Carter, Ann Moran and Mary Williams—all loved her. There was something magical about a beautiful woman, who just happened to be world-famous, doing her best to be seen as just one of the folks. Father Brew recalls that at those dinners (he was often in Carrollton) it was rare for Susan to make the slightest reference to her movie-star status. She usually allowed Eaton to lead the conversation.

Her language had become immaculate, devoid of all profanity. Eaton never swore himself, for, as he said to Father Brew, "I'm just a half-assed Catholic, but I'm going to keep my foot in the door no matter what." "The worst Eaton would ever say is 'hell' or 'damn,'" says Father Brew, "and Susan made a real effort to eliminate that kind of talk. She could talk like the best of ladies, and most of the time when she was with Eaton she did."

After a few months, Carrollton grew used to seeing Susan Hayward on its streets and in its shops. Susan, who only a short while before had been walking in and out of Beverly Hills women's shops with her dark glasses and her eagerness to run from friend and foe, was now donning slacks and scarf and driving a pick-up truck into the center of Carrollton; casually walking into McGee's Bakery off Adamison Square and carrying out white bags and boxes; waving to people she had met with her husband as she walked through Griffin's department store looking for kitchen items. Her supposed myopia had suddenly vanished. She would get folksy with all the tradesmen, who always called her "Mrs. Chalkley."

Susan worked to become just one of the townspeople, although, for the townspeople themselves, her transformation from glamorous movie star to Southern housewife was always a tinge bizarre. But everyone was game. She bought raffle tickets, went to church functions with Eaton, waited her turn on line for the fried-chicken buffet. She became great pals with Mary Williams, one of the town's leading citizens, a mischievous little lady who was a kind of mother figure for Susan. Susan spent hours sitting in Miss Mary's kitchen, gossiping at its big table, enjoying Miss Mary's antics, which included a one-woman tango. Susan joked that the kitchen was as much her as Miss Mary's and had a plaque designed for it which reads: THIS IS THE KITCHEN OF MISS SUSAN I AM THE BOSS IF YOU DON'T BELIEVE ME START SOMETHING. (It still hangs there.) The Chalkleys hired two housekeepers, Katie, a small, round black woman who reminded people of Hattie McDaniel, and Curlee, a tall, attractive black woman of whom Susan grew quite fond. Despite the help, Susan insisted on cooking Eaton's meals herself, unskilled as she was, and doing her own gardening and canning.

Occasionally, Carrollton found it all a little much. Not long after she moved to town, the town electrician stopped a neighbor in Griffin's depatment store and exclaimed: "I just came from Susan Chalkley's house and you know what she was doing? She was freezing vegetables."

"She is just like you and me," confirmed the neighbor.

Everyone knew who that woman in blue jeans was, as she went in and out of shops. However, one shopkeeper who apparently never went to Carrollton's movie theater was confused by the newcomer's soft, lolling, deep-throated speech, a kind of Hollywood-cultivated Brooklynese.

"Are you from England?" he questioned her.

"No, I'm from a place called Brooklyn."

"Whare's that?"

"That's up north."

"Oh, I see. Well, I knew you weren't from anywheres around here."

Through Eaton, Susan made another good friend, Ann Moran, the best cake-baker in town, who would visit Susan at the Sunset Boulevard house, shoot the breeze, have cake and coffee. Susan became just like one of those gossipy heroines in a soap opera. She would give Ann all sorts of clothing for resale at the church charities. Ann Moran, like the rest of Carrollton, was anxious to accept Susan on her own terms, cooking and canning included, but when one day she saw the super-star pasting supermarket green stamps in a booklet, she suddenly heard herself say, "Susie, you've got to be kidding." Susan shot back with, "Well, I need things, too.... Listen, don't you save stamps?" Ann had to admit she did.

Susan was developing almost a mythology for Carrollton. She was the goddess who desired to become mortal. J. Carl's, the local cleaning establishment, got a call from the Chalkleys to make a pick-up. Mr. Carl drove over himself and rang the bell. Susan answered the door with a towel wrapped around her head, explaining she had just washed her hair. Mrs. Carl examined the load of expensive gowns and velvet slacks that her husband brought back from the Chalkleys' and immediately called Mrs. Chalkley to tell her that she was fearful of cleaning such wonders. Susan instructed her to treat the clothes just like everyone else's. Word of the incident got around.

The town talk was about one thing: how down-to-earth the goddess from Hollywood was, how she was just folks, how utterly strange it all was. But had Red really changed? Was it all really just play-acting on the part of an accomplished actress or a true transformation brought on by the power of love? The question is legitimate, but Susan's hybrid identity makes a simple answer difficult. She had spent her previous years in Hollywood in one form of play-acting or another. Susan Hayward, movie star, had been a construct, an illusion. Only the slumgirl from Brooklyn had been real. What Edythe was doing now was simply modifying the original Hollywood illusion to suit a new environment. She was much better and quicker now at changing than she had been two decades earlier. The proper question is now whether Susan was play-acting, but what new form her play-acting was taking.

The woman underneath the role was always visible if one looked hard enough. Susan would, for example, drive a might too fast through the small town of Ranburne, Alabama, on her way to Carrollton. The police had posted signs with a very low speed limit and the Highway Patrol always stopped her. Susan finally got out of her car, slammed the door and shook her fist, shouting: "If you stop me one more time, I'm going to buy this goddamn town and build a bridge over it!" Eaton was not with her.

But if there was any real change in Susan, rather than a superficial adaptation to small-town Southern living, it was in her passionate devotion to a person, as opposed to career and money. She was deeply in love with Eaton Chalkley; it was an obsessive love, the kind she had not had for Jess or any other man, and it required of her an absolute commitment of time, effort and emotion.

The best evidence of Susan's love is the town of Carrollton itself, which remains today almost one remembering entity of a woman's devotion. Ask any of the shopkeepers or residents who circulated about Dixie Street or Center Street or Harris Street or Adamison Square, and they will tell of the ubiquitous pick-up truck that pulled up to curbs. Out of it would emerge the handsome, tanned man and the woman in jeans, sunglasses and bandana. The man would pick the woman off the ground; she would laugh; he would kiss her, raise her high over his head, then let her down. She would dash into the cleaner's; he would go off to the hardware store. Time would pass. She would wait patiently for him to return for her. They would re-enter the pick-up truck, waving to at least one passerby that they recognized.

Said the counter girl in McGee's Bakery off the Square: "She followed him around like a puppy. So he wouldn't run off, I guess. No matter where he moved, she'd have to be with him."

Said Ann Moran: "She would go into town with a babushka tied around her hair, which she did herself. She'd wear a hat and sunglasses, and off she'd go. Nobody had to deliver anything; she went after it. I spotter her in Bohana's store one time and I walked in and said, 'Susie, you stranded?'"

Susan said, "Yeah! Eaton's down the way."

"Do you want me to take you home?"

"No. When he gets through, he'll pick me up."

"The heck with that...no sense waiting here. I'll give you a lift," Ann offered.

"I couldn't do that to Eaton. He'll come and get me sooner or later."

She was more than just comfortably in love with Eaton. She was a woman reborn, charged with a sort of patient vitality. On their three hundred acres, Susan would stand among the steak cattle with her hands on her hips just watching Eaton in the fields as he did daily chores, such as making repairs or putting up concrete fenceposts. In their home, she pampered him almost unreasonably. "Anything he wanted, he got," says Ann Moran. Once she called Susie and asked if Eaton would like some "city chicken" that evening (it's mock chicken: pork and veal put on a skewer, dipped in egg and cracker meal and baked). Susan was already half-finished making her own gourmet curry dinner for Eaton, but when she heard that he liked city chicken, she insisted that Ann rush over with it and bumped the curry dinner.

In public, they were demonstrative, holding hands, reading the same menu in restaurants. They developed a strong nonverbal communication. They would always exchange looks, whether of disappointment or affection. Susan had at last found a home for her restless spirit.

In every physical way, she made an effort to improve that home. She had long before suggested to Eaton that they build a new house on the Sunset Drive acreage. The old farmhouse was too small for them, and so accessible to the town that teenagers from Carrollton High School would frequently come to her door asking for autographs (the only real interference Susan had from the populace). They decided to build a ranch-style house a half-mile from the old one, well into the property for added privacy, as well as add a fifteen-acre lake behind the house where Susan could fish. The building plans were elaborate and would involve granite from Stone Mountain, which one could see from the property, various forms of marble, tongue-in-groove logs for the walls, and black-painted slate for some of the flooring. A sumptuous fireplace would divide the living room from the master bedroom. The house and landscaping took nearly a year to complete.

Susan chose not to reveal that she was paying for everything, except to members of her own family, perhaps because there had been such bitterness between her and Jess over the disparity in their incomes. By himself, he could not have afforded such expensive building. The lake alone cost a fortune. Of course, Susan, who had just liquidated her California properties for seven figures and had already been cash-rich, could cover it all.

When her mother, living in an apartment back in Los Angeles, heard how much money her daughter was spending to renovate and build in a place so strange to the Marrenners, she grew quite upset. She could never understand how her millionaire daughter could have been mean enough to refuse to buy a little house for her own mother in California while eagerly spending many hundreds of thousands in Georgia. Wally, too, did not understand.

The new house, completed late in 1957, was a marvel. Stables were constructed nearby for the Chalkleys' horses, which, apart from fishing in the new man-made lake behind the house, became one of Susan's passions. (She and Eaton had previously been parking their horses in stables they rented on Mary Williams' estate. Susan had learned to ride during her early days at Paramount.) A cabin was built near the lake to hold Susan's trophies. The old red farmhouse now served both as a guesthouse and as an office for Eaton. The new house had a special room for the twins, who were still in their California boarding school. Susan was petitioning the courts to let her bring the boys to live with her in Georgia as soon as they finished their current term, while Eaton simultaneously filed for joint guardianship.

The great living room, dominated by a massive fireplace, and the spacious foyer were decorated with French Impressionist paintings. The walls were dark wood, the carpets were gold and white, and one wall, dividing the dining room from the living room, was all brick. The living areas projected naturalness, solidity, endurance—above all, security. But the *pièce de résistance* of the long, one-story building, the pat of the original plans that Susan had truly fussed over, was the master bedroom.

When Ann Moran first saw the enormous yellow room, with a huge bed at its center floating like an island, and a pink dressing room the size of Ann's kitchen off one end, the only thing she could think to say was: "What are you doing with two bathrooms in the bedroom?" Susan explained that Eaton was worse than a woman in the way he lingered in the bathroom and she needed to have one for herself. Then Ann spotted all the bottles of perfume and cologne in the dressing room; they seemed out of place in Carrollton.

But, then, Susan did bring something of Hollywood with her to Georgia—namely, her skills. Years later, she recounted to a friend, the sort of ritual which often took place in and around the new bedroom. She would *dress* to go to bed. After spending the whole day in blue jeans, she would choose one of her many sheer negligees, in a color appropriate to her mood, and lay it out on the bed. She reclined in a scented bath, sipping a scotch, while Frank Sinatra records played in the background. The bedroom lighting was soft and sensual as she would slip into satin mules, brush her (now) auburn hair, make herself up, put on earrings, dab on Joy and arrange herself on the gigantic bed, surrounded by pillows. She would sip another scotch. By the time Eaton came up from his office, she had set an exquisite mood, becoming Messalina in *Demetrius and the Gladiators*. It was a lovely game which always thrilled Eaton. "She should have received an Academy Award for all that sighing in the bedroom," said a relative of Susan's who had been an overnight guest. One thing is clear: she no longer needed a sex therapist or an analyst, for she and Eaton shared a healthy, powerful sexual relationship which kept them inseparable.

Late in the fall of 1957, Susan still had not agreed to do a new film, even though she had, almost a year and a half before, committed herself to six films for Twentieth Century-Fox. Too much involved with Eaton, all the new building and her new life, she had been sending one script after another back to her Hollywood agent, Jack Gordean. When Walter Wanger, who had virtually made her a star in *Smash-Up* and *Tulsa*, now asked her to help him by starring in his new film, Susan agreed to read the outline, but as soon as she received it she tossed it into Eaton's office. She was in no mood to work.

Walter Wanger, onetime millionaire producer, had gotten himself into deep trouble. He had invested his last dime on his own production of *Joan of Arc* with Ingrid Bergman, which flopped badly at the box office when the married Bergman had her scandalous affair with Italian producer/director Roberto Rossellini. Washed up and broke, he went into a deep depression which resulted in his belief that his actress wife, Joan Bennett, was having an affair with agent Jennings Lang. In a fit of rage, he shot Lang in the groin, in a parking lot. He spent ninety days in jail. Afterward, Graham Kislingbury, the Hollywood publicity man whom Susan had always liked, gave Wanger a brief scenario from a docudrama about the first woman to be sent to the gas chamber in California. The scenario was written by Pulitzer Prize-winning journalist Ed Montgomery, who had known the executed B-girl, Barbara Graham, and had covered her story. Montgomery's outline portrayed Graham as innocent and cried out for an end to the cruelty of capital punishment. Wanger had been upset by his own prison experience and thought that his film could become his statement about the prison system as well as a comeback.

Eaton found the outline in his office, read it, made Susan read it and began to lecture her, as he would often do in the future, on the importance of returning favors to old friends like Walter Wanger. When Wanger finally called her for an answer, she found herself in a generous mood and said she was interested. She and Eaton flew to Hollywood and met Wanger and Ed Montgomery in a restaurant, where for three hours Wanger and Montgomery pitched the story of the B-girl who was accused of the pistol-whipping murder of elderly Mabel Monahan, railroaded, as they believed, to a conviction and executed in a San Quentin gas chamber. Wanger was anxious to get Susan for the film and offered her a juicy 37.5 percent of the movie's profits. After the offer, she received quietly approving glances from Eaton, so subtle as almost to constitute a secret code between them, and told Wanger that she would be happy to do the movie.

Susan began work on the film on March 24, 1958, on the Goldwyn lot, using a mobile trailer for a dressing room. Inside it, on a table, Eaton kept a vase filled with fresh, long-stemmed yellow roses. He gave Susan unflagging support during the difficult months of filming and was, as far as everyone around the set was concerned, the ideal movie-star husband. "Eaton would sit off to one side on the set, quietly observing and never interfering," says Ed Montgomery, who was often on the set as the film's consultant on Barbara Graham. "Susan would ease up and smile when she looked his way. He was a good listener. He asked questions, but he didn't talk a lot. When he did say something, it usually made sense. He wasn't running around the place letting everybody know that he was Susan Hayward's husband."

The part of Barbara Graham in *I Want to Live!* was every bit as grueling as that of Lillian Roth in *I'll Cry Tomorrow*, but this time Susan did not have to suffer in the same way to reach her performance peak. She did not have to moan and groan or writhe in her sleepless bed or take sleeping pills. Wonderful, cavalier Eaton became the cushion she needed for all the draining emotions of the part, which could have been, without him, quite dangerous for her. He took the chill off Susan's inherent coldness toward the people around her. Quite under Eaton's influence, Susan grew interested in Ed Montgomery's family and one day showed his wife and their three children around the studio, explaining everything. Few people had been so pleasantly treated by her during any of her movies.

Yet, even with Eaton around, her working method still required her to remain aloof from her fellow workers. The film's brilliant director, Robert Wise, quickly sensed that don't-come-near-me quality about Susan and not only kept others from interfering with her on the set, but accepted the no-socializing-with-Susan rule himself. At the end of the day, she would leave her director and co-stars, enter her trailer and close the door. She was, naturally, guarding her creative mood and her energies, for the work on *I Want to Live!* was particularly difficult. But, as always, she was also hiding herself from those peers who might see right through her. Only once, with Robert Wise, did she let down her defenses for a few seconds to reveal something genuine. They were filming a scene in downtown Los Angeles. "See those kids over there?" she said, pointing to a group of tough-looking street kids. "They're like Park Avenue kids compared to the gang I grew up with." Moments later, she changed back to her sullen, efficient *persona*. It was the only glimpse Wise ever had of who Susan really was.

Hardly three weeks into filming, on a Monday morning, April 15, 1958, Eaton walked onto the *I Want to Live!* set and asked Bob Wise to stop shooting. Susan's mother had just died. Ellen Marrenner, aged sixty-nine, had suffered heart failure at Mount Sinai Hospital after a few days of what appeared to be routine confinement. Eaton told Susan. She said not a word. She lit a cigarette and stared toward an empty spot on the soundstage. Her look was clearly one of anger, obviously toward Eaton for stopping the scene. The movie's hair-stylist, Carmen Dirigo, recalls that after she resumed work that day she seemed to be brooding, although she did her scenes as well as ever.

The three surviving Marrenners, Wally, Florrie and Edie, went to the Beverly Hills funeral, which was particularly hard on Florence. It was the end of something that she had not wanted to end. She had always felt that her mother had been devoted to her children, and that life had treated her harshly. Florence also felt that her younger sister had not cared about any of them, including their mother, after fame and fortune came.

At the chapel of Pierce Brothers, Susan's heart appeared to harden. There was no big reconciliation scene between the two sisters, and Florence was taken aback that Susan showed so little grief. "She came in with a group and I was with my friends, too," said Florence. "Susan stayed about an hour and a half and then said to me, 'Well, I've paid my respects. What more do you want me to do?' And then she left."

There were others who felt some of what Florence felt. Stan Musgrove, who was working on *I Want to Live!* as an assistant to Robert Wise, observed: "When Susan's mother died, it was like the closing of a door to her. She was *not* inconsolable. I can tell you that."

Ellen Marrenner was cremated and the ashes were supposed to be shipped back to Brooklyn and stored in a special place where her husband, Walter, was buried. Instead, Susan allowed them to be stored in a cardboard box in the Chapel of the Pines while Florence tried in vain to get through to Susan to have the ashes sent to Brooklyn. Susan appeared to be using their mother's death as an excuse to end their already tattered relationship. She refused to communicate further with her sister.

Susan did not miss a day's work on *I Want to Live!* because of her mother's death, which, if anything, seemed only to fortify her performance. It was indeed one of the most remarkable of her entire career. For the first time in any of her movies, she was able to rid herself of mannerisms, deleting all those extraneous body movements which had become her trademarks. Instead, she found simpler modes: a mere look of defiance to the district attorney, a slow-building display of her emotions as her character learns more and more horrifying news, minimal self-choreography during the most terrifying scenes.

She had reached a pinnacle of technical growth, proven in take after take on *I Want to Live!* She was able to display the most suspenseful sort of torment without inducing observers to wonder at the actress behind the emoting: a rare creative objectivity that audiences had never seen in her before. So many scenes in this movie leave one wrung out with empathy and awed by her fully developed skills. In one of them, Barbara Graham, who has already received one reprieve from the gas chamber, meets reporter Ed Montgomery (played by Simon Oakland) while she is sitting in a prison dentist's chair. He tells her that the psychologist who had championed her has just died and that her execution date has been rescheduled, but there is some hope. Susan's sudden outburst that she can't bear any more and why don't they simply kill her and be done with it, all the character's defenses dissolving in a fearful breakdown, wrenches one's nerves and keeps the heart pounding. Later, after she has been prepared for execution, she is given another postponement only minutes before the pellets are to drop, and she turns to the priest who has heard her confession and cries out: "Oh, Father, why do they torture me!" The effect for the audience is the same, utter terror and heartache.

Robert Wise's careful direction and Nelson Gidding and Don Mankiewicz's masterful scripting had much to do with the powerful effect of this movie, but it was Susan's genius that dominated it. A replay of the breakdown scenes and others shows the spare but advanced choreography that Susan employed to achieve the depth of realism. But, beyond technique, one is also aware of Susan's accurate sense of the B-girl herself, especially in the film's early scenes. Many times, Susan asked Ed Montgomery to join her in her dressing room and asked him, "Am I getting this right? Is that the way Barbara Graham would have acted? Is that the way she would have done it?" After a while, she had developed such a strong feeling for the woman that she began to suggest bits of business to Wise, who usually agreed to them.

Susan, Bob Wise and Walter Wanger were all concerned about the final execution scene. From the pro and con noises that were being made by the police departments and other groups, the general feeling was that *I Want to Live!* would be shocking and influential. No film had so dwelt on the details of capital punishment or shown an execution at such documentary length. To sustain the film's credibility, the gas-chamber sequence had to be not only dramatic but authentic. Wanger was especially bothered by the fact that the audience might not believe that a beautiful thirty-two-year-old woman, the mother of a little boy, was actually taken to the gas chamber to die on three separate occasions before she was finally executed. The torment had to be exquisite, but unmarred by any sort of romantic ending with a choir of angels.

As preparation, Bob Wise witnessed an actual gas-chamber execution and Susan questioned Montgomery about Barbara's death. By the time of starting the execution scene, which was long and exhausting for everyone involved, Susan felt she had a good understanding of what the experience was like. Blindfolded, with only a few lines to say in the final walk to the chamber, Susan was forced to communicate the interior drama solely with her stance, her walk, small movements of her head. (Her one line in the gas chamber, as she is being advised to take a deep breath of the cyanide gas to make her death easier, "How would *you* know?", is quintessential Susan.) Her simulation of death was masterful, chilling. People on the set felt as if they had actually watched someone die. The director was terribly touched. Ed Montgomery saw her later in her dressing room, as she was smoking her cigarette to relax. He could see she was drained, but he was impressed that she began talking about something completely unrelated to the film. She had come a long way since *I'll Cry Tomorrow*.

As expected, the film's release later in 1958 caused commotion. Audiences were shocked by the execution scenes, but flocked to see the film. In some parts of the world, the film was either banned or cut. In England, it was both: first completely banned, then shown in a watered-down version. Albert Camus thought the whole world should see the movie and that future generations would view it as a document of prehistoric cruelty. Eleanor Roosevelt publicly praised it. *Life* devoted an article to the film.

The reviews were startling, filled with acclaim for the movie and for Susan. The *New York Times'* Bosley Crowther, who had been mean to her countless times before, called her performance "vivid" and "shattering" and deserving of "our most respectful applause." Other critics fell over themselves in describing the searing effect of Susan's Graham. The language of her peers throbbed with even greater praise. Walter Wanger couldn't say enough about her to the press. Bob Wise compared her with Sarah Bernhardt and Garbo. People came to her personally to congratulate her on what was probably the best peformance of the year if not the decade. Stan Musgrove, the publicist for *I Want to Live!*, told her what he believed: that she was sure to win the Oscar. "She wouldn't say, 'I know it,' but she felt pretty good about her chances. So I said, 'What are you going to say when you win?'

"'I know what I would like to say,' she said. 'There is one person I would like to thank above all—*me*!'"

While *I Want to Live!* was still on the editing moviolas, Jeff Chandler asked her if she would do a Western with him to help revive his failing career, which had never been all that sound. He needed her name to get back on his feet. Encouraged by Eaton to do professional favors for old friends, Susan agreed to appear in *Between the Thunder and the Sun*, a terrible film about Basques shot in Oklahoma. In it, she affected a French accent that fooled no one and did an unskillful flamenco dance. The film was later released as *Thunder in the Sun* and received poor reviews.

Near Thanksgiving of 1958, around the time *I Want to Live!* was released, Susan, with Eaton as her constant escort, went on tour with Ed Montgomery to promote the film in twelve major cities. Ed Montgomery has only the fondest memories of the Chalkleys on that trip. In New York, he and Eaton met Susan and Walter Wanger, who were just stepping off a plane at La Guardia Airport. Eaton handed Susan a big box with a mink coat, which she tried on the minute she entered the airport. In Carrollton, where they all stopped off on Thanksgiving day, Montgomery remembers Susan trying hard to prepare a turkey dinner in the new house without the help of servants: "Frankly, she wasn't the best cook in the world, and she knew it. She said, 'You know, I just haven't done enough of this sort of thing, but I'm learning.' Eaton laughed and went on dicing up some celery for the stuffing. She said, 'I'm glad you're here. I wouldn't have remembered to put that in.' They had fun. It was a nice family occasion and she was genuinely in love with him. Later, Eaton did all the washing and I dried. Her two boys were there and helped. They were very well behaved and very quiet. I can remember Susan, after dinner, sitting on a sort of stool at one side of the room, having a cigarette and just kind of shaking her head as if to say, 'Thank heaven this is over with.' Then we went to the cabin by the lake. She liked to pump the player piano there and change the piano rolls. She would sing and Eaton would sing along."

The Chalkleys continued the tour in France, Germany, Italy, Argentina, smiling prettily for the press, receiving awards from photographers, such as the Golden Globe, Sicily's David di Donatello, Berlin's Silver Bear, Argentina's Golden Gaucho, and loving every minute of their time together.

In love with her new success, Susan violated her own rule against press intrusions and allowed television cameras into her home for an Edward R. Murrow "Person to Person" interview. Millions of Americans saw her house, her trophies, her handsome husband, as she went through the famous show-and-tell ritual.

Back in Los Angeles, where she and Eaton touched base several times, Wally spent time with them. They went to Santa Anita racetrack, where he worked as a page, and he would arrange to get them a table through his connections. "When I would visit them at their table, she'd say, 'Here's twenty bucks, Wal. Go bet it for us and we'll split.' So I made her a little money. But I'd tell her she'd have to take care of the *maître d'* and the waiters, and she said, 'Don't tell me about all that. Eaton takes care of that.' 'Okay,' I said, 'but remind him, will you, because you're putting me on the spot!'"

Wally liked Eaton as Susan's husband because, as he says, "they got along well together." But on a more personal level, one suspects that Wally found him a bit foreign: "I didn't look too closely at him."

Susan began work on a new film for Fox called *The Snow Birch*, another one of those confusions concocted by the studio in the hope that it would magically hold together by release time. Susan played a widow and mother who marries the wrong man, with lots of outdoor action. The director, Henry Hathaway, never particularly liked working with Susan and was not known as a good director for this sort of woman's film. Susan obviously accepted the film to fulfill her contract to Fox and for Eaton, who loved to see her at work, no matter what she was making. It was released as *Woman Obsessed* the following year, 1959, to dismal reviews and box office.

But *I Want to Live!* was clearly headed to be one of the year's big money-makers. While Susan and Eaton were on their way back from another day at Santa Anita, they heard on the radio that she had been nominated for Best Actress—her fifth time up for the Oscar.

The night of the Academy Awards on April 6, 1959, might well have been a replay of the 1957 ceremonies, in which Susan had lost not a professional prize but a popularity contest. But this night there was one difference: Hollywood no longer perceived her as the same woman. In marrying a man like Eaton and moving to Georgia, from where her name seldom made headlines, Susan had physically and spiritually left the colony. If the audience was still filled with people who recalled only her coldness, they were now forced to acknowledge her brilliant triumph over the claustrophobia of Hollywood and the contract system. With *I Want to Live!* Susan Hayward had become an independent artist of the first order, a money-making star who had proven herself a great actress. She was no longer just another member of the family whom they could chastise with a mere vote.

As she waited in the audience for the ceremonies to proceed, she carried a gold medal which had just been given to her by Walter Wanger. On one side, it had a figure of St. Genesius, protector of travelers, with the words, PLEASE GUIDE MY DESTINY, and on the other side, a fresh engraving, TO SUSAN—BEST ACTRESS AND BEST FRIEND—WW. Susan's performance had helped put him squarely back on his feet. Meanwhile, master of ceremonies Bob Hope joshed from the stage: "Movies are becoming so realistic, I was surprised to see Susan Hayward here tonight." Finally, as Red sat glued next to her man, Jimmy Cagney and Kim Novak read off the list of nominees for Best Actress: "Susan Hayward for *I Want to Live!*, Deborah Kerr for *Separate Tables*, Shirley MacLaine for *Some Came Running*, Rosalind Russell for *Auntie Mame*, Elizabeth Taylor for *Cat on a Hot Tin Roof.*"

Even before the line "The winner is Susan Hayward for *I Want to Live!* was finished, the audience erupted into deafening applause. The name of the film could barely be heard. Susan kissed her husband, sprang from her seat like a suddenly released coil, gathered and lifted slightly the folds of her black satin dress and ran as prettily as a ballet dancer to the stage. One hundred million television watchers saw how long it took her to run from her seat to her Oscar, nearly twelve seconds. It had taken her, indeed, a very long time to get to her Oscar, and when she reached it, she clutched it heartily. She had very little to say, uttering the obvious, thanking the Academy, thanking Walter Wanger and forgetting to thank Bob Wise. But that great big smile on her face was all anyone needed to see or hear to know all about Susan in that instant.

The vote had been a long time coming and the feeling of approval was unanimous. A roaring, cheering crowd ganged the entrance to the Pantages Theatre. The police had to extricate the departing Susan and Eaton by carving a pathway through the wall of people who were trying to touch her, and later, as the Chalkleys entered the Beverly Hilton ballroom for the Academy's annual dinner dance, another crowd surrounded them. Susan and Eaton were seated at a table on the perimeter of the dance floor with Joan Bennett and Walter Wanger, and Bob and Dolores Hope. The table was bombarded with round after round of blinding camera flashes from surrounding photographers. Eaton tried to duck out of range and let Susan take the spotlight, saying, "I didn't win anything."

She cried out: "If it hadn't been for him, I wouldn't have either."

A photographer asked her to pose kissing her Oscar statuette and she quipped, "I don't kiss anyone but my husband."

Strangers jammed the dance floor to congratulate her and get autographs. She and Eaton became flustered and started to leave. A reporter asked, "What are you going to do next?"

"We're just anxious to get home," she said, turning wearily to Eaton.

Back at their Beverly Hills Hotel suite, they packed the statuette and flew to Carrollton the same night.

CHAPTER 7

Role

ARROLLTON was in a dither. The day of the ceremonies, a benign conspiracy took place, involving phone calls to and from the mayor's office, the offices of various other local officials, the homes of the town's leading citizens, Eaton's friends. Arrangements had to be rushed. That night, hardly a soul in town wasn't pinned to his television set. There was tribal unity for Susan. Hearts pounded. The two boys, given special permission to stay up late at their school, watched along with everyone else. At about half past eleven, when Susan was named winner and everyone could see her kiss Eaton on those small screens, Carrollton went into quiet frenzy. More phone calls. Gasps. The next day, a congregation, headed by Mayor Stewart Martin, met Mr. and Mrs. Eaton Chalkley as they stepped off the plane in Atlanta. They were driven in a two-and-a-half-mile-long motorcade the full fifty miles to Carrollton, where throngs waited to greet them. In the city, a great cheering parade with four bands honored them, banners flying everywhere. They were handed the keys to the city and a special edition of the local newspaper. Susan, who was not wearing her glasses, could not make out any of the writing, but she didn't need to. It was oh-so-wonderful for Susan and Eaton.

Yet, forty miles away in Cedartown, in the Catholic church over which Father Charles Duke presided, stormclouds were brewing. The day before, while officials had been making hurried preparations to give Susan and Eaton a motorcade and a parade in the event that she won the Academy Award for *I Want to Live!*, Father Duke had addressed his congregation, made up mostly of Catholics from Carrollton. He spoke of the Chalkleys and of the great fuss being made over them. He alluded to the fact that

Eaton's marriage was not sanctioned by the Church. Then, as Father Richard Marrow, who later headed Duke's mission in Carrollton, notes: "Father Duke told them their relationship would have to change toward Eaton because he had done the wrong thing.... Instead of being the great white father of that parish, Eaton had given a bad example.... [He said] that these people would always be welcome to the church, but they were not to get extraordinary attention."

When word of what Charlie Duke had told the Catholic congregation in Cedartown got back to Eaton, he was upset, mostly with himself. He and Charlie had been on the outs since his marriage to Susan and he knew how badly the priest had been hurt. Eaton looked upon Father Duke as his conscience and took everything he said to heart. The day of the festivities for the Chalkleys, Eaton was well aware of the distance his old friend was keeping. On several occasions afterward, Eaton and his friends in the Church invited Duke to important events but were turned down. Duke was reported to have once said, "If I came, it would look as if I were patting Eaton on the back for what he did." Indeed, Father Duke was a man with an excellent, strong character who could not equivocate when it came to his faith.

Eaton had the same sort of character: that was the difficulty. He would sometimes joke about his religious problem by calling himself, as Father Brew said, "a half-assed Catholic" who was trying to keep his foot in the door. But it bothered him terribly. He attended mass without fail, keeping that foot in the door, driving eighty miles round-trip when he wanted to go on weekdays, but he knew, as did all the Catholics around him, that it was all less than real. Even a lot of Carrollton's Protestants knew about Eaton's dilemma. He couldn't go to confession, couldn't receive the sacrament of holy communion during mass. He was, in effect, no longer a Catholic. But nothing was ever said by him or others, except for Father Duke's clarification of Eaton's position in church. It wasn't necessary. Eaton already knew, just as Susan did, but he kept his pain to himself.

For Susan, it was a hard position to adjust to. Church-going had never meant much to her, but there was no way she was going to have a happy marriage to Eaton without acquiring some of his fervor for religion. They tried to work it out in different ways. On Sundays, right after she first moved to Carrollton, she would attend the local Baptist church while Eaton went to the Catholic church. However, after she learned about a group that waited for her at the church waving autograph books, she decided she couldn't attend alone and began going with Eaton to his church. That only made her feel uncomfortable, since she wasn't Catholic and was as out of place as even Eaton was beginning to feel; and so she wound up making infrequent token visits with him to Sunday mass.

Susan was equally aware of Eaton's distress over family problems. He was virtually estranged from his two daughters, who, ever loyal to their mother after the divorce, would not visit him and Susan in their Carrollton home. No one remembers him ever saying an angry word toward them behind their backs. He saw a good deal of his twenty-two-year-old son, Joe, for whom he had high hopes. Joe Chalkley was attending St. Joseph's Academy in Bardstown, Kentucky, and was barely making passing grades, much to his father's regret. High-strung and nervous, Joe talked a lot about getting away from books, maybe going to flying school if his father would permit it. Eaton pressured him to do something more academic, making his son continually uncomfortable.

There was little Susan could do to help Eaton with his children, although she did ingratiate herself with his charming mother and sister, who often came for visits. The one important thing Susan had decided to do for Eaton was to help him win back his feeling of being a true Catholic and to mitigate the prejudice on the part of some Catholics in Carrollton that Eaton had done "the wrong thing" by marrying her.

A full year passed before Susan accepted another film role under her loose but lucrative Twentieth Century-Fox arrangement. It was *The Marriage-Go-Round*, a celluloid version of one of those light and sexy Broadway comedies which only got worse on film. On Broadway, it had starred Charles Boyer as an anthropologist who attracts the interest of a young woman, played by Julie Newmar, who wants to "mate" with him to produce superior children, while his wife, Claudette Colbert, quietly protests. Susan now played the wife, James Mason the anthropolgist and Julie Newmar had the role she had created on Broadway. The picture turned out to be worse than merely dreadful. Susan looked old and was boring and unbelievable in the part. She did the picture for the same reason she was doing all of her roles these days; because Eaton encouraged her to work, no matter what.

This was an odd time for her, professionally. She went through all the technical motions, but her heart wasn't in her work. As Tom Tuttle, who was still in touch with her, says, "Work was her whole life until she met Eaton." He replaced it almost totally. Right after she finished *I Want to Live!* Susan told him that she intended to retire, to make up for all the years spent in "that dungheap," as she called Hollywood. She had developed a great love of fishing and pressured Eaton into buying a "retirement" house in Fort Lauderdale, not far from the canals, where Susan had three boats: the *Oh, Susannah*, the *Big Susannah* and the *Little Susannah*. She dragged Eaton down to the house every chance she could and they would while the hours satisfying her new nautical passion. She was happy just being with him.

Eaton, however, was restless. He talked to her a lot about doing more films, "because I don't want her to waste her talent," he told his friends, although it is possible he was getting to like the trips to movie sets, the attention of clamoring reporters, the moderate kind of jet-set glamour the Chalkleys had. He also made good use of all the publicity in his diverse business interests, which included a baseball stadium/shopping center he was investing her money in. Susan was tremendously in love with the man, and so permitted him to have inordinate influence over her professional life. She set up a corporation with him to develop and produce movies, although she would have much preferred to keep on fishing.

After she had received her Academy Award, Walter Wanger had told everyone: "We can all relax now. Susie's finally got what she's been chasing for twenty years." But, in fact, it was Susan herself who was doing the relaxing, standing in front of the cameras these days, in film after film, with her mind not on creativity but on Eaton and Carrollton. She was appearing in movies strictly to please him, and it showed in her choice of roles and in her acting. But even Eaton had to admit that Walter Wanger's offer for her to play Cleopatra in a giant spectacle was slightly mad. Susan suggested that Walter make Elizabeth Taylor Queen of the Nile, which is apparently how Wanger got the idea.

Timothy and Gregory had been spending their summers and holidays in Carrollton and now entered Georgia Military Academy. The courts had long since granted Susan permission to bring them to Georgia, as long as they could pay regular visits to their father. On weekends, the two fifteen-year-olds came from their military school to stay with Susan and Eaton at the Sunset Boulevard house. With young Joe Chalkley also coming and going, the house was, in those days, filled with family activity. In summers, the twins lived there full-time and worked in town at the local gas station, with their mother's encouragement. She wanted them to learn the value of a dollar. She had already had too many experiences with members of her family expecting handouts.

Eaton had often told Susan of his exasperation at having to travel to Cedartown when he wanted to go to church on weekdays. He thought the Carrollton church, open only for Sunday mass, in awful shape. The oldest structure in town, it could hold only sixty people and tended to sway in several directions. When church-goers prayed, the kneelers gave under the weight of bodies. It had always been his thought to build Carrollton a brand-new church. Late in the year, Eaton made a call to the diocese and invited the head, Bishop Hyland, to pay him and Susan a visit. The bishop came to the house, along with Monsignor Regan, who had been in the area since the early fifties. Eaton told the bishop that in a dream he had just received a vision of a new church for Carrollton. He saw in the dream exactly how it would look. He told the bishop that he and Susan were willing to donate fourteen acres of their land as a site for a new church, which they would finance. They expected the cost to go a little over $100,000 and would oversee the construction. The bishop delightedly accepted the offer. Not long after, he designated Father Richard Morrow as the future pastor of the new church and wanted him to work with the Chalkleys on building plans.

Father Morrow, an attractive, tall, dark-haired man, had only just taken charge of the church in Cedartown, which Father Charles Duke had left some time before. Father Morrow had already heard about Eaton and Susan from others in the church—how they were outsiders who always wanted to be insiders. No one in the church truly knew how to treat these two people, whose relationship to Catholicism seemed unorthodox. Eaton, eager to establish good relations with the priest, met with him before Susan did, and discussed his marriage. Eaton told Morrow that Susan's religious conscience had grown since they were married. His own had rubbed off on her. Both men realized, of course, that that did not make his marriage to her any more acceptable to the Church.

Father Richard Morrow first saw Susan in the Carrollton church, wrapped in furs and looking every bit like the woman he had seen in movies. He didn't speak to her then. "It was two or three days later," says Father Morrow. "I was in Carrollton and this pick-up truck came along. There was this lady with a scarf over her hair, slacks on and a nondescript blouse and jacket. She blew the horn and said, 'Hey, Father!' and pulled the truck over to where I was and started to chat right away. For the first minute or two, I wondered, 'Who are you?' Well, that was the way I always saw her afterwards. She said she felt badly that there were no introductions."

Soon Father Morrow became a frequent visitor to the Sunset Boulevard house, and dined with the Chalkleys in restaurants. He and Eaton were forever going over building plans for the new church, which would be constructed on the highest piece of land that Eaton owned so that he and Susan could see it from the house. Morrow became quite close to the Chalkleys. Sometimes, when Susan was alone with the priest, she would tell him how rough her childhood in Brooklyn had been, and how different life now was with the cattle and the farm and the green trees. She blurted, "Father, we are never going to leave here!"

For Father Morrow, the close involvement with the celebrated Chalkleys was wonderfully exciting. He received frequent invitations to join them at their Fort Lauderdale retreat at 220 Nermi Drive, where he relaxed with them on their boats, in their long, air-conditioned, one-story house adjoining a canal. The atmosphere was casual, yet charged with fascination, for Susan was, after all, an Academy Award-winning movie star, still one of the most popular in America. Morrow saw her in between roles, when she allowed herself to gain weight, baking brownies for him and Eaton, and just before she made a movie, when he always knew that she wouldn't offer him any more brownies. In restaurants, he saw the love in her eyes for Eaton as she held his hand while they read a menu; but he also saw the star in her. "She would say to a waiter on walking into a restaurant, 'No, we don't want that table, we want *that* table.' She had *that* voice in dealing with the plumbers or anyone on the farm, as if to say you're not getting her money until the work is done right. There was no softness in dealing with people like that. Susan was always afraid of somebody taking advantage of her."

Theoretically, Morrow always had access to the Chalkleys. He could call them up night or day. Even when they went out of town, Eaton would arrange for his number to be given to the priest, "just in case." At the same time, Morrow was perpetually reminded that these were not ordinary people whose main concern was the activities of the parish. He got used to the voice of Curlee, Susan's housekeeper/companion, on the telephone. "I would call up there and Curlee would say, 'They just flew to Florida' or 'They just flew to New York.' I would say, 'But I was supposed to meet with them today,' and Curlee would say, 'Oh, Father, you know how it is.'"

Early in the church-building project, Eaton conveyed to Father Morrow, who conveyed to Bishop Hyland, his conviction that the new church should become the center of the parish. The relocation of the parish headquarters from Cedartown to Carrollton did make sense: the Carrollton Catholic population was bigger. With money flowing from the Chalkleys, Hyland quickly agreed to the change. He was, in fact, so concerned about his relationship with Susan and Eaton that he had asked Father Morrow to become the pastor of the new church after it was built because Morrow had been getting on so well with them. For Susan and Eaton, the relationship with Morrow was important. They genuinely liked him as a man and as a priest, but he was most certainly also part of the grand design to strengthen Eaton in the Catholic community, to forge a psychological bridge to the Church, if not a spiritual one. Susan and Eaton were eager to win back what he had lost by marrying her.

During the following year, 1961, while Eaton delighted in the little details of the construction of the church's foundation and basic structure, Susan spent most of her time away from Carrollton, out in "that dungheap" and in Europe, making the movies that Eaton helped her choose. For lack of scripts, she and Twentieth Century-Fox mutually decided to abort her six-picture deal after only two films. Important vehicles for female stars of the fifties, like Susan, were becoming extinct. Instead of making the *I'll Cry Tomorrow* and *I Want to Live!* docudramas that had brought Susan to her peak, the studios were now concentrating on steamy

Top: She was quite fond of gentlemanly William Holden in *Young and
Willing,* 1943. *(Gene Arceri collection)*

Above: Jess and Susan and the two-month-old twins, Timothy and Gregory.
(Courtesy of Wally Marrenner)

Top Left: "Mr. and Mrs. Jess Barker (former Edythe Marrenner of Brooklyn)" was what Susan scribbled on this shot. *(Courtesy of Wally Marrenner)*

Top Right: Florence, her seven-year-old son Larry, and Ellen Marrenner—in Hollywood, 1951. *(Courtesy of Florence Marrenner Dietrich)*

Above: Susan and Marsha Hunt, in the famous powder room cat fight from *Smash-Up*. *(Universal Pictures)*

To Wally — from his little sister Susan also known as "Edythe" "mama" "movie actress" "Mrs Barker" "Miss Hayward" and "Hey Red!" Love and kisses

Top Left: Susan sent this photo of herself to Wally while he was in the armed services. It kept him out of a lot of K.P. *(Courtesy of Wally Marrenner)*

Top Right: On August 28, 1951, she pressed her hands and feet into wet cement in front of Grauman's Chinese Theater. *(Courtesy of Cleo Miller June)*

Above: Tulsa, 1949, was Susan's most important film of this period. *(Doug McClelland collection)*

Top: Susan played courageous Jane Froman in *With a Song in My Heart* in 1952 and the same year helped Froman accept a USO citation. *(Doug McClelland collection)*

Above: Dan Dailey, Sam Jaffe, Susan, and Tamara Shayne in *I Can Get It for You Wholesale,* 1951. It was a perfect vehicle for her. *(Doug McClelland collection)*

With a Song in My Heart established Susan as a top money-maker. *(Doug McClelland collection)*

st before Susan's breakup with Jess in 1953, she posed with, from left, lly, Martha Little, the boss of Robert Emslie, and Robert Emslie—an old xt-door neighbor who had put a dime in Susan's fist when she was an ant. *(Courtesy of Wally Marrenner)*

Top: Violence, much of it against herself, was brewing in Susan all through the very public 1954 divorce trial. From left: Jess Barker, his attorney, S. S. Hahn, and Susan. *(UPI/Bettmann Newsphotos)*

Above: Lillian Roth, *I'll Cry Tomorrow*'s producer Lawrence Weingarten, and star Susan, who fought to get the role of Roth. *(Doug McClelland collection)*

Left & Above: She rushed from the courtroom to Utah to make Howard
~~gh~~ghes' (now) high-camp classic *The Conqueror.* Above photo, from left, at
~~~~une 30 birthday party for Susan: director Dick Powell, John Wayne, and
~~s~~san flanked by Gregory and Timothy. *(Doug McClelland collection)* Wayne,
~~s~~san, and choreographer Bob Sydney, whom Susan adored. *(Courtesy of
~~~~ Sydney)*

Right: Now it was the King's birthday, on the 1955 set of *Soldier of*
~~~~une. *(Doug McClelland collection)*

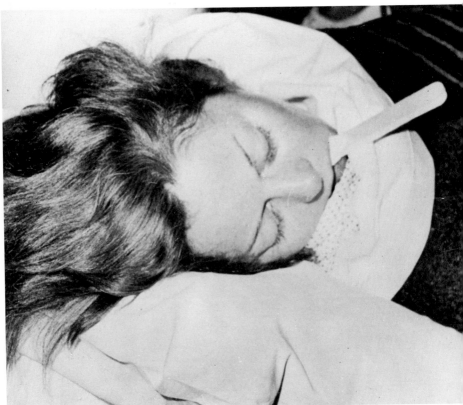

Distressed by her divorce, Susan took three bottles of pills the night of
April 26, 1955. The next day the whole world saw these two gruesome
photos. In top photo, from left, are Wally Marrenner and Detectives
G. W. Wilkerson and K. L. Brondell. *(UPI/Bettmann Newsphotos)*

spectacles, like *Peyton Place* and *By Love Possessed*, that would make people leave their television sets for a few hours. Susan made a concession to the new trend when she agreed to star in MGM's *Ada* with Dean Martin. Based on a novel called *Ada Dallas* by Wirt Williams, the film cast Susan as a prostitute who winds up married to a Southern governor and ultimately wields all the power. *Ada*, which Susan and Eaton probably accepted because Daniel Mann was directing, had a number of scenes in which Susan could display her fiery temperament, but it was not a good choice for her. Audiences preferred to stay in front of their tubes rather than see her as a prostitute who makes good.

When Ross Hunter sent her what was probably the most mawkish, sentimental script ever penned, for a remake of the remake of the popular Fannie Hurst novel *Back Street*, Susan had her doubts. But after she and Eaton discovered that she would be wearing hundreds of thousands of dollars' worth of Jean Louis creations, would be suffering in a lavish New York apartment, a garish Italian villa and a boutique in Paris—in other words, given the full Ross Hunter tear-jerker treatment—the Chalkleys were seduced into saying yes.

For the film, Susan dieted down to barely over a hundred pounds and looked, in front of the cameras, positively radiant: no, more than that—for cameraman Stanley Cortez captured a glow in her that everyone agrees was strictly for Eaton. She did very little real acting in this movie, which didn't need it; what she did was play the part of herself that was in love. That wasn't hard, with Eaton forever around the glamorous European locations. In the opening scenes, as Rae Smith, an aspiring clothes-designer, she looked every bit the twenty-year-old that the script suggested and not at all too old for the thirtyish John Gavin, who the role Charles Boyer had once played.

Back Street was utterly trite, a woman's film that seemed not so much to be made for women as to pander to them. The characters were plastic people in a fairytale for childish adults. There was also a good deal of unintentional campy humor. Susan was supposed to be seen as suffering (as Margaret Sullavan had done before her) because of her tragic love for a married man. But Susan's character, as one of the world's most successful dress-designers, pulls up in front of chateaux in racing cars, accepts a lavish villa as a gift from her married lover, romps around in superb gowns and coats, and suffers so little that the situation almost seems like a comedy takeoff on the 1941 movie. Susan and John Gavin have inane dialogue like:

RAE: "When you love somebody—that's it."
PAUL: "Just that simple."
RAE: "It is for me. How about you?"
PAUL: (No answer.)
RAE: "Oh, Paul, I know this is crazy—but I love you, I love you."
PAUL: "As simple as that and as wonderful."
RAE: "We'd better be going. You've got a plane to catch."
PAUL: "There'll always be another plane to catch, but never another picnic with Rae Smith."
RAE: "Don't say it, please. Never is such a long time." (They clinch in the grass.)

It was all great silliness. Not long after the movie's release, *Mad* magazine gave Susan a worst-actress award. But nothing in this movie, not the cardboard performances, not the soaring romantic music, not the foolish clichés, mattered as much as that glow of love in Susan's face. Audiences seemed to feel that, too, and made *Back Street* one of the top-grossing movies of the year. Of all of her movies, it is the one most often played on television. Once in a great while, a local station will run *I Want to Live!* at three a.m.

When Susan married Eaton, she adopted his family, his friends, his town, his life, and had little more to do with her own family and the few friends she had made in Hollywood. She and Wally had always been on good terms and continued to be, although Wally didn't appear all that interested in visiting Susan in her Georgia home. He couldn't leave his at the racetrack; he saw her when she came to Hollywood and talked with her on the phone. With Florence, not a word had been spoken, on the telephone or in person, for three years. Susan's pattern, for decades, had been one of moving away from her family.

But while Susan was fulfilling her destiny, Florence, now fearfully on her own, was still searching for her own identity. Unlike Susan, Florence didn't find the breakup of the family any sort of liberation. She took the death of her mother and the final loss of her sister's affections badly. Nearly fifty, she had little money and had to support her seventeen-year-old son, Larry, without a husband. Wanting finally to make a home for herself and Larry, she married a mining engineer named John Dietrich, who claimed to be the brother of Noah Dietrich, Howard Hughes' chief aide. He took her to his lavish home in Nevada, but she says he had a temper and, as with Udo Zaenglin, she left him within months after the marriage. (She paints a vivid picture of Dietrich running after her and Larry at the train station, while Florence would only say to him, "I'm leaving!" That was that.) Suddenly alone again, she scraped up $175 by selling an Exercycle and went back to Hollywood with Larry, then discovered she was pregnant with Dietrich's baby. To support herself, she took a domestic job, but had to quit in her seventh month. With nowhere to turn, Florence went on public assistance, receiving $40 a month for rent, enough to pay for a one-room apartment for her and Larry, and $8 a month for food, which she cooked on a hotplate. In December of 1960, she had her baby, a beautiful daughter whom she called Moira (after Moira Shearer), in City Hospital, while Larry was put temporarily in Juvenile Hall. For a while, the authorities were threatening to take little Moira away from Florence for possible adoption because of Florence's inability to support her baby. Moira turned into a darling little girl with light red hair and a cute turned-up nose just like her famous aunt's. The resemblance between little Moira and the way Susan looked as a child was remarkable. The family remained on welfare, but there was never enough money and so, as a child, Moira made some by shining shoes on the streets of downtown Los Angeles. "When the welfare people found out about it," says Moira, "they threatened to take her to court to cut us off. You weren't supposed to make any extra money." At the time, they were living in an apartment at Beachwood and Franklin, in the heart of Hollywood. Moira says that as a girl she only heard of her famous aunt, Susan Hayward, but never met her, as had Larry. "And I wasn't sure that I wanted to."

To raise some money to help support her baby, and possibly as a last-ditch effort to communicate with her sister, Florence gave a story to *Confidential*, that legendary scandal magazine, about how Susan was allowing her to live on the public dole. MY SISTER SUSAN HAYWARD HAS MILLIONS...BUT I'M ON RELIEF, blared the cover of *Confidential* in April of 1961, along with a photograph of Florence that showed an unmistakable resemblance to Susan. There were other stories, in *Modern Screen* and the *Los Angeles Mirror*. When called for their reaction, Susan and Eaton issued a terse statement via their lawyer: "This has been a long, drawn-out situation, and Miss Hayward and her husband, Eaton Chalkley, prefer not to discuss it."

Why Susan wouldn't help Florence is still a mystery. One suspects that there was an element of mystery in it even to Susan herself. Right after all the articles came out, she brought the subject up with Ann Moran.

"What would *you* do?" Susan asked her.

"Let her go to work," said Ann.

"Let her go out and get it the way I got it," chimed Susan. "Let her work for it."

Susan's explanation of why she was permitting her sister to live on the public dole, without regard for her infant niece, sounded somewhat like those complaints against Jess for living off her and not working. But with Susan there was always some hidden terrain underneath her long-standing grudges. Her actions had as much to do with Ellen's earlier domination of Susan's private life as with that old childhood rivalry with Florence. Susan could not make peace with the memory of her mother, who certainly would have wanted her to help her sister.

A few months after the flurry of Florence articles appeared, Susan learned that Jeff Chandler was in a Los Angeles hospital suffering from a ruptured spinal disk and serious abdominal bleeding which occurred, apparently, after an operation. The original disk problem had come about after he injured his back while filming *The Marauders* in the Philippines. He was wasting away to nothing in his hospital bed. His ex-wife, Marjorie, and his divorced parents, Phillip and Ann Grossel, rushed to his bedside. Susan, who had been intimate with him a decade before and had loved him, phoned the hospital every day, only to hear that his condition was worsening. After a series of operations, Ira Grossel, alias Jeff Chandler, Susan's casual childhood friend and her affectionate adult friend, died of septicemia on the night of June 17, 1961. He was forty-two. Grief-stricken and irate, Susan joined some of Jeff's friends in calling for a complete investigation of the circumstances of his death.

Engulfed by a series of bad reviews for her most recent films, Susan chose *I Thank a Fool* simply because the filming was to be done in England and Ireland, instead of taking *Sweet Bird of Youth*, which would have brought the Chalkleys to Hollywood. She hadn't even bothered to read the script. If she had, she would have realized that this strange story of a Canadian woman doctor who is convicted of the mercy-killing murder of her lover and then is accused of murdering the wife of her second lover, played by Peter Finch, was abysmally unclear. The film flopped and Susan's reputation began to suffer.

It was as if Susan had lost her ability to select parts, Eaton's influence having undermined that ability. Whenever she had a professional meeting, Eaton was usually there, giving her his quiet signals, steering her in the way he preferred. Even in social gatherings, she let Eaton do most of the talking for them. But, and this was the point, Susan was happier than she had ever been.

Eaton continued spending her money. After her bad experience on *I Thank a Fool*, Susan decided to quit films for a while and bought a six-hundred-acre ranch/farm in Heflin, Alabama, for him. It cost her $50,000 to renovate the main farmhouse and another $25,000 to build an air-conditioned barn according to Eaton's design. He wanted the barn for his offices; it was also to be used for entertaining and for barn dances. They also redid a small studio house on the ranch so that Susan could work on her new hobby, creating mosaics. The ranch, where the Chalkleys intended to spend a good deal of their time, had 225 head of cattle roaming about. Eaton had trucks emblazoned with the insignia: CHALKMAR (for Chalkley-Marrenner) FARMS.

Susan was also paying the bills that were piling up for the new church in Carrollton, though not always in the most generous spirit. Around this time, she would poor-mouth to Wally: "If Eaton keeps spending my money like this, I'll go broke." Far from it: all the building didn't make a dent in her total assets, which were accumulating large sums of interest. Her one-third ownership of the profits of *I Want to Live!* alone had made her a half-million dollars.

As the church neared the final phase of construction, Susan became more than just the bill-payer and began going continually to Eaton and Father Morrow about the details of the interior design. She had grown interested in decorating during the construction of the main Sunset Boulevard house, in which she had helped choose the interior finishing materials, the color scheme and the Impressionist paintings. The architect had called for a modern-looking church with light pine beams and a green carpet. Susan had no qualms about Morrow's desire to see the beams a dark brown and the carpet a maroon. But Morrow also wanted the interior to reflect the recommendation of the Second Vatican Council that churches be simplified and not cluttered with a lot of statues and pictures which would distract from the altar and the pulpit. Susan, an Episcopalian who had only her idea of Catholicism as "theater" to guide her, fought Morrow for statues. Morrow, with Eaton's encouragement, held his ground. He wanted only two paintings for the wall behind the altar, which he commissioned from the director of the Atlanta School of Art, Joel Reeves. One of them was of Jesus of the Sacred Heart and imparted a modern tone to the altar. During a trip to Europe, Susan and Eaton walked in and out of old churches, saw all the wonderful statues of Jesus and the saints, and Susan once again told Morrow that she wanted to buy some for the church. When Morrow politely refused to accept them, Susan, who squeezed full value out of every dime she spent, said: "Father, you won't be pastor here always. I'll get my statues in."

Early in 1963, Susan signed for United Artists' *Stolen Hours*, a remake of the 1939 Bette Davis triumph *Dark Victory*. It was to be filmed in England at the Shepperton studio and in the countryside. Susan had been reluctant to do it. Morrow remembers Eaton saying to him that he thought the two of them might be going on location with a new movie "if I can get Susan to really do it."

"But why have her do it?" asked Morrow, who had already heard Susan talk about not wanting to make movies anymore.

"Because," said Eaton, "she has such a gift. She should make them."

Stolen Hours did not have a bad script, but couldn't possibly be as good as the original, no matter how hard Susan and the director, Daniel Petrie, tried. It featured the handsome British actor Michael Craig in the old George Brent role of the doctor who performs a brain operation, then falls in love with his terminally ill patient; and Diane Baker in the Geraldine Fitzgerald role, but this time playing a sister/friend instead of a secretary/friend. The filming went well, and for the most part what was caught on film was pleasant if not riveting. No attempt was made by the scriptwriters, the director or Susan herself to imitate the high-strung nature of the original *Dark Victory*; instead, all the movement of the original play by George Emerson Brown and Bertram Bloch was slowed down, focusing attention on an attractively calm Susan. The second half of the movie, in which Susan, as Laura Pember, has only months to enjoy her new love-life in the country, was beautifully acted and serenely touching. One believed in the courage that Susan was showing on screen.

But it is hard to watch *Stolen Hours* today; hard to separate what finally happened to Susan and the fiction of the dying woman who at one point has her head shaved for a brain operation. One part of the film, in the beginning, stays in the mind. Susan is attending a car race and a sudden accident occurs. Susan (as Laura) rushes in with the crowd and discovers that an innocent bystander has been critically hurt. An ambulance driver takes his pulse and proceeds to cover his body and head with a blanket. Susan shouts, "Stop! He's still breathing." The attendant says that he won't be for long and that the blanket should be put over his face. "Not while he can still see!" she says. "Let him see life for every second he's got left." Susan could not have realized how horribly real that dialogue would become.

She was beginning to look her age in *Stolen Hours*. That youthful look of love that she had had in *Back Street* was now gone. She looked older, more tired, perhaps for no other reason than that the clock could not be held back much longer. Nevertheless, she was as happy as ever with Eaton around. In her dressing room at the Shepperton studios, she spent quiet hours knitting Eaton a sweater. Next to his always-present yellow roses on the dressing-room table, she kept her favorite picture of him in a silver frame. On her days off, during the concluding scenes for the picture, she and Eaton drove along the Cornwall coast. They even talked about buying property there.

After filming, they went to Rome and met with Father Daniel McGuire, a friend of Father Brew's who was then with the Vatican Jesuits in Rome. Father McGuire introduced them to his friends in the Church, people whom Eaton, always entranced by clerics, could never have met on his own. Eventually, Eaton and Susan had an audience with the Pope. Eaton's application to have his marriage to Susan recognized by the Church was still being processed. There was really little he could do to speed things up.

The new Carrollton church, Our Lady of Perpetual Help, was completed and dedicated late in 1963, but the joy of the Chalkleys and their friends was marred by Eaton's sudden loss of health. He had a recurrence of the serum-hepatitis infection which he had first come down with more than ten years before in Chicago. Eaton, a big, strapping man, had always exercised and kept himself in top shape. Lately, however, he had begun to drink more heavily and the assault on his liver apparently brought back the old infection.

Father Brew was now coming to Carrollton frequently, to install Georgian stone as backdrops for the twelve stations of the cross in Our Lady of Perpetual Help. He was worried by the hepatitis, the drinking and the general state of Eaton's health. Only a few years before, Eaton had been hospitalized for a kidney infection.

Martin Rackin was now head of production at Paramount Pictures, which was planning to film Harold Robbins' novel *Where Love Has Gone*. Rackin, who had already put Susan in one of her worst movies, *Top Secret Affair*, wanted her to star in this potboiler, an obvious fictional transformation of the Lana Turner–Johnny Stompanato manslaughter case of 1958. The trial was better than the book, and the book was better than the film script. Marty sent the script to Susan's agent, but then called her directly.

"My husband was a great salesman," says Helen Rackin. "Before she knew it, he had talked her into saying she would do it. She read the script, but a week before starting she had second thoughts about it and called Marty.

"'Marty, I don't know if I want to do this,' she said.

"Suddenly, she decided it wasn't right for her and she wanted to get out of it. That's where Eaton came in. He said, 'Listen, Susan, you did promise Marty you would do it. It would put him in a bad spot.' Then he said to my husband, 'Marty, Susan will do it.' I must say, Eaton is the one who talked her into doing it."

All of Susan's instincts told her that an actress who had achieved the performance she had given in *I Want to Live!* should not now be rolling in the cinematic gutter. The script would have Susan playing a promiscuous sculptress whose jealous daughter is put on trial for killing her mother's lover; later, it is revealed that the daughter really meant to kill her own mother. Eaton, with his strong sense of loyalty and his lack of understanding of his wife's talent and reputation, was motivated only by the fact that he had gotten to know Marty Rackin. Eaton believed himself to be an insider, and could not see the extent of Rackin's self-interest.

For the part of Susan's antagonistic mother in *Where Love Has Gone*, Rackin chose Bette Davis, knowing full well that Davis and Hayward could never hit it off. Says Helen, "I asked Marty why he didn't get Barbara Stanwyck for the mother and he replied that Bette Davis was hot right now. [Davis had just had a comeback with *Whatever Happened to Baby Jane?*] I think he realized he had made a mistake because, had he used Barbara Stanwyck, she would have been far superior."

Susan and Eaton flew to Hollywood in early 1964 and stayed at the Beverly Wilshire Hotel during filming. At a contract-signing press conference, Susan and Bette showed up for reporters and spoke pleasantly to each other, but the niceties disappeared soon after. Some thought the war that occurred on the set between the two Academy Award winners was caused by Susan's having recently done a remake of one of Bette Davis' most famous films, *Dark Victory*. ("Some pictures should never be remade," Davis later told reporters, and she was right.) But the problem between the two was really caused by a rotten script which made both women insecure. It caused Bette to insist on rewriting her own death scene, which she now wanted to run for two pages, and Susan to fret about Davis possibly stealing the movie. Susan finally went to the front office and demanded that the script be shot as originally written or she would pull out of the film. Eaton tried to calm Susan throughout, while Bette Davis felt that Susan was being mean to her. In a finale to all the dissension, one which reflected the utter triviality of the script, Bette and Susan flipped a coin over which one of their characters was to die on screen. Susan won (lost) and had to plunge a knife into her own stomach.

When *Newsweek* said, "One watches *Where Love Has Gone* in disbelief, wondering how, in a movie from a major studio, there could be such universal and serene ineptitude," it was being kind. Bosley Crowther rightly tore Susan to pieces. She had betrayed all of her most ardent admirers from the fifties. Much later, she made the excuse that she had done *Where Love Has Gone* only for the money. She didn't need it; the reason was Eaton. But Susan hadn't disillusioned only her fans from the fifties. Today, because television airs *Back Street* and *Where Love Has Gone* so often, and seldom runs her most important films, many young people associate the name of Susan Hayward with lavish Hollywood trash. That is a terrible injustice.

Everyone believed that Susan had a wonderful marriage. After six years, the side of their union that was indeed wonderful was the obvious, external one, the part of the Chalkleys that was surrounded by friends and good fellowship and the joys provided by unlimited resources. They were forever on planes between Carrollton, Fort Lauderdale, Hollywood, New York and various European locations. They stayed in the best hotels, ate in the finest restaurants, always held hands. People thought they were completely in love; of course, they were.

But on some important level there was an inappropriateness to the match. Eaton was incapable of understanding the world in which Susan had gained her fame. Perhaps that is why, unintentionally, he did such damage to her career. She, on the other hand, had fallen in love with a fantasy out of *Gone with the Wind*, the movie she would have given all of her roles to star in. Eaton was a Brooklyn girl's comic-book Ashley Wilkes: Southern (with a twang not much stronger than Leslie Howard's), genteel, independently outgoing. The brilliant Joseph L. Mankiewicz, who had met Eaton several years before while they were all touring for *I Want to Live!* (Mankiewicz owned an interest in the production company), offered the following insight when reached by telephone: "Susan wanted to become the Southern gentlewoman. I could see her as an *actress* wanting Eaton Chalkley, but I couldn't think of Susan as a woman wanting him. The actress in her wanted him." She had loved the fantasy. What Susan at first did not understand was that the real Eaton was a man whose charming affability was mired in tremendous guilt which threatened only to get worse.

And worse it got. One day in September of 1964, the phone rang. Joe Chalkley, Eaton's firstborn and only son, had been killed in an accident near Louisville, Kentucky. Joe was twenty-six.

If the Lord had suddenly decided to turn Eaton into Job, He couldn't have invented a more efficient means. Eaton's grief seemed normal—at first. Father Brew, at the time on retreat in Detroit, remembers the terrible call from Eaton telling him that his son had just been killed while flying an airplane. There had been a thunderstorm. Joe had rammed into a mountain and died instantly. Eaton would be taking his body back to Washington, D.C., for burial near where Joe's mother and sisters lived. Brew expressed sympathy, but couldn't be definite about whether he could attend the funeral.

Susan begged Eaton to let her come to Washington, but Eaton said no; it would be too awkward. Meanwhile, Brew finally broke away from his retreat, and when Eaton met him at the Louisville airport, he told his best friend soulfully: "This is more than I hoped for." Eaton and Thomas had the grim task of taking Joe's body from Louisville to Atlanta, where Harvey Hester joined them, and then on to Washington, D.C.

In the months following, Eaton began to drink much more heavily, for Joe's death marked a kind of turning point for him and Susan. What disturbed Eaton was that his son, although polite, had never accepted Susan as his father's wife. That was why, as Eaton explained to Brew, Joe wouldn't stay around home, had gotten restless and wound up flying planes. Eaton grew permanently depressed. He looked at Joe's death as a punishment for the wrong he and Susan had done.

The loss of the sacraments. The loss of Joe. Susan's love for Eaton was at the center of his guilt. What could she do? She had spent so much of her time and money trying to make Eaton happy, and yet there was that oppressive sense of wrongdoing which was destroying the foundations of her marriage. Her ability to communicate with him spiritually was limited; her understanding of his faith, not great. Her private solution to the problem was superficial but the only one she had: to try to please him at every turn, even more so than before, to make him aware of her love on every possible level. At times, her love was cloying. To Eaton, it all seemed like make-believe. Her response to the incredible obstacles he was placing before her should have been to smash bottles, slam doors or slap him in the face. That is precisely how she had reacted to the great frustrations in her marriage to Jess. Instead, she mothered Eaton, bought him more property, invited his friends to the house. He sensed the artificiality and concluded that her behavior wasn't coming from the heart. That she was playing just another role.

In a moment of utter terror over what his marriage had become, Eaton turned to Father Brew and asked: "Where does the acting stop?"

The drinking was bringing on more hepatitis attacks. It seemed very deliberate on Eaton's part. Brew sensed what Eaton was doing to himself and spoke continually to his friend about his health. Susan always liked Brew, but she didn't hide from him the resentment she felt because her husband would often listen to him but not to her. She also didn't like his solicitousness; Eaton was *her* problem.

The bouts of hepatitis began to take their toll on his energy and physical appearance. Susan took him to the Fort Lauderdale house for the sun to bring health back to his jaundiced face, but whatever good all the boating and the lounging and the warmth did was undone by the drinking. Once during this period, Susan flew to Hollywood with Eaton on business and met with Helen and Marty Rackin. Helen says, "There was a big change in Eaton. He had gotten very, very thin. He laughingly said that on the boat he had tripped and hurt his leg and that the leg was giving him trouble, and my husband said, 'My God, Eaton, you've lost a lot of weight.' Susan was very defensive and cut in, 'He looks marvelous.'"

She knew that she was losing Eaton, the love of her life, but she remained the steely stalwart, denying all of her fears. She said not a word to anyone about how her world was coming apart, not even her brother. Her fans from her movies of the fifties would have been especially moved, but because Susan had dropped out of Hollywood, this tormented part of her life was lived virtually in secret.

The Christmas of 1964 was filled with the ghosts of Christmases past.

It was a tradition that the Chalkleys spent every Christmas in Carrollton. The good side of their marriage was highlighted at Christmas, for it was the time of year when Eaton's natural gregariousness and his strong religious feeling found complete expression. It was always the happiest time for Susan. The change in season brought cold weather, warm kitchens and a fire in the living room. Amid the snow-covered countryside, they scurried here and there buying presents and a pine tree and extra ornaments for it. Ann Moran was asked to come to their home every

Christmas. She remembered: "We always went in on Christmas Eve for a holiday drink, right after midnight mass. They had a gorgeous tree with golden angels, red ribbons and silver bells. The fireplace was ablaze, casting a golden glow on her Oscar on the mantel, and there were silver trays heaped high with food and silver coffee urns filled and placed around. She told me, 'If ever you need them for a church affair, come over and get them.'" And Father Morrow remembers previous Christmases with the Chalkleys. He recalls that sometimes Father Brew would come by and often there was corpulent Harvey Hester, "not very pleasant to look at" but his adorable heart was always showing. Cautious Susan displayed various levels of ease with Eaton's friends; with Harvey, the only friend who had known Susan and Eaton separately before they were married, she was uninhibited and would gag with hysterical laughter. One Christmas, Father Morrow came for lunch and found Harvey sitting in the living room. "Eaton used to egg me on to get Susan and Harvey to come to mass more often. 'They're pagans,' Eaton would say. When I saw Harvey on Christmas Day, I said, 'I sure missed you last night in church.' They all started laughing like mad because Harvey had spent the night in the pokey. He had been going around with his bottles of liquor as Christmas gifts, having a drink with everybody, and he drove out for a celebration by way of Buchanan, and I guess he was weaving and he ended up in jail. He couldn't get anybody to get him out until he finally got ahold of Eaton."

Susan must have known that it was all gradually ending, that all her happiness with Eaton would soon become the domain of the past. She tried her best to make the Christmas of 1964 jolly, but Joe's specter haunted Eaton.

Now there were other issues besides creating good times. He spoke to her often about going to mass regularly. She felt she couldn't simply attend without being a true Catholic. That was of course the huge problem which was destroying their marriage: the Church wouldn't permit her to convert because she was "living in sin," and the Church denied Eaton the sacraments. It was the conundrum that was partly driving Eaton to self-destruct and left Susan frankly mystified. She confided in Brew that she considered her marriage to be perfect—"There's nothing missing," she told him. So why was Eaton so distressed by these rules? she asked.

"She never really understood Eaton's situation," assesses Brew.

She only knew how bad things were getting. She absolutely refused to work while Eaton was sick, spending most of her time taking care of him in Fort Lauderdale. But a few months after the New Year, Susan's agent, Jack Gordean, called to ask her to come to Hollywood to discuss a part in Joe Mankiewicz's next film, *Anyone for Venice?*, a sophisticated retelling of the *Volpone* story to be shot in Venice in the fall of 1965. Eaton insisted that she consider the part: Italy would be good for both of them, despite his illness, and she hadn't worked for a year. Besides, Mankiewicz was a genius. She had already worked with him on *House of Strangers* and trusted him.

Susan accepted, but as the time arrived for their departure for Italy in the fall, Eaton was weaker and yellower. He knew he was dying; his liver was being progressively eroded not only by the infection but by an insidious sclerosis from the drinking. He called all his old friends from the corner of Sixth and B Streets in Washington, including his precious friends from the Renroc team, and invited them to a reunion at the Carlton Hotel in the capital. As many of the old gang showed up as could be reached on such short notice. Brew says: "Everyone there was shocked by Eaton's appearance. This big, strong guy was wasting away. He did not look like himself.... He was looking for a life he had lost somewhere between his two marriages." They all talked about the old times; they gagged about the time when, during a previous reunion in Washington, they were presented with a $350 damage bill from the hotel.

In Carrollton again, when Susan saw how bad he looked, she offered either to quit the film or to go to Venice alone. No, he didn't want her to break her business commitments, which were nearly sacred to him, and he didn't want to face all alone what might soon happen to him. So in September of 1965 they flew to Venice.

Shooting had already been in progress a month on *The Honey Pot*, the movie's final title. Mankiewicz says he is still angry today about what the studio cutters did to his film. He had imagined an elaborately developed and witty tale of a millionaire, played by Rex Harrison, who pretends to be dying in his Venice mansion and invites his three wealthy ex-wives to visit him, presumably to test their affections. Besides Harrison, Mankiewicz had hired a

truckload of talent. The three wives were to be Edie Adams, Capucine and Susan, who played Texan millionairess Lone-Star
Crockett Sheridan. Cliff Robertson was Ben Jonson's original Fly
character, essentially a kind of master of ceremonies for all of his
boss's schemes. Maggie Smith was Lone-Star's secretary. In the
released "brutalized" version of the film, Lone-Star was murdered
and the whole second half became an ordinary murder mystery
with a pat resolution. But Mankiewicz says that what he had filmed
was quite different. He had done a fantasy dream-sequence, later
cut, in which Susan, as Lone-Star, leaves Cecil Fox (Rex Harrison)
to die in the desert after stealing his gold, "a satire on Westerns."
Anyone for Venice? was intended to be one of those mythic, rarefied
jewels that Mankiewicz was famous for, like *All About Eve*, but, as
The Honey Pot, it wound up just a talky stage piece. (Mankiewicz
says that his original uncut film is currently being pieced together
and will eventually be shown.)

Filming continued for an arduous eight months, filled with
tragedies and dangers. "It was a very, very unhappy period," says
Mankiewicz. Edie Adams concurs: "We all had a bad time. It was
a hard-luck picture. Our cinematographer, Gianni di Venanzo,
died suddenly during the shooting. The movie was plagued with
so many misfortunes, even though it read beautifully—a clever
satire."

While Susan ministered to Eaton in their hotel room and at
poolside whenever she was not filming, Venetians were, ironically,
alerted to a widespread hepatitis outbreak. Edie Adams arranged
for gamma-globulin shots for the entire cast, but Susan refused
to have one. "I'm not letting any doctor near me!" she snapped
to Edie.

Susan, as usual, didn't join in with the cast on any social level.
Joe Mankiewicz was the only one Susan seemed comfortable with,
although the two of them had never developed any real cama-
raderie. Edie Adams read the stand-back signs: "I would have
liked to have gotten close to her. But she let nobody near her; we
all kept away. She was a small, gutsy lady and she was under a
strain."

During the months that Eaton was in Venice with Susan, she
never discussed his physical suffering with the other actors. Edie
had heard that Eaton was drinking a lot, but didn't know the

extent of his problems. Susan kept it all bottled up. When Eaton was feeling up to it, they visited Father Daniel McGuire in Rome. Eaton was always happy to be with priests.

In Rome, he grew weaker with the disease and in the first week of December came down with the most severe attack of hepatitis ever. Susan was terrified. He was receiving treatment by Italian doctors, but neither she nor he wanted him to stay in Rome any longer. After making arrangements with Mankiewicz, she flew with Eaton to Fort Lauderdale, where he went into Holy Cross Hospital. His illness was very bad this time. She immediately called Father Brew.

An amazing thing happened before Brew arrived at the hospital. The chaplain at Holy Cross had been a priest at Mount St. Mary's, the Catholic college Eaton and Brew had attended. Although the chaplain had never met Eaton, he knew of his reputation and all about his invalid marriage to a famous movie star which made it impossible for him to receive the sacraments. But Church rules are clear: in such a case as Eaton's, the sacraments may be administered if there is danger of death. While Eaton lay suffering, the hospital chaplain absolved him, heard his confession, annointed him and gave him holy communion. Eaton had been waiting nine years.

By the time Father Brew found Eaton and Susan in the hospital room, his friend was heavily sedated. Brew already knew of the chaplain's absolution and that Eaton was making final preparations. Susan just assumed that Brew was there as Eaton's friend, but suddenly Eaton said to her: "Would you please step out of the room." Father Brew will never forget the look of irritation on Susan's face in that moment, just before she left the room. What really bothered her was that she had been asked to leave almost the second Eaton had set eyes on Brew. He heard Eaton's confession and gave him communion; later, they talked in private. Afterward, Susan asked the priest what her husband had said to him. Brew, of course, couldn't tell her. He politely said: "Eaton will let you know."

Eaton didn't want to die in a hospital and asked to be taken home to the Nermi Drive house. Brew moved in. Nurses tended Eaton around the clock. Then Eaton began to insist that Susan go back to Venice to finish the picture, telling her, "I'll be all right. You agreed to do it." She always did what Eaton told her to do.

She flew back to Venice, while Brew agreed to stay on at the house and to phone her the second there was a change or if Eaton should need her.

"The next few weeks were difficult," says Father Brew. "She was calling up every day, asking how he was. What can you tell a person on the telephone? He wasn't getting any better and there came a point when his doctor said, 'You have to tell her.'"

One can only imagine what Susan endured on the flight from Venice to Fort Lauderdale. It was right after New Year's Day, 1966. She had spent the loneliest Christmas of her adult life.

After she arrived home, she called Father Morrow in Carrollton. "You've been talking about coming down," she told him. "You better come down soon or you won't see Eaton again."

Morrow says: "She was so gentle with him. I remember I took a cab to the house and after I arrived she said, 'He's excited about your coming, but he's sleeping. Suppose we wait awhile. He'll wake up later. I'll take you out to the boat.' She wanted everything quiet. Then she said, 'I don't want to leave him alone too long,' and we came back in."

Walking back, she told Morrow, "Father, you know he is receiving communion now and it is making him so happy."

Morrow said, "What about you?"

"I started instruction," she said, "but I am more concerned about easing him through this. Then I'll look after myself."

Eaton was awake now. Morrow asked Susan about a rosary Eaton was clutching and Susan said, "Oh, he's constantly got those in his hands." Father Morrow remembers his visit with Eaton as pleasant, although difficult because Susan, who was doing most of his nursing now, kept running in and out of the bedroom with water and medicines. Later, when she and Morrow were alone, she mentioned something which concerned her. From the day she and Eaton had talked about building a church for Carrollton, Eaton had hoped the church would have a cemetery where he could be buried. But when Morrow had previously mentioned it to the archibishop, the prelate had resisted the idea because running a cemetery was a good deal of bother. But Morrow believed that Eaton should die exactly as he wished.

He said to Susan, "Do you mind if I use your phone?"

"I didn't tell her, but I called the archbishop and I said, 'Eaton Chalkley is back receiving the sacraments and is entitled to a full

Catholic funeral. He would also like to be buried at the church. Susan wants that, too. Why can't we?'

"The archbishop said, 'Yes, but when you get back you should announce that the parish is going to have a cemetery, so the announcement will precede the announcement that Eaton Chalkley will be buried there.'"

Brew, who had to leave the house briefly, came back to be with Eaton during his last week. Brew would say mass at a nearby church and then bring holy communion back to Eaton. Eaton was greatly comforted by his friend. They prayed together hourly while Eaton held a black onyx crucifix given to him by Brew, who in turn had gotten it from a priest friend, Father Robb, before the priest died.

Eaton now had the sacraments, the Church's forgiveness, the burial he wanted and a great closeness with his best friend. He believed wholeheartedly in the afterlife he was going to. Brew felt the restlessness in Eaton's soul subside. It was almost as if Eaton were choosing the time of his going, not really as though death were taking him against his will.

On January 9, while holding Susan's hand, Eaton told her that he was concerned about her soul. She promised to achieve the sacraments, too. Then Eaton died. He was fifty-seven.

It was a wonderful Catholic death. Eaton had not been afraid or demoralized. He had made his peace with his church and with himself.

CHAPTER 8

After

SUSAN was calm and brave, meticulous in all the preparations. Eaton's wake, she decided, would be held in Washington, D.C., so that his hordes of friends could come to see him; she also wanted to spare his first wife and his two daughters the awkwardness of having to come to Carrollton. While Eaton was laid out, Susan showed little emotion, and in Carrollton, where she brought his body for the funeral mass, she was much the same.

The winter sun was filtering thinly through the windows of Our Lady of Perpetual Help. Susan was dressed in black, standing erect, looking straight ahead during the service conducted by Thomas Brew. He eulogized his friend. He only told the truth. What bad could anyone say of Eaton? The small gathering in the church moved outside in silence to the open grave, where Brew intoned a final blessing as the casket was lowered into the ground. Morrow thought he saw a few tears in Susan's eyes but nothing more.

Mary Williams walked Susan back to the Sunset Boulevard house, where she had invited everyone to come for refreshments. Harvey Hester had the employees from his restaurant, Aunt Fanny's Cabin in Atlanta, bring all the food to Susan's. After a few hours, the guests left. Mary Williams didn't want to leave Susan alone, but eventually she left the house, too.

Brew had been staying at the guesthouse near the gate, as he usually did when he came to Carrollton. It was almost dusk when he thought to leave the house, cross the road and pay a farewell visit to Eaton in the new cemetery. "It wasn't until I got over there a little distance from the grave that I saw Susan lying on the grave, crying, holding her arms as if to cradle the grave. It was the only time that she really broke down." He picked her off the grave and held her in his arms, trying to comfort her. "She was a very sad, distraught and heartbroken lady." For all of Brew's reservations about the marriage, he never once doubted her love for Eaton.

Susan had loose ends to tie. She returned to Venice to finish *The Honey Pot*, then came back to Carrollton to try to live in the house alone. She couldn't. Some nights became so unbearably sleepless that she would go to Mary Williams, her substitute mother, and stay with her for a few days, sleeping in the upstairs bedroom. In the daytime, in between discussions with lawyers, accountants and real-estate people over her money and property, she began drinking to relax.

She went to Father Morrow to ask about beginning the process of conversion, which she hoped could be completed by her birthday, June 30. But something in her manner alerted Morrow to a phenomenon that priests often see in people who wish to convert quickly to Catholicism: an irrational belief that simply signing a few papers will turn their lives around. Morrow had to say to her, "You try to see what the reasons are behind your decision." Then he questioned her at length about her intentions. Why was she doing it now? Was it only because Eaton was Catholic? Morrow was only doing his job, but Susan became impatient: "I always wanted to, but the Church wouldn't let me."

"You know what it will mean," he said. "You will have to be very circumspect about whom you might marry in the future."

"Never, never will there be another man," she said. "I could never meet a man like Eaton Chalkley."

Eaton had just died. Her eagerness for conversion could have been pure emotionalism. Morrow suggested that Susan continue with the instruction she had begun while Eaton was alive. "It will take a while," he said, but that was the only way to do it right.

Dissatisfied with Morrow's answer, she went to Brew, who was no more encouraging: "When she told me she was going to do it, I didn't get overly enthusiastic because I thought she was going too fast. I wanted to be sure it was a calm, reasoned judgment. I also wanted to be sure she had an understanding of the Church's laws on marriage lest the whole thing come up again."

Susan, though, was determined to become a Catholic by her

birthday. Part of the rush was that she feared that if anything happened to her and she were not a Catholic, she could not be buried in consecrated ground next to her husband at Our Lady of Perpetual Help. In no time, Susan located Father Daniel McGuire, the Jesuit who had been so kind to her and Eaton in Rome and was now pastor of Sts. Peter and Paul Roman Catholic Church in Pittsburgh. In Father McGuire's estimation, Susan was ready and sincere, and she began instruction for her conversion. On the evening of June 29, 1966, Susan flew to Pittsburgh to sign the proper documents, and the next day, June 30, her forty-ninth birthday, she came to noon mass at Sts. Peter and Paul, stood before the altar and was baptized into the Catholic faith by Father McGuire.

A few days later, she received her first holy communion at the same church. Suddenly, it all became very Hollywood. A few people at the mass recognized her and approached her after the service. Then the press was alerted.

She left straightway for Fort Lauderdale, where she strengthened her ties to Timothy and Gregory, now attending Auburn University; then she went to Carrollton. For her first time at holy communion at Our Lady of Perpetual Help, she asked Mary Williams to walk behind her for support. Susan still hated being alone in the house (the maids didn't spend the nights there) and Mary spent a god deal of time with her there. Three months later, telling all of her friends in Carrollton, "I don't want anything to remind me," she sold the farm in Heflin and the Sunset Boulevard house. Because of her rush to get out of Carrollton, she took well below what she could have gotten for the main house and property. All the furnishings went to the new owners. She relocated permanently in the Nermi Drive house in Fort Lauderdale.

For months, she sat and stared at the canal next to her house, which she rarely left. She smoked up to five packs of cigarettes a day, and drank Jack Daniel's and Johnnie Walker Black Label and Beefeater martinis in large brandy snifters. Curlee had moved with Susan to Fort Lauderdale and became her constant companion. As Susan drank, she rambled on and on about her life with Eaton, while Curlee, who had endless loyalty to Susan, listened patiently.

Wally and Susan often talked on the phone. "I know she was depressed," he says; the terrible thought occurred to him that she might try to take her own life "because she loved Eaton so much."

Holed up with Curlee and her liquor, she only occasionally left the house to do some solitary fishing, but anything she tried to do alone that she had done with Eaton became painful. It was especially hard for her to meet new people, not only because of her prolonged grief but also because she had gotten so used to Eaton's gregariousness pulling people into her life. Her normal posture with people was still: "Leave me be."

Nevertheless, in the fall of 1966 she accepted an invitation to the home of Dr. Leonard Erdman, the physician who had cared for Eaton during his illness. At the dinner was Ron Nelson, a charming, thirty-eight-year-old Southerner who was the executive director of the Fort Lauderdale Heart Fund. Nelson had been a great fan of Susan's and knew that Susan and Eaton had lived on the same "island" as he did, but he never met them. Now that Susan was alone, he wanted Erdman to introduce him to her. "I suspected that there was something there between us." He was right. She, inhibited, vulnerable, responded to Nelson's outgoing Southern manner and his wit: some of the Eaton Chalkley fantasy all over again. Nelson's grandmother had even been buried in Carrollton. After they left Erdman's, they spent the night together.

Her life changed immediately. She accepted his invitations to Heart Fund charity benefits, becoming his constant companion in that tiny retirement community. The local papers quickly picked up on the romance/friendship. Under his influence, Susan learned to relax and joke, but without the slightest letup on her drinking. Ron was far from a teetotaler himself and joined her. As they sat sipping in her living room, she told him endless stories about Eaton, Jess, her childhood in Brooklyn, the rivalry with Florence. Ron Nelson, her fan, occasional lover and best friend, listened with unbroken interest.

Susan had met Ron Nelson none too soon, for it was positively unsafe for a woman of Susan's fame to be living alone with another woman. Once a young and apparently disturbed Viet Nam uniformed veteran traced Susan to the Nermi Drive house. Her celluloid image was his great love; he wanted to meet her and tell her of his passion. He stood outside the house, yelling and demanding to see her. Curlee looked out from behind the jalousies and went rigid when she saw that the young man was holding a gun pointed right at her. She screamed for Susan, who came running and shoved Curlee out of the line of fire. She whispered to Curlee to phone the police, while with great bravery she stood in front of the jalousies herself and began to talk sympathetically to the vet. She eased his tension. He said he loved her, had seen her films repeatedly, then talked about the war. Susan played her role as beautifully as any plainclothes policewoman could have, not showing fright or budging from the window. The police, meanwhile, came in a boat on the canal beside Susan's house and carefully made their way around the house. They lunged at him from both sides and he gave up quietly. Susan walked outside and told the young man not to worry, she had only called the police for his safety, and did not press charges. Later, Susan would inquire about him and wrote to him while he recuperated in the hospital.

Susan was still not interested in making movies. By now, most of the studio heads who would have jumped at the chance to have her in a film were either dead or retired. Walter Wanger had been knocked down a second time by his failure to bring *Cleopatra* in on budget. Twentieth Century-Fox's Darryl F. Zanuck, who had thought so highly of Susan that she was invited to lunch in his private dining room, was gone. Susan was frankly terrified to return to Hollywood and learn that she was just another aging movie queen. And she wasn't anxious to do with her career what now had to be done: modify her image away from the old-guard glamour to fit the concepts of new directors like Mike Nichols. Nichols was seriously interested in Susan for the part of Mrs. Robinson in *The Graduate*, but, repulsed at the semi-nude hotel-room sex scenes she would have to play, she did not consider it. The movie revived Anne Bancroft's career and would have done the same for Susan's.

Her view of her career these days was strictly short-range. Hollywood was her money factory, the cash cow she could milk for some extra change. That attitude had been developing ever since her Eaton period began; it had a good deal to do with Eaton's own belief that movie-making could be reduced to negotiating the right deal and journeying to pretty locations, as well as Susan's first reason for staying in the business: financial survival.

In May of 1967, Susan received a phone call from her agent, Jack Gordean. Just before the phone rang, Susan and Ron Nelson had been drinking heavily. After Gordean said something on the other end of the line, Susan covered the mouthpiece and asked Nelson: "Did you ever hear about this book *Valley of the Dolls*?"

"Yes, of course," he said.

"Any good?"

"No, but it's very popular."

She uncovered the mouthpiece and said to Gordean, "How much?...Okay, it will pay for some gas for the boat."

That was the way Susan thought about her movie appearances these days. Before reading the script, the idea of only two weeks of work in a walk-on cameo role for $50,000 was enough to convince her. (It also didn't hurt when Gordean told her that Mark Robson, with whom she had made *My Foolish Heart*, was to direct.)

The lucrative offer had come about because Judy Garland, who had originally been hired to play the role of the novel's aging Broadway singer, Helen Lawson, had been abruptly fired. Susan's old friend Bob Sidney had been assigned to choreograph Judy's song-and-dance number for the film, and recalls: "Poor Judy—it was very sad. I auditioned the 'I'll Plant My Own Tree' number for Judy that Susan finally did. I had it laid out for her and we already had it arranged. We had the chart done in Judy's key. We had five days of Judy's locking herself in her trailer and not coming out till six p.m. The first time I sang the song for her, I had to get under the table—she did the most outlandish things. Then I had to do it for her and Roger Eden, her musical director. Judy liked it. She liked the excitement of it. But then she would lock herself in. They had people there just to see she had no booze. Her daughter Lorna was a teenager then. She came running out of the dressing room one day, saying, 'Mommie's strange. Mommie is taking something.' They had to dismiss Judy. Nobody could handle her."

There may have been an artistic explanation for Judy's bad behavior. She held up productions only when she felt insecure about her work, and there was every reason for her to feel insecure about her part in *Valley of the Dolls*. She would have been playing an aging musical-comedy actress who had survived only because of her claws, and who now coped with threatening younger actresses using cut-throat tactics. The meanness of her role would have left Judy's fans confused and disappointed. Susan, however, had grown less sensitive than Judy Garland about damage to her image.

Susan insisted that Judy be paid in full before she would come to Hollywood. Back amid the glitter, she told curious reporters that she loved fishing in the sun but was happy to be back, and for a while she really was. She ran into many of her friends from the old days, including Stanley Musgrove. They had an odd meeting. Stan thought she was "slightly mad" and found her "very sweet, too much so," not at all the Susan he remembered.

"I'm just in agony over Eaton's death," he said.

"Oh, I'm not," said Susan. "I just have joy for the time we had together. I don't resent it. I'm not bereaved. I don't think of it that way. I just think of the wonderful times we had together. A lot of people don't have the times we had."

"Susan," he asked, "what do you do in Fort Lauderdale?" It was the same question that nearly everyone in Hollywood was asking her.

She gave Stan Musgrove the standard response: "I go fishing all the time," and went on about how she had caught a seven-foot-one-inch sailfish just before flying out, and all those boats she had. Stan couldn't help thinking that this was all a figment of her "madness."

Susan and Curlee had a suite at the Beverly Wilshire Hotel, from where, one Sunday, she wrote Ron Nelson a thank-you note for a gift:

Dear Ron,

The book is just charming. Thank you! Worked this past Friday, and very happily too. Of course it was like old home week when I went on the set. Know most of the crew from years back and they all like me—and I like them. Hope to be back in time for your birthday—but also want the musical number to be as good as possible so might ask for more rehearsal time. Will keep you posted, my friend.

Best,
Susan

Susan was the only veteran actress in a cast which included energetic Patty Duke, untried Barbara Parkins and Sharon Tate as girls who make it in the show-business world of New York and Hollywood and get hooked on pills ("dolls"). For the first time in her life, Susan found herself the visiting movie star who had to endure a smattering of awkward veneration from young starlets. Barbara Parkins may never live down the fact that at a press conference she introduced Susan Hayward as "my co-star." Bob

Sidney was delighted to be working with Susan again: "She came on the set a real pro. She arrived absolutely letter-perfect. Everybody was impressed. Patty Duke was there and she was flip and all that, but the minute she met Susan she knew she was a strong lady and it was no nonsense. None of the four-letter words. Susan was a stickler for that. She never held up anyone. I can never remember them holding the camera for her. If they said, 'Let's go,' she was there."

Bob Sidney and Susan resumed their dynamite relationship from days gone by. He still adored that scrapping, fightin'-mad quality about her and she still loved to banter with a clever guy who was obviously on her side although he pretended not to be.

"She was a big star when she left to go live in Fort Lauderdale," says Sidney. "She realized she had paid her dues and she wanted some personal happiness. Wherever she met this Chalton Chalk, whatever the hell his name is, he had to be a strong man. Susan would not respect a weak man. I asked her if she was as strong as he was.

"'You really are a problem,' she said.

"She was delighted that I was on the picture. The first thing she said to me was 'When do we do the exercises?' Every damn day, I used to get black and blue because she never stopped."

The exercises were for the "I'll Plant My Own Tree" song-and-dance number, which Susan would do while mouthing a prerecording by Margaret Whiting, one of Susan's four scenes in the film. Susan wore slacks and a mere midriff while limbering up. As soon as Bob Sidney started watching her, she tied a shirt around her waist.

"A bit of a belly there?" he said.

"I didn't ask for your anatomical opinion," she snapped, but later asked him what he really thought about her condition.

He expected her to burn his ears off with questions about Judy. Everyone else wanted to know the dirt. "She's the only actress I know who never had any comment about any other actress. When we did *Valley* and we were alone, she never once discussed Judy Garland."

Bob did have a question for Susan he had been dying to ask for years: "Didn't you dunk Barker in the pool?"

"What do you mean?" she spat back.

"I believe you did the dunking. You're stronger than he was."

"I could do it!" she boasted.

"What do you do down there in Florida?"

"I look at the water," she said. "I have my fishing fleet."

"Oh, come on! What kind of fishing fleet? What kind of crap is that? Really, don't you miss it here?"

"Miss what?" she said. "This is the place to work. I'll always come back if the price is right. I don't have many friends here. I love living down there."

Susan's big scene in *Valley of the Dolls* was the one in which she has a fight in the ladies' room with Patty Duke, as Neely O'Hara, and her wig accidentally falls off, exposing a head of white hair underneath. Susan wanted them to bleach her own hair white for the take. Sidney, appalled, warned: "When you keep changing your hair color, isn't that bad?" He knew that Susan had been dying her hair red for years. She replied that if she wore a white wig underneath a red one, it wouldn't look authentic and, in her own mind's eye, the scene wouldn't go as well. Bob stayed on the same tack: "Oh, wear a wig!"

Then Susan dragged out the big cannon, one of those irrefutable Hayward arguments: "Don't worry. I'm not paying for it."

She generally looked good in *Valley of the Dolls*. That scene in the ladies' room, if run a few times on the video tape recorder, reveals a Susan Hayward who is almost too good for this movie. She plays three different kinds of anger, shifting with great ease from one to another, and employs a body choreography (such as staring at the ceiling at exactly the right angle seconds after her young rival enters the powder room) which Patty Duke cannot match. Duke tears off her wig and soaks it in the john, forcing Susan's Helen to consider rushing out the back exit. Susan's reading of the line "I'll go out the way I came in" was a reading only three decades in the business could create: at first embarrassment, melting into an ironic smile, melting into hard-core determination. No other performance in the movie comes close to Susan's.

In her two weeks of work, Susan left a fascinating glimpse of herself for future audiences. It was the only time she allowed her Brooklyn accent to surface, especially in that powder-room scene, and the only time her street-fighting quality came through without the camouflage of glamour. It was not the Susan Hayward that Eaton had loved, for she had put on many layers of the movie star's façade for him and then stripped off only some of them to become a Carrollton housewife. It was the Susan that only her own family had seen, which may be why she kept her distance from them.

The movie was Twentieth Century-Fox's highest-grossing film ever, but, aside from Susan's powder-room scene, it was of no artistic merit. But *Valley of the Dolls* did bring Susan back to Hollywood and got her talking to agents about new career ventures, such as television movies.

While in Hollywood, Susan learned that her brother, Wally, had secretly married a woman named Carole, whom he met the day he led a circus parade in Los Angeles. Why didn't he tell his sister he was planning to marry? "I'm like Susan that way. It was a kind of quiet thing. We took off and went to the justice of the peace. Later, when Susan met Carole, they hit it off right away." It was Wally's only marriage.

Susan returned to Fort Lauderdale and told Ron Nelson about the Hollywood adventure. That fall, she began meeting Southern politicians, including Republican leader Ed Lahey, who was running for governor. Attracted to Lahey and his circle of political friends, she gave a speech for him on September 16, 1967. She also started dating other Southern politicians, such as Tom Shelton and Claude Kirk. When Father Morrow visited her in Fort Lauderdale, he mentioned that he had read about her dating Lahey and the others. She became defensive: "Yes, but, like I told you before, there will never be another Eaton."

She went to Carrollton to visit Eaton's grave and to see Ann Moran and Mary Williams. Carrollton's phone lines burned up every time a newspaper item about her appeared. Once, while Susan was staying at Mary's house, Ann and her twelve-year-old daughter, Judy, took one of Ann's famous banana cakes to Susan. Susan and Judy chatted for a while and then Susan asked her: "Did you hear Mrs. Chalkley is going out with another man?"

"Yes, Mrs. Chalkley," Judy said.

"You know, Mrs. Chalkley has to go out with a man once in a while to these Oscar shows and these big things."

"Oh, that's all right," said Judy.

"You know," said Susan, "if Mrs. Chalkley ever marries a man, he is going to have to be exactly like Mr. Chalkley. Is that okay with you?"

After the flurry of newspaper articles about her boyfriend

politicos and Lahey's election as governor of Florida, she withdrew from all her political involvements as quickly as she had taken them on. She told Father Brew that she had felt used by all the politicians: "I've had enough of this! Dealing with these people!" She stopped dating.

Again she found herself with much time on her hands. When William Holden, of whom she had always been fond, called to invite her to join him on safari in and around the vast animal sanctuary he owned in Africa, she accepted; but Holden later became furious when Susan shot a big cat. She even had a picture taken of herself with her kill. The whole point of Holden's sanctuary was to preserve the lives of animals.

Back in Fort Lauderdale, there was still only Ron Nelson, Curlee, her dog Matey (from Carrollton), her fishing and her liquor; she only occasionally saw her twenty-three-year-old sons. Tall, lanky, blondish Tim was now at Fort Bennington, Georgia, in intensive training for the Green Berets, while redheaded, freckled-faced Greg was hard at work getting a veterinary degree at Auburn University.

Between drinks, she expanded her interests. One day, she heard jazz organist Jack Frost play in Fort Lauderdale and thought he was good. Soon, he was giving Susan lessons in her home on her own Hammond organ. She sent an album Frost had made to her agent in Hollywood, Jack Gordean, with instructions to forward it to "The Joey Bishop Show," her favorite TV talk fest. Bishop agreed to have the organist on, but only if Susan appeared with him. Without hesitating, Susan flew to Hollywood with Jack Frost and his wife and made a rare appearance on a talk show.

On the Bishop show, she talked about fishing, of course, and about catching her first glimpse of a white marlin, and about her boats moored right behind her house, one for daily use, another just for Sundays. She quickly reviewed her whole career in Hollywood, summing it up as a dream come true. She told how proud she was of her twins. Of Eaton's death and her new life, she said: "I've learned to live again and I've learned to live alone."

One can debate how much Susan was living these days while the depressed grieving for Eaton continued.

CHAPTER 9

Vegas

ONCE AGAIN, Marty Rackin talked Susan into the wrong part. He owned a big interest in Caesars Palace in Las Vegas and wanted her to star in its second 1968 show, *Mame*. *All* that would be required of Susan, who hadn't appeared on the stage for thirty years, was to sing herself hoarse and dance like Ann-Margaret seven nights a week, two shows a night. Rackin stood to make a fortune from Susan as Mame if she didn't collapse on the stage after two weeks. He didn't tell her that, of course; his technique was to use the old buddy-buddy approach that they still teach in salesman training courses. "Hey, Hooligan!" he shouted over the telephone wires from Los Angeles to Fort Lauderdale. "How long you gonna sit there with the old folks in Sun City? How about coming to Vegas to do *Mame* for me on the stage?"

Any sensible person could have told her that *Mame* was certain to be hellishly difficult. She wasn't equipped. But she didn't have sensible people around her; too-trusting Eaton would have wanted her to do the show for an old friend; and, as Rackin knew, she was lonely, bored and vulnerable. After several calls from him, Susan flew to New York to see Angela Lansbury perform in the Jerry Herman musical, to Hollywood to listen to more "You'll be great! They'll love you!" hype from Marty Rackin, to Caesars Palace for a meeting with the hotel people and a glimpse of the stage. The producers did not ask her to audition, as they had Judy Garland, who was subsequently turned down because of her instability. (This had been the second time Judy had lost a role to Susan. Judy had wanted *Mame* so badly that she used to stand in the wings of the Winter Garden to impress the producers with her sincerity.) In Las Vegas, Susan gave Rackin an insecure yes.

She knew she wasn't ready, but she was assured of three months' intensive preparation before the six-month ordeal began at Christmas. If it occurred to her that ready she could never be, given her inexperience and the exhaustion of two years of steady drinking, all the encouragement and ballyhoo drowned out the last-minute voice of her Marrenner logic.

She flew to New York in late September. *Mame* company members remember her frightened manner as she entered the rehearsal hall for the first time. They had all been waiting tensely for the legend, La Hayward, wondering what she would be like, what gems she would offer for opening lines. Neither of the two previous Mames, Lansbury and Celeste Holm of the national company, had been nearly as terrifyingly important. What they saw in the first few moments was a tiny creature, bekerchiefed, no makeup, sweater over slacks and blouse; a very plain little doll striding toward them, as far from the steely giant of *I Want to Live!* as they could imagine. Before she had a chance to speak, the *Mame* people stood and began to applaud her.

"Hey, wait a minute," said the legend. "Hold the applause until you see if I can do it."

Laughter broke out and the tension spilled like so much milk. *Mame*'s cast warmed to a friendly, soft-spoken woman who made no effort to hide her enormous fright. Susan ingratiated herself deeply. When greeting an individual for the first time, she stretched out her hand like a man to say a forthright "Hi there." Her little self-deprecating comments drew instant "Oh, sure you can do it" responses. The cast quickly grew to adore her.

Choreographer Onna White and director John Bowab were a little more technical in their first appraisal of Susan, for, after all, they had to convert her into something approximating Angela Lansbury in three months. Both of them were shocked by her physical appearance. Onna White thought she looked like "Humpty Dumpty, with no waist at all" and her legs looked like "matchsticks." John Bowab preferred to compare her figure to "an avocado or a round pear": "The lady was dissipated, bloated. The body that all of us knew and loved, the great walk and look, wasn't there." One look at Susan and these experts knew that she had become a drinker. Women who drink tend to lose muscle tone in their legs, which become spindly (Susan's were always too thin anyway), and display improperly proportioned waists. Judy Garland's body in later years is a classic example of the effect. John Bowab was especially worried about how Susan's legs would look. Onna White decided that the only solution would be to put Susan through a horrendous regimen of exercises to bring her body to the level where it could be exposed onstage.

Susan responded to her heavy work load with childlike obedience and enthusiasm. She was jolly with choreographer Onna, calling her "Boss Lady": "Okay, Boss Lady, what do you want me to do next?" Onna White started calling her "The Big Sue" because tiny Susan was so *big* in her efforts and spirit. When Susan first opened her mouth to sing, Onna was floored; it was an enormous, deep mezzo. *Mame*'s creator, Jerry Herman, attended a few rehearsals, heard the same voice, and thought it "throaty" and "just perfect." She endured grueling muscle-building exercises that had young, agile John Bowab reflecting, "God, *I* would never do them."

Onna assigned Diana Baffer, the dance trainer, to put Susan through these exercises. Baffer says, "She was in such bad shape that it took me two weeks to get her to do a *plié*." Susan would lower herself to her haunches—not easily, but she could do it. Then she was stuck. She would groan, struggle to rise from the deep knee-bend, but could not return to a standing position. The muscles simply weren't there.

Meanwhile, the Winter Garden Theatre stage was housing Angela Lansbury and company for regular evening performances. As much as he could, Bowab would have Susan rehearse on the Winter Garden stage during the daytime, for he was painfully aware that she had had no prior musical stage experience. On Saturdays, Bowab had no less than three future Mames rehearsing on different parts of the same stage: Jane Morgan, Janis Paige and Susan.

"I'll never forget Susan sitting on the floor of the stage," says Bowab. "She was changing her shoes. Jane Morgan was on one side of her and Janis the other. They were both in awe of Susan. Jane did a back flip with a couple of the boys. Susan's face went absolutely green. She said, 'What is that?' She thought it was something she would have to do, that we were holding back on her."

Susan was game, but not crazy.

Susan's own dancing assignments were awkward if not impossible for her, and little real progress could be made until her muscles were strengthened. Her general lack of energy was also a problem. Onna White thought it best to send Susan back to Fort Lauderdale, where she would be somewhat more comfortable, accompanied by Diana Baffer, who would continue to see Susan through the bone-cracking physical ordeal.

Diana Baffer was a mere twenty-one, pretty and sweetly genuine; and she was awestruck by Susan. As a youngster, she, like millions, had agonzied in darkened theaters over Susan's tormented characterizations in the late fifties. She could not make small talk with such a goddess, so in the beginning Diana overcame her nervousness with strictly work talk: *pliés*, stretching exercises, what was good for the leg and tummy muscles, the difficult "Bosom Buddies" dance routine: "and now you do this." Susan appeared to understand Diana's worshipful nervousness. During the five-minute breaks between deep knee-bends, Susan, like Diana, talked only about the show. But as work progressed and the two women grew at ease with each other, the little chats at break time became friendlier. Susan began remarking on Timothy and Gregory and her number-one subject, Life Without Eaton. By the time the two were holed up in the Fort Lauderdale house, they would while away the hours, after the day's work and Curlee's fine dinner, talking about the most personal matters. Susan, who disliked women almost as a rule, took to this appealing, unthreatening girl without reservations. She seemed to be opening up completely.

Susan's conversation had all been heard before by others: Gregory was such a wonderful son, Timothy caused her some concern, she should have won the Award for *I'll Cry Tomorrow*, she should never have married Jess, she had been manipulated by the studios, Catholicism had changed her life. On the subject of Eaton and her great loss, she came up with the following cheap paperback cliché: "When you're in love, ten years passes like a moment."

But in manner she was far from a cheap novel. Diana vividly recalls sitting with Susan, magnetized by her slow, purposeful voice; there was toughness and vulnerability in it; and drama, as the Hayward head and body moved in just the right ways to emphasize the haunting speech. Diana felt that she was experiencing Susan's very heart and soul, and the experience, for a twenty-one-year-old, was unspeakably thrilling.

Then something strange happened. Timothy, on leave from the military, was in and out of the Fort Lauderdale house. Diana was finding her evenings in the company of a great actress just heaven. Furthermore, she had a steady beau in New York, and Susan knew about him. It was therefore curious when Susan, one evening, began to insist that she go out on a date with Timothy. Diana showed little enthusiasm.

Susan became strident: "Come on! You've been working here with me every day. I'm an *old lady*. It's time you went out with some *young* people and had a good time. Now, I want you to go out with my son Timothy tonight." Before Diana could pose another objection, Susan just went on with this bossy railroading, which Diana thought so unlike her: "Timmy's coming over to pick you up and you're going out with him!" Diana felt she had no choice.

Timmy took her to a very young party, and they came back to the house quite late. The enormous living room was dark, except for the light of a single small lamp. Sitting under it, at a table, was Susan. The effect was eerie chiaroscuro. She was the only thing in the vast darkness that was lit, like those solitary figures in darkly moody Rembrandt paintings. Susan was wearing an exquisite negligee, sitting perfectly straight-backed in a chair, her profile stunningly illuminated. A director might have worked a week to photograph her so provocatively.

She was holding a glass, had been drinking alone and was obviously quite drunk. When she saw Diana and Timmy, she said, in a slur, "*Wellllll*, you're home. *Oooooooh*, come on in. I'm just having a drink. Would you like to join me?"

Timmy, Diana recalls, suggested that his mother go to bed. Susan instantly became vicious, lashing out at her son on different matters, gratuitously ugly in tone. Timmy, although not pleased, did not seem surprised or angry. He was gentle and answered his mother's tongue-lashing in an appeasing tone. Diana, shocked, excused herself and went to her bedroom in the adjoining wing.

Her room was too far away for her to be aware of how long the scene continued. As she readied herself for bed, she couldn't help but dwell on the mysterious episode. She had had no idea that Susan was a drinker. Before she dozed off, Diana thought, over and over: "There's a lot I don't know about that lady."

Vegas' Caesars Palace, a twenty-five-million-dollar circus of gilded grotesqueries, was big enough and opulent enough to distract the bigtime losers from their depression. As a palace of delirious delights, it competed with the gaudiest of them on the Strip: thirty-four acres of mindless amusement, more than a thousand employees donning togas and other Roman drag, a chandelier costing in the six figures with 100,000 tinkling crystals, and an untold number of expensive Italian statues. On any day, the serious gamblers, who needed all this insanity to make their own compulsive self-destruction seem ordinary by comparison, could expect the most unlikely things—nuns in black habit frenetically jerking one-armed bandits, or conservative businessmen threatening to divorce their wives unless they got another chance at blackjack, or even posters announcing a high-caliber Academy Award-winning actress soon to traipse across Caesars' stage.

Susan arrived in this new Sodom-and-Gomorrah just before Christmas, along with the rest of the *Mame* people. She had not been drinking or smoking during the whole of her rehearsal time in New York. On the plane, Onna White offered her a reward: "You've been such a good girl, I'm going to let you have one brandy after dinner." Once in Vegas, they went right to Caesars Palace. Before Susan and Onna could get to their rooms, they were scurried into the Greco-Roman dining room and seated. Frank Sinatra, who was singing there, introduced Susan and, Onna says, "the whole room just fell apart." As Marty Rackin had known all along, Red was still hot and Vegas would pant for her.

All the attention was more than well deserved, Onna knew. She felt such admiration and love for Susan, after watching her achieve the impossible over the past months. Who else could have done what that little redhead had done? It was sheer Irish guts!

For two months in a New York rehearsal studio, Susan had jumped and squatted and toe-touched and sung and emoted until numbness overcame pain. She complained only in jest; never begged off. There had been spectacular progress. John Bowab and Onna White would come to the rehearsal studio, point right at Susan's legs and say to her, "Look what's happening!" Susan felt such pride when she began to see muscles building in her legs and her waist flab melting. Just before she left for Vegas, her body looked absolutely gorgeous, as in the old days.

She was still terrified of appearing in front of a live audience. *Mame*'s producer had arranged a special one-night benefit performance with Susan at the Winter Garden before the Las Vegas opening. They wanted to see how a tough audience would react to her. Susan agonized over a tryout in New York City, of all places. She did finally agree, but union snares made the benefit impossible. New York gossip then had it that Susan was either too liquored, or too ill, or too scared to go on. The producers, nevertheless, received some idea of how the public viewed Susan the night she came to the Winter Garden with Diana Baffer and her beau to see Janis Paige as Mame. Usually, she dined out or went to the theater in a nondescript dress, minimally made up. This one night, Susan had done herself up like a movie queen. She had on a close-fitting, narrow-waisted, snow-white dress, cape to match; her longish hair, coiffed ornately; makeup, Hollywood perfect. Susan and her group went backstage after the show to talk to Paige. When they attempted to leave the theater using the backstage exit, hundreds of people were milling, waving autograph pads, trying to grab Susan. Somehow, perhaps through the show's publicity people, they had found out that Susan was backstage. A limousine was waiting at the curb. Susan and her two friends pushed and shoved their way through the swarming mob and managed, after some tense grappling, to shut the limousine door behind them. Even then, people were jumping on top of the car to get a look at her.

Susan's first week in Vegas was strenuous. Few things went right during the mayhem of the final dress rehearsals on the Caesars Palace stage, the last of which occurred on Christmas Day. The show, which had Mame aging and changing styles over three generations, required innumerable costume changes. Susan had to twirl off the stage, get unzipped, stripped, redressed and twirl back onstage hurriedly, so often, that a great deal of the time parts of her costume were missing or a strap was hanging. The clothes were not the theatrical type, and had millions of tiny buttons and countless little zippers to fasten and later undo, forcing Susan into panicky near-delays at every entrance. Her shoes lacked the rubber guards that dancers wear, causing her to slip ungracefully during the routines that she had practiced so doggedly. All of the dancing, heavy costumes and lightning-fast changes caused her to perspire profusely. By the third scene, her long hair was soaked and difficult to keep away from her face.

She was scheduled to open the night after Christmas. On the afternoon of December 26, 1968, she previewed *Mame* for a houseful of Air Force personnel. When Susan made her sensational entrance sliding down a banister blowing a bugle, the men, packed so thickly that all you could see were eager faces and beige uniforms, went wild. Susan couldn't make a move onstage without "ooh's," "aah's," laughs, carrying on and other signs of male appreciation. If she was making mistakes, they worshipped her even more. It was like those throat-knotting scenes between Susan, as Jane Froman, and the fighting men she entertains in *With a Song in My Heart*.

That night there was semi-hysteria backstage as word got out that the room, which seated thirteen hundred, was loaded with movie stars who had flown in from L.A., and columnists, syndicated in most of the major newspapers, all waiting wide-eyed. An army of telegram-carriers and flower-bearers scurried to and from Susan, who was in the eye of the backstage storm of confusion. She held up astonishingly well, although dying of fright.

Her greatest fear was not that she would trip and look silly during the dancing, but that she would forget her lines. After more than half a lifetime of having to learn no more than three pages of dialogue a day for the cameras, the idea of having to recall so many words, especially lyrics, overwhelmed her, even after months of preparation. She got a bug about one song, "If He Walked into My Life"; she thought there was no way she would remember it. She asked Ruth Gillette, the show's Mother Burnside, to stand in the wings and whisper each line before she had to sing it.

The curtain rose; she came sliding down the banister into George Tregre's arms, to great applause; she didn't forget "If He Walked into My Life" or anything else; didn't trip; and she looked simply glamorous, the most glamorous Mame ever. With her hands on her hips in the legendary Hayward way, and in her light beige "Bosom Buddies" dress, turban and stone-marten furs—the Mame getup redesigned for Susan—she was breathtaking.

Her dancing and vocal work was ordinary, but she herself was, every moment onstage, captivating; as everyone agreed, she was a dreadful Mame Dennis but a scintillating Susan Hayward. Writer Robert C. Jennings, who was there that night, right afterward observed: "She was never the Mame we have come to know, with the 'cockeyed nincompoopery' called for in the script. She lacked stage authority, and her timing was terrible. But she was a curiously affecting Mame. I was even moved by her scenes with Patrick. Having cursed and cried through countless miles of celluloid for so long, she was best, it is not surprising, on lines like 'Oh, hell' and 'That word, darling is *bas*tard' and 'Who gives a damn about money, I've lost my child. Oh, Vera, what are we gonna do?' Hokey, sure, but just glutted with Susan Hayward's own very special brand of sexiness and suffering. I guarantee you will never see the likes of it again."

Susan was far too vulnerable in her portrayal of the gutsy, sassy Mame. When she sang "My Best Beau" to young Patrick, there were misty eyes all over the room, and the song she was so worried about, "If He Walked into My Life," came across with such desperate sincerity that people were convinced she was thinking of Eaton, causing heavy breathing in the audience. Robert C. Jennings noted, "When Susan Hayward grabbed both thighs hard and with moist eyes and pouty lips told us that we need a little Christmas right this very minute, she was Barbara Graham pleading for her very life." With this Mame, the audience wanted to rush up onto the stage to protect her, not marvel at her nuttiness. It wasn't right, but positively wonderful. Reviewers and columnists sang hosannas, almost unanimously, to Susan's musical debut in Vegas. There was no doubt in anyone's mind, after the opening, that Susan would be playing indefinitely to a sold-out room.

She received an ovation that night and at almost every performance thereafter. The opening-night backstage scene of flowers and telegrams was, similarly, repeated nightly. After performances, droves of people waited in line, asking to see her, and all were turned down except for friends from Hollwyood like Charlton Heston and VIPs whom the management thought Susan should see. It was like holding court: someone would say, "Miss Hayward, this is Mr. and Mrs. So-and-So," and a tired Susan would endure the few awkward minutes of trying to be friendly to strangers, a skill which was thoroughly foreign to her nature even when she was rested.

She settled into a workaday, difficult routine. She and Curlee had taken a house in the desert, where mornings Susan slept late to recover from the previous night's athletics. She spent the rest of the day indoors, taking hot baths to soothe her stretched and aching muscles, and saw only a few people: her new press agent,

Jay Bernstein; company member Ruth Gillette; and Ron Nelson, who paid several extended visits. She refused most invitations because she could hardly move prior to show time. Much later in the day, she would feel refreshed and would drive to the hotel, ready, or almost so, for another three-and-a-half-hour assault on her nerves, muscles and voice.

She arrived at Caesars in her usual Shannon-green slacks-kerchief-blouse-sweater-dark glasses disguise, always adorned with the radiance of her emeralds. They were perfect for her small face and set off her hair, which she had changed from the strawberry of Fort Lauderdale to a lush henna-brunette. As she walked from her car in the parking lot to the hotel, any Vegas thief could have spotted the emeralds and known their enormous value. Cast members, who thought Susan soberly sensible, were surprised she wasn't more cautious and chided her continually.

Ruth Gillette scolded, "Somebody's going to hit you over the head."

"No, darling, I don't think they ever will," chirped Susan stubbornly. "I don't want them in a safe deposit box because I wanna use 'em."

Her dressing room would drive her stir crazy, and when she wasn't too fatigued she would wrap a chiffon kerchief around her head, slip on her dark glasses and take Curlee into the casino. While Curlee held a cupful of quarters, Susan would drop them into a hungry one-armed bandit, hurriedly pull the arm and watch with child's delight as the lemons and oranges spun to a halt. She was a delicious sight: jerking away, inserting quarter after quarter from the cup, eyes darting and her tiny figure swaying daffily. Luckily, patrons standing next to her hadn't the foggiest who this dizzy green apparition really was.

After the New Year's show, the Caesars audience had a great treat. Timmy had just married and Susan hadn't been able to attend the wedding. So, unknown to Susan, Timmy and his bride from Germany, Ilse, flew to Vegas and took a front table to see his mother do her first stage show. While Susan was taking her final bows, the manager threw a spotlight on the newlyweds. Susan, delighted, insisted they join her on the stage. Mr. and Mrs. Barker stood up on their table, leaped over the footlights and hugged and kissed Susan to joyful applause.

* * *

The triumph of opening night, with all the excitement of compliments and kisses, had been bliss for her, but after only a few weeks she grew, predictably, quite bored. In theory, the challenge of becoming a theater actress had been appealing, but in practice the exertion of fourteen shows a week was an empty grind. Susan, who had built up her stamina during the New York rehearsal period, might well have gotten through many months of *Mame* if she had continued the stoic discipline of those months in New York, but without a man like Eaton around, there was no way that she could fight the loneliness. So, instead of resting quietly in the daytime, she went back to her heavy drinking and her two packs of cigarettes a day. She ate minimally. She became difficult. She threw figurines and dishes across the living room of the desert house to vent her frustration. Arriving at the hotel sloshed, she would fall down into her seat at her dressing-room makeup table, feel disgusted and clatter all the vials, tubes, boxes and bottles to the floor with one sweep of her arm: "What's all this *junk* doing here?" Curlee, as always, stood by, trying to calm her.

People ran around backstage trying to cope. The actors, who at first believed she was simply over-exhausted, did their best to buoy her. There would be near-insanity minutes before Susan was to make her entrance. Someone would rush over with coffee and pour it down her throat while the dressers struggled to get the costume and jewelry on her. To her credit, Susan, drunk as she was, seldom betrayed her true condition to the other actors and never to the audience. As soon as she was pushed out onstage, she found her spot instantly and became, just as on opening night, her own special, dramatic Mame. She would be superb. Then she would go limp again as soon as she left the stage, falling like an unstringed marionette into the dressers' arms while they lifted a half-comatose Susan by the armpits, redressed her and shoved her out on the stage when her cue came.

Susan's work exhaustion quickly became extravagant. The liquor was undermining her new strength and the smoking was killing her voice. By the end of the second show, she was pale, breathless, dripping wet and hoarse. The producers and hotel management tried to make things easier for her. They asked Betty McGuire, Susan's standby, to become her new dresser, for, from the national company, she knew the proper change methods cold.

She had the millions of tiny buttons and dozens of little zippers removed from the costumes and replaced with big theatrical zippers so that Susan could be changed more quickly. McGuire had Susan's shoes sent to a shoemaker to have rubber grips put on the bottom so she wouldn't slip, along with securing straps to keep the shoes from abrading Susan's tiny, overworked ankles. The perspiration problem, too, was quickly diagnosed; Susan was talked into allowing Charles LaFrance to "restyle" her long hair. He didn't dare tell her that he intended to shorten it to a near pageboy to keep it from getting soaked and bothersome during the dancing. In "The Man in the Moon Is a Lady" number, handles were placed on the rising moon so that Susan, who was often unbalanced, could hang on to them for dear life.

Everything that could be done by the management to lessen her exhaustion was being done. But none of these well-meaning changes had much effect on the overall impossible situation. Before Susan could continue comfortably in *Mame*, she had to dry out; she wouldn't do that. When Ron Nelson came to Las Vegas to help Curlee get Susan through her performances, Susan told him that the show had become nerveracking and she couldn't wait to get back to the peace of her yacht and Fort Lauderdale.

The more she tried to do what so much of her didn't want to do, the more her anger surfaced and the more she drank. Her tantrums became worse. She screamed at Ron before a show, "I'm not going on tonight with that son of a bitch!" referring to an actor who she believed was stealing her scenes. Another time, she decided that she disliked the precocious child actor who played Patrick. Then it was the actress who played Vera. Ron would laugh it all off and tell her that, yes, she was going on, help get the coffee into her, and Susan would go on.

Curlee was growing numb with all the madness of Susan's struggling both with herself and with three and a half hours of the hardest work imaginable. The backstage hurly-burly had been unbelievable. Sometimes, Curlee would stand in the wings and try to find a peaceful oasis in the tumult by singing quietly the same words that Susan sang onstage. But peace wasn't easy to find backstage for very long; Curlee would soon see Susan panting and desperate when she exited. Once, to Ron Nelson, Curlee, in her quiet, understated way, summed up her reaction to Susan's self-destructive world: "Ain't it exhaustin'."

* * *

Nelson was perpetually backstage. The actors used to wonder about this tall, outgoing, ingratiating man who had the privilege of helping the star through her most difficult moments. Was he just a friend of Susan's? Her paid publicity man? Susan's obvious attachment to him made him all the more intriguing to the cast. One of the young actresses thought him "kinda cute," as she told Ruth Gillette, and played up to Ron, who felt both squeamish and flattered. He coaxed her into joining the little Vegas coterie, which included Susan, himself, Ruth Gillette and hair-stylist Charles LaFrance. When the young actress would hint to Ron about going out on a date, Ron, embarrassed, would switch to discussing books. Charles LaFrance thought that Ron's perpetual sidestepping was ticklishly funny and started calling him by the pet name "Books." Susan didn't think any of it funny and made it clear that she didn't like the young actress hanging around him. Susan's jealousy was a revelation to Nelson. Up until now, he had believed that she saw him merely as a good friend.

Ruth Gillette was a perfect Mother Burnside and, in her own right, was warm, trusting, with a sweet smile and nice white hair. Susan who saw the show-business toughness under the lovability, admired Ruth and often invited her to dinner in the rented desert house. Among the *Mame* people, especially those not close to Susan, gossip spread about Susan's drinking. Ruth became one of Susan's staunchest defenders, denying to others practically everything said about Susan's excesses. Much later, in Hollywood, Ruth would remain a friend of Susan's and would be disgusted to hear the irresponsible stories circulating about Hayward the Wild Dypso-maniac.

Susan dreaded aging, and the spirited Ruth Gillette, older than Susan, seemed like its perfect foil. So did Mame, who was ageless and forever beautiful; Susan had fun impersonating her offstage. She became uncharacteristically solicitous with her "kids" (the company), and made calls beginning with, "This is your dear old Auntie Mame," or left with answering services such messages as "Just tell him Auntie Mame called." Calls to Ruth Gillette began with an ironic "Hi, darling! This is Mother Goddam." Susan was so fond of this little "older woman's" in-joke that later, when *Mame* was but a bad memory, she would begin all her calls to Ruth in the same way.

Susan never had to make good on her drunken threats not to go on at the last minute, for the inevitable happened early in her run. She had been found in her dressing room futilely trying to force her stage boots onto her feet, which had, through the relentless exertion of the dance numbers, swollen to nearly twice their size and become excruciatingly tender. Betty McGuire went on for her that night and for the next nine performances, the better part of a week, while the painful swelling subsided.

This was the first time in her life that Susan had the experience of being replaced. Her reaction was one of self-loathing and at first a kind of loathing of Betty McGuire, too. McGuire, who was as Irish as Susan, with big eyes, freckles and red hair, danced with ease and sang, Susan marveled, without straining her voice. One of the papers gave McGuire a great review. Susan came into Betty's dressing room with the clipped review crumpled in her fist and threw it at the dressing table, telling Betty, "Here, put this in your scrapbook. They loved you and they hated me!"

Nevertheless, she knew that Betty was no threatening Eve Harrington. Betty was asked to replace the actress who played funny, competitive Vera Charles. Previously, during the "Bosom Buddies" dance routine, Susan had thought herself continually upstaged by the actress who first played Vera. But Betty always deferred to Susan during the scene. One time, during the complex "Bosom Buddies" turning and zigzagging, Susan tripped and fell into Betty. Betty, who could have been oh-so-perfect and shown the star up by just going on like a trouper, instead tripped and went one better by falling on top of Susan. Betty and Susan started howling with laughter while the audience applauded wildly. After the show, Susan called Betty into her dressing room and jovially said, "I've never had so much fun onstage." All of Susan's coldness was gone; she saw Betty now as helpful and adorable.

As the weeks passed, the situation grew hopeless. Not Ron, not Betty, not any of the many concerned actors around her could prop her. Even if Susan had quit the booze and the cigarettes, it wouldn't have helped, so drained and ill was she.

On the brink of losing Hayward and a jammed box office, Caesars was in a state. Marty Rackin, who had been shuttling between Hollywood and Vegas during all the trouble, was babying Susan and conniving at ways to keep her in the show. He proposed that Betty McGuire do *Mame* on week nights and Susan do it on

Friday, Saturday and Sunday. Susan was fed up, but didn't know how to say no to Marty. She had never walked out on a role, so she agreed to Rackin's changes, enduring more of the torture.

Something about the dry air in Las Vegas plays havoc with singers' voices. The condition is known in the business as Vegas Throat. Everyone thought Susan had it, but she suspected something more serious. A specialist came from Hollywood and found that she had developed nodes, or little tumors, on her vocal cords. Within the past year, she had had a hysterectomy because of a benign tumor; this, then, was the second time that she had shown herself prone to growth formation. The specialist warned her that unless she quit the show, the damage to her voice might be permanent. She felt almost relieved.

Ron Nelson, by now, had flown back to his job at the Heart Fund in Fort Lauderdale. Before he left Vegas, however, he had spotted something he thought wonderfully amusing, and couldn't wait to share the fun with Susan, who needed cheering up. While walking near the Strip, he had noticed a crowd of people standing around a store window. He went closer. Behind the glass, he saw a man painting on a huge canvas a life-size portrait of Susan. The figure in the painting was like a Barbie Doll with a Susan Hayward face superimposed, plastic and unreal, but so large that it could hardly be dismissed out of hand. The Barbie-Doll Susan was dressed in the costume of the closing number of *Mame*, a white gown with a white fox collar. The cleavage was copious. The nose and mouth had exaggerated pertness and cuteness. The face loomed against a turbulent nocturnal sky, which, as Ron later learned, was the artist's representation of Susan's "private life"; threatening the sky were stormy clouds, her "emotional sweep"; moonlight spilled on restless waters, symbolic of her astrological sign, Cancer; and, lo! rising mysteriously in the background was the Rock of Gibraltar, Susan's "great strength." The artist had been given permission by Caesars Palace to attend numerous performances of *Mame* in order to sketch Susan from real life. Every day, he painted his mural as crowds gathered to watch his progress. Ron thought it *so* absolutely Las Vegas, and rushed back to tell Susan, thinking it would crack her up.

But Susan didn't laugh. "How dare they permit that!" she exploded.

"You've got to see it. It's very funny. Let's go."

"I won't see that garbage."

Ron gave up. She could be such a spoilsport, he thought. But curiosity got the best of her and eventually, in her dark-glasses disguise, she went to the store front with him to see the opus. Dozens of people milled and glared at the life-size fake Hayward while standing in their midst, unrecognized, was the life-size real thing.

Ron persisted in telling her how fascinating the whole happening was, but to deaf ears; Susan was ready to throw a brick through the window at the artist.

"Look at that candy-box crap!" she seethed.

Susan was deeply hurt when Curlee gave notice. She was going back to Carrollton to marry Frank Crowder, who had proposed to her some time before. Susan loved Curlee and knew she would be losing one of the few truly loyal people in her life, but that was not what she said when she called Ron, filled with rage and sarcasm. He flew right back to Vegas to help the situation.

When he arrived, Curlee was already preparing to leave for Georgia and Susan, far from angry, was unnaturally happy because Caesars had released her from her contract and her return to freedom was imminent. She planned several big events to mark her departure: a news conference to make the official announcement and an expensive party (her very first cast party) for all sixty in the *Mame* group.

To the gathered reporters and actors at the news conference, she appeared shattered. Her tears streamed, her voice became a whisper and she said, "My doctors insisted I leave *Mame* and do nothing but rest my voice for several months. I love the show and the cast and I hate to walk out on Caesars Palace. What really breaks my heart is I've never copped out on any role or anybody in my thirty years as a performer." Her agonized manner was convincing in that singular Hayward style. Betty McGuire responded to Susan's tears with tears of her own. Others choked up. But right after the news conference Susan went back to her rented house and her tears dried up instantly. She said she felt wonderful at the thought of returning to "real living" in Fort Lauderdale.

Of her planned farewell shindig for the cast, she told Nelson,

"I want to go out in style and say thank you in style." It was held at the hotel in one of the ultra-Roman rooms. Blinding white leather covered circular dining booths; two orchestras played; waiters floated around, pouring champagne; glasses clinked; a delicious dinner was ready to be served. Everyone was waiting for the star.

Deliberately delaying her arrival for maximum impact, Susan finally made a sensational entrance. The two orchestras swelled to Jerry Herman's big "Mame" number and the actors and guests lavished applause on Susan, superstar, as she sashayed through the room in a spectacular sequin-sprayed beige-and-lavender gown. Her full breasts drew attention. Her emeralds flashed, but not as brightly as her eyes. She had never looked so beautiful, nor, from the fire in her eyes, so dangerous.

She wasted no time in belting down her liquor and before long was flying. She and Nelson sat in one of the white leather circular booths while dinner was served, although Susan was more interested in liquid than solid intake. While they sat in the booth, Susan suddenly saw Celeste Holm enter. She was appalled. She couldn't bear the thought that competent Celeste Holm would be replacing her.

Celeste Holm was not crashing Susan's private party. The Caesars management had instructed her to come down from her room so that publicity pictures could be taken of Susan and her together. Moreover, she was told she had to rush, not to bother fussing with her appearance lest Susan, who was supposed to be sick, decide to leave early. A trouper, Celeste did as she was told and came to the party dressed in ordinary street clothes, intending to stay just long enough for the pictures. She came over to introduce herself by name.

Susan cooed, "Celeste *whoooo?*"

Holm got the message, but persisted with dignity: "Holm... I'm Celeste Holm." Forced to stand, she smiled nervously.

Ron, who had already sensed what was coming, sat helplessly.

Then Susan rapid-fired, "I didn't invite you. It's *my* party. And, look, if I ever hear of you mistreating any of my kids, I'll kick your ass all the way back to Toledo, Ohio." (The idea of the cast being *her* kids after only two months was somewhat absurd; Holm had worked with most of them for much longer.)

All the eyes in the room had gravitated to the scene taking

place between Susan and Holm, who must have been greatly upset. A Caesars public-relations man somehow managed to get Holm seated in the same booth with Susan. The publicity shots were taken while a smoldering Susan sat as far from Holm as the booth would allow. After the cameras stopped clicking and the feigned smiles vanished, Celeste excused herself and walked out.

Not long afterward, while Susan was having, or seemed to be having, a riotously good time, the artist who had executed the life-size Barbie-Doll Susan in a store window approached Susan. The party was becoming unreal, Ron thought, and he quickly told Susan that her favorite painter was about to accost her. Ron asked if she wanted him to stay and help.

"I'll take care of it," said a resolute Susan, and Ron quickly vanished from the battle zone.

The man went through a long and elaborate introduction, while Susan manufactured a slight disarming smile to keep him going.

"I'm such a devoted fan of yours, Miss Hayward, I've seen every film you ever made..."

"Uh-huh," she egged him on, still smiling.

"...and you're my favorite actress. There's no one else..."

"Uh-huh."

She was shoring up for a splendid detonation, sans the equipment she would have needed twenty years before: hands on hips, hair flying, good lighting.

Never suspecting, the artist finished his worshipful peroration by saying that he had spent many thousands of dollars in paint, canvas and time. He had been offered $25,000 for his labor of love, his portrait of Susan Hayward. He could not part with such a personal treasure for any price. Yet he would give it as a gift to his goddess, for a mere $10,000 to cover costs.

"Really?" said Susan. Then her posture straightened regally, her arms swayed stylishly and she began yelling for the guards.

"I want this man thrown out! Throw this man out! I want him thrown out!" She was pointing toward the "villain."

While the room went into an uproar and the guards came flying over, she finally addressed her horrified victim.

"I saw your candy-box crap, your little Susan Hayward doll that looks like if you wind it up it will cry tomorrow."

She drew in on a cigarette, the guards grabbed him by the

arm, she waited a few beats and then said, "Throw the bum out."

Susan was pleased. It was the second perfect "take" tonight. In a movie studio, the director would have yelled "Cut!" and hugged her, the grips would have applauded. The only problem here was that this was not a movie and people were getting hurt.

Susan took off her emeralds and gave them to Curlee, who was standing nearby, quite stiffly. Ron, near Susan again, believed that Susan had been taking Curlee for granted far too long; he could see that Curlee was having no fun while everyone else was jolly. He offered her a drink and asked her to sit down. No, she said, she was not there to party with the others but to look after Susan.

Susan spotted Ron chatting with her defecting servant and rushed over. She grabbed him and insisted he dance with her. He refused, knowing that she was riding high and might try for a third "take" on the dance floor. But with Susan like this, there was no resisting. Once on the dance floor, she began leading him roughly, forcing him this way and that to the beat of a rhumba. He knew they must look odd: little Susan pushing and shoving awkward, big Ron.

"Come on, move! What's the matter! Dance!"

He was terribly embarrassed.

It was a markedly different Susan on her very last night in the show, after her triumphant party. She had arrived backstage at Caesars and said, quite hoarsely, "I'm going on!" She had to make one last spectacular impression. While she began putting on her costume, one of the management went to Betty McGuire and told her to get ready. A child could see that Susan couldn't perform. Susan was not only voiceless but visibly quite ill. At best, using a microphone, she might have gasped her way through the first scene and gotten no further. However, no one would tell her that she couldn't go onstage on her last night. Shaking badly, but determined, she had barely finished dressing when the overture began. She tried to move toward her dressing-room door, then collapsed in Curlee's arms. Betty was waiting in the wings, in costume, hoping that Susan would make it. When she got the word that Susan just couldn't do it, she began to cry. Moments later, Betty made her entrance in turban and furs. A frustrated Susan angrily got out of her costume and began redressing.

Her work on *I'll Cry Tomorrow*, finished under enormous stress, was the best of her career to date. Top photo: with director Daniel Mann. *(Courtesy of Daniel Mann)* Bottom photo: in a cathartic scene with Eddie Albert. *(Doug McClelland collection)*

Susan wed Southern gentleman Eaton
Chalkley on February 8, 1957, in Phoenix,
Arizona. *(UPI/Bettmann Newsphotos)*

At the 1956 Academy Awards ceremony, Susan was with her sons and
Eaton Chalkley, who made losing the Oscar easier. *(UPI/Bettmann
Newsphotos)*

o: Susan and the family of Ed Montgomery on the set of *I Want to Live!*
om left: Ed Montgomery, sons Douglas and David, Susan, and Ed's wife,
lene. *(Courtesy of Ed Montgomery)*

ove: Robert Wise directing her as Barbara Graham in *I Want to Live!*
urtesy of Ed Montgomery)

Susan didn't waste the bat of an eye in her scenes in *I Want to Live!* Every movement and word had maximum impact—she had reached the top of her art. The film was greatly successful both as polemic and drama. *(Top left photo: Gene Arceri collection . Top right and bottom photos: United Artists)*

Top Left: Wally and Susan at the Santa Anita race track, where he was a page, in 1964. Eaton, just out of camera range, was intermittently ill these days. *(Courtesy of Wally Marrenner)*

Top Right: She got it at last—at the Oscar ceremonies of 1959! *(UPI/Bettmann Newsphotos)*

Above: Susan and Eaton played horses in the Bahamas, March 1960, among their other endless recreations. *(UPI/Bettmann Newsphotos)*

As *Mame*, 1968, at Caesars Palace in Las Vegas. First her voice gave out, then her spirit. *(Doug McClelland collection)*

Susan replaced Judy Garland as Helen Lawson in *Valley of the Dolls*, 1967. *(Doug McClelland collection)*

She moved back to Hollywood in 1972 and the same year starred in a television pilot called *Heat of Anger*, with James Stacy. *(Doug McClelland collection)*

...ith Darren McGavin in *Say Goodbye, Maggie Cole,* her second TV movie. ...few months later, doctors identified twenty tumors in her brain. *(Doug ...cClelland collection)*

Top Left: In one of her red wigs, about a year before her death in 1975. *(Doug McClelland collection)*

Top Right: Susan took a great risk in becoming a presenter at the 1974 Oscar ceremonies. That night, she was total illusion and total courage. At left, Charlton Heston and producer Melvin Frank. *(Doug McClelland collection)*

Above: Florence and her daughter Moira in a 1984 photo taken in Los Angeles. *(Photo by Robert LaGuardia)*

Just then, Nelson entered and found her scribbling with her makeup erase stick, gashing in big letters across her mirror

CELESTE WHO???

and boldly signing it

SUSAN HAYWARD

She wanted to insult Holm again. Nelson became concerned about the hysteria he saw brewing through her exhaustion.

"They say she's a perfect bitch," Susan said. "But she's got it and I haven't." She suddenly began pounding her fists on the mirror that held her graffiti, crying, "I am not beautiful! I'm not!" He took her in his arms to mollify her.

Says Nelson, "There was a very sad little girl in Susan."

No matter how many times she had said that she couldn't wait to leave *Mame*, tonight she couldn't bear to leave the theater at seven. This time, it was no act.

Four days later, back in Fort Lauderdale, Susan received a glowing letter from Caesars Palace that only a Sarah Bernhardt could expect: they were honored to have had such a great actress on their stage, and as a memento of that historic time they had shipped, Express Mail, a painting of herself as Mame by "that great unknown artist..."

Susan was beside herself. Apparently Caesars had paid the artist his $10,000, believing they were pleasing her. When the painting arrived at Nermi Drive, she called Ron with vicious glee, telling him to come right over and to bring a pair of big, strong scissors. "I'm going to cut it into little pieces and throw it into the canal."

Ron was delirious at the thought of the painting actually being in Fort Lauderdale. On the way to Susan's, he schemed different ways to keep her from destorying the portrait. Then he realized there was only one way to do it: appeal to her sense of humor. Susan had so little that when it was finally coaxed into surfacing, she was surprised, happy and pliant. After Ron arrived at Nermi Drive, he and she had a few drinks, as was their custom, and he began to talk about how campy the painting was. Campiness was a subtlety that both eluded and intrigued Susan, for it held that badness could be interesting if viewed in a certain light. Oh, just look at the silliness of the nose and big, big eyes, and the tits were *so* big, and the Rock of Gibraltar! God, it was just so tacky and wonderful. Susan had another drink and yes, she saw it, too. She began to laugh and laugh with Ron. Once she started to laugh, Ron knew he had won.

He asked for the painting. Sure, he could have it, she said, laughing, but only on the condition that if he ever wanted to get rid of it or if he died, it was to be burned. Ron agreed, but he had no intention whatsoever of fulfilling his promise. He genuinely loved the painting, for it said something profound to him. He hung the enormous mural-size painting on his living room wall and had a big light placed over it. In the evenings, the light over the painting was always kept lit, even when he was out of the apartment. When visitors came to call and walked into a dark living room illuminated only by a life-size image of Susan Hayward standing before the Rock of Gibraltar, they were stunned. In this way, of course, everyone who came to know Ron found out instantly the identity of the most important person in his life.

CHAPTER 10

Mania

ON THE DECK of the *Oh, Susannah*, the hot sunbelt winds streamed through her hat, hair and blouse, dramatizing the shape of her substantial breasts and drawing glances from others. At the parties Nelson took her to, male eyes would linger too long on her, inquiries were made by the more confident men, dates attempted.

Susan was, in early 1969, back in Fort Lauderdale, as appealing as ever. That drinker's body had disappeared after the rigors of *Mame* and at fifty she was magnificent, looking hardly more than forty. While her look was not glamorous, it had great feminine strength. A slowly forming smile, a riveting stare, a deep voice, a haunting profile, straight and sure posture created a voluptuousness more magnetic than mere youthful glamour.

Men, however, had scant chance with her, for she would not let go of Eaton. What had been understandable grief several years before was now abnormal and prolonged. It prevented her from making important decisions about her life. It kept her in a debilitating state of fantasy and sad reflection. She could not find love. She could not find herself. Her tiny body was lost in that spacious house on Nermi Drive overlooking a canal. She moved about without energy on the cream-colored high-pile wall-to-wall carpeting. Sat drinking her neat scotch on one of the exquisite lounges of the conversation area where she and Eaton had entertained. Watched movies from the fifties in another part of the living room where she and Eaton had done the same. Often, she would look out the windows to see her swaying yacht. It had been her passion to bide the hours with him on the *Susannah*. Her spirit was restive.

* * *

She did have occasional relationships, with men who were almost always the wrong type: younger and Midwestern. They did not last long and she was not happy with the way she was living. Her mainly solitary nights were as restless as they had been during the few years before she had married Eaton. The only way she could face the nights and, increasingly, the days was with liquor, her only true companion, along with Nelson.

The bond between them grew stronger. What had been a friendship advanced to another stage. Call it a sort of marriage. Left finally by Timothy and Gregory and Curlee for marriages of their own, Susan called on Ron ceaselessly to fill the emptiness. They drove around Fort Lauderdale together, spent afternoons on the *Susannah*, went shopping for groceries as she and Eaton had done. Susan bought liquor in endless cases. She and Ron drank from the moment they met until the moment they parted, which was often in the wee hours. Many a morning, he'd wonder, hungover, if he'd make it through the day. Yet he matched Susan drink for drink, the price he was willing to pay for her friendship.

Nelson continued to take her to parties, his wonderful extroversion allowing her to break through the walls of her saturnine, suspicious nature and to enjoy the company of perfect strangers. Liquor was a great help, too. This was a *quid pro quo*: for she in turn took him to the most exclusive VIP events. President Richard Nixon sent Susan an engraved invitation to the White House, which also bore Nelson's name. One can imagine Ron's emotions, sitting next to Susan Hayward and the President of the United States in a White House dining room, hearing Richard Nixon confess to Hayward, with grave candor, "You know, you have always been my favorite actress."

Susan aided Ron's career by accompanying him to various Heart Fund benefits, bringing much prestige and publicity to the events. She made several sizable donations of her own. Nelson became a minor celebrity in Fort Lauderdale and a not-so-minor one at the Heart Fund. She was changing Ron Nelson's life in every conceivable way. When they had first met right after Eaton's death, he had been slightly overweight, almost puffy, with a Buster Brown boyish look about his clean-shaven face. He had dressed conservatively, for his conservative job, in solid suits, or the standard tux for benefits. But now he was dressing up to all the glamour that Hayward was bringing into his life. His suits became natty, weaves or white, or were replaced by fancy Florida dress jackets of brocade or linen, with very contrasting pants; he wore French and Italian shirts, left open at the collar; he flashed necklaces, bracelets, rings. He lost a great deal of weight, allowed his hair to become fashionably long, grew a goatee and mustache. His boyish face now resembled that of a Continental *bon vivant*.

Add to the drastic changes in Ron's life, wrought by Susan, a sometimes comic but more often unsettling mania. She adored her boat, and if Ron were free when she had a yen to sail, he became her crew. From his point of view, it was a good thing that he was matching her drink for drink, for otherwise, unsedated, he might have fainted from fright. She would speed the *Susannah* recklessly through the canals and waterways, paving dangerous wakes, chanting as some drunken Norseman might have centuries before, "This is my ocean!" Other boats, spotting the by now familiar devil-may-care actress at the helm, gave her wide leeway. More than one Lauderdale boater cursed after getting ensnared in her frenzied wake, sometimes after averting a collision with the *Susannah* by only a few inches. Once, she did have a serious smash-up.

Susan's eyesight was poor, and Ron, convinced that these outings were somehow half-hearted attempts at suicide, was always sick with terror when he was on the boat, especially during her dangerous night cruises. Perversely, Susan was thrilled at Ron's wan, doubled-over look and would become even more reckless to see it get worse. She would laugh: "Hi ya! Captain Tuna, Chicken of the Sea!"

She cherished the singing brass mechanical bird in a gilded cage given to her by Bill Holden in 1942, and brought it on board the *Susannah* so that while she ripped through the waters she could hear it play "Let's All Sing Like the Birdies Sing." In her deep contralto, she sang the "Tweet...tweet, tweet...tweet, tweet" part, and demanded that Ron sing along. He did, reluctantly, and she laughed at him for having a voice higher than hers.

The wickerwork of Fort Lauderdale's canals was spanned by many bridges with low ceilings that required boats like the *Susannah* to lower their high antennas and fishing lines for safe passage. On drunken kicks, she refused to lower them as she sped under the bridges, and the antennas and fishing lines would scrape the bottoms of the bridges. These maneuvers were not so much dangerous to life as destructive to property and attention-grabbing. Susan was asserting her power, defying someone to tell her that she couldn't do exactly as she pleased.

No one ever did. All the authorities knew of her maritime escapades; but there was an understanding among Fort Lauderdale officials that Susan Hayward, the city's most important celebrity-in-residence, someone who brought excitement to its otherwise dull retirement-community image, was to be given special freedoms. Although she was a great danger both to herself and to other boaters, reprimands were never given. Nevertheless, she was watched like a hawk. The police, spotting her on the canal, would warn the Coast Guard, who would then keep an eye on her. The irony is that Susan, from her fishing days with Eaton, always knew how to be a good boater. Her boating excesses were quite self-conscious.

The police were continually aware of Susan's other Fort Lauderdale antics. Her house had an easily triggered alarm system. Coming home late and high one night, she and Ron slammed the door of the long black Cadillac limousine driven by the chauffeur and walked toward her front step. She wore mink over a white pants suit, which had been hot and tight and so she unzipped the sides to let her legs breathe. She began groping with her keys and clutching her loosened pants underneath the mink. Struggling between the keys and the pants, she accidentally set off the shrieking alarm. The neighbors awoke. In minutes, the police arrived, car lights swirling, guns out, aggressively rushing. Ron and Susan, caught in a spray of light, threw up their hands. Susan's pants dropped around her knees. After a moment of stunned silence, the soused couple broke into spasms of laughter. It looked like a gag routine from a Mabel Normand silent. The policemen recognized Susan Hayward immediately, pretended not to be amused, gave a tepid be-more-careful-next-time reproach and left, while Susan sat on the doorstep, still gagged with hysterics.

Susan's mania during this period took the form, for the most part, of destructive and/or childish play, but there were times when it turned deadly serious in the cause of righteousness. She and Nelson had been leaving a supermarket when Susan spied a Cadillac speeding away from a parked car it had just sideswiped. She shoved Ron inside their car and yelled, "Follow that car! Get her! Faster! Faster!" Nelson dutifully chased the Caddy until they caught up with it and she could read the license-plate number. She grabbed a piece of scrap paper, copied the plate number and then wrote next to it: CULPRIT, in big capital letters, underlining it so angrily that the paper tore. He drove her back to the super-market parking lot. On the same scrap of paper, Susan wrote the damaged car's plate number and then, in big capital letters, the word VICTIM, again underlining angrily. Once home, she obtained the "victim's" telephone number from the police and called her, explaining what had happened, giving the "culprit's" telephone number and license number. The grateful woman asked with whom she was speaking, for she wanted to send a little gift. Susan wouldn't identify herself, then signed off, saying (as sailors say, meaning to repay a rescue effort by saving someone else's life one day): "Throw someone a lifeline."

While Susan and Ron drank and boated, they talked, by them-selves, hour after hour. He became the ears for Edythe, not Susan, the part of herself that she had been hiding for years. She would spill her soul, running on about her past in epic style, slowly probing her relationships with the main people in her life. Ron recalls a multitude of snippets from these liquorous, languorous journeys.

About her mother: "Susan was very critical of her mother. She used to tell me that she was an emasculating, cold-hearted woman. She told me, 'I could never get over the way she treated my father; it was just ridiculous. She was selfish and cold and cruel and she wanted what she wanted and didn't give a damn how she got it.' She said that her mother had never given her encouragement, never told her that she loved her, that she was pretty. It was always 'Florence is pretty, Florence is the one.' She told me that she thought her mother was frigid and that she never wanted anything but money." Nelson could not help but note that her discussions of her mother might really have been veiled discussions of her-self.

About Eaton: "She had a great suspicion that Eaton Chalkley was less than the macho male that she told everybody he was. She would say to me, 'He should have been a priest. He loved the priests. He really didn't care that much for women.' Then she would correct herself later and say, 'That's not what I meant.' She felt that she had contributed to his suicidal drinking. She had a need to believe that she was so irresistible that he couldn't help himself."

About Jess: "She told me that the marriage was a shotgun affair, that the studio made her marry him. She said that she had ruined his career by talking against him to all the studio heads during their divorce, and she felt guilty: 'I was never very nice to Jess and he deserved better.'"

In between saying such things, she would go on jags and moan to Nelson, "Christ, I'm no good. I never was," laying on him all the accumulated guilt of a lifetime.

Ron became fascinated with the relationship between Susan and Florence, who seemed always to be on Susan's mind, even though she hadn't seen her older sister for twelve years. She kept coming back to Florence, saying that Florence had had all the advantages when they were younger and lorded it over her, and then later "when I made it—and I made it in spite of her and not because of her—she spilled her guts about me to some gossip columnist that I didn't know, about an affair I was having, and it damned near ruined me." (Florence doesn't recall such a happening, unless Susan was referring to the *Confidential* interview.) He had the impression, from Susan's ever circling references to her sister, that she hadn't really disposed of Florence, in her mind, as thoroughly as she pretended.

If only someone could have thrown Susan "a lifeline"—for she was hurting terribly. Her needs remained unfulfilled, and rather than return to Hollywood for more of what she'd had before she married Eaton, she was more determined than ever to find solace and temporary diversion in her liquor. As the months passed, the Nermi Drive house grew lonelier and she, more isolated. A solitary, drinking woman was an easy target for intruders. Susan may have been smashed much of the time, but her sense of logic and survival had not been dulled. She made up her mind to move to a condominium, which seemed safer for a woman alone, and far more convenient. She put Nermi Drive up for sale and bought a splendid penthouse apartment at the Four Seasons, a blue-and-white Art Deco building located on Sunset Boulevard, not far from the ocean and right on a Fort Lauderdale waterway.

While waiting to move into her new apartment she lived in a

suite at the nearby Pier 66, where she was a regular at its restaurant and where she and Eaton had stayed many times. Louie Sanchez, a room-service waiter, remembers that she ordered a turkey sandwich and was so outraged, upon discovering that it was filled with turkey roll instead of fresh-cut poultry, that she called the management and raised hell. There was more hell to come: Red opened the door of her suite and flung the tray down the hall along with a few epithets, then dashed back into the room, packed her bags and checked out in a flurry.

Susan had been so proud of Gregory when she attended his graduation at Auburn University in June of 1969. He moved to Jacksonville, Florida, to practice veterinary medicine, with his new wife, whom Susan liked. About Timothy, however, she fussed and clucked. She had been proud of his stint in the Green Berets and his swimming expertise, but wondered where he was going professionally. And she was a bit of an irritable mother-in-law with Ilse, his gorgeous, buxom, blonde wife. When Jay Bernstein, Susan's handsome young press agent, offered Timmy a job in Hollywood, Susan was delighted. The only problem was that the new job would keep him three thousand miles away, and she needed family closeness these days.

Wally was still living in Los Angeles. Sometimes in the wee hours of the night, when the walls would begin to close in on her, she called her brother. After a few hours of listening to Susan's liquorous gab, Wally would put Carole on the phone, and Susan would go into an irritating concerned-sister routine: "Are you taking good care of my brother? Are you feeding him right?" Carole yessed her sister-in-law good-naturedly, but as the solicitous interrogation continued, Wally could hear his wife's tone changing to anger. In an aside, she said to him, "What does she think, I'm neglecting you?" Carole had not realized, at first, how depressed Susan was, for Susan had always seemed a bulwark. Wally would take the phone from Carole, and Susan would talk to him for several more hours. He knew her well and, sensing the despair, made no attempt to end the call. She would beg him to move to Fort Lauderdale, get a job at the racetrack, like the one he had in Los Angeles. They could all be together. "Maybe," he said, not daring to say no.

She also made long and late phone calls to Ruth Gillette, who had been strong and motherly toward her during *Mame*. "Hello, dear. This is Mother Goddam." She was trying, in this bleak time, to reach out, but Susan, the distrustful loner, had garnered so few friends during her lifetime that now, when she wished to communicate, there was mostly silence.

Barred from outlets, Susan was experiencing dreadful emotional upheavals. Her roller-coaster-like drunken manias were accompanied by a series of accidents that were surely related. On the January 21, 1971, after drinking for days, she fell asleep in a chair holding a lit cigarette. While the chair smoldered, she awakened, changed into a nightgown and moved to her bedroom, where she passed out again. The thick smoke awakened her, for, luckily, even when drunk, she slept uneasily. Choking and coughing, she ran to the bedroom door and found herself trapped by a wall of flames. She called the fire department, then ran to a feature of her apartment which eventually saved her life: the balcony, nine stories high. The smoke and heat would have killed her, even before the flames entered the bedroom, had the outdoor balcony not been there.

"Fire! Fire! Help!" she screamed from the balcony.

Sure she would be dead before the firemen got to her, Susan ran back into the hot, smoky bedroom to gather her silk bedsheets, then came back out and began tying them into a long rope to lower herself to the balcony of the apartment below, where Mrs. Russell Carson lived. By now, the firemen had arrived on the street and they saw the danger in what she was planning to do. Fire Lieutenant Phil Brewster, from the street, screamed that she shouldn't do it; the sheets might not hold; his men would be up to rescue her in a minute. Susan kept on tying the sheets. She wasn't about to trust anyone, and she was panicky. Then Mrs. Carson chimed in: "Don't do it! Wait for the firemen!" Susan decided to wait a little longer. In no time, Lieutenant Kenneth Nation, leading a seven-man squad, was battering down Susan's apartment door. It was then that Susan, hearing the sounds of her rescuers, felt safe enough to become sassy and call Ron.

The brave firemen, wearing gas marks, raced into her bedroom, found her on the balcony, quite collected, and immediately gave her oxygen to prevent further damage to her lungs. They put out the flames in the living room with hand extinguishers, and escorted a sooty Susan to Mrs. Carson's apartment, where Ron later found her. It was already daylight by then.

The apartment was quickly repaired and refurbished. Several months later, she fell and broke her arm. She had been blotto, as always now, insisted on waxing the kitchen floor herself, poured the wax, walked on it and slipped. Shortly after that, she broke her foot. The penthouse, where she had moved for safety and convenience, was becoming a disaster zone.

Nelson tried to be the best friend he knew how to be, to meet Susan's demands and to be available to drink with her any day or hour. They had a relationship that included sometimes sleeping together (usually only after they had both been drinking; it was the only way she could, he says), but most of the time they were merely affectionate with one another. "There was a great deal of touching and kissing." If they did sleep together, Ron would allow her to control the circumstances (as apparently Eaton had). Once, things did not go as she had wanted and she was irritated for days. He took her to an elegant Fort Lauderdale party, and in the midst of a group of people a soused Susan looked at Ron and cried, in a particularly vicious way, one of her favorite sexual curse words, which amounted to an attack on his manhood.

The guests were stunned. Ron was at first aghast, then deeply hurt and angry. He went into a brooding silence for the rest of the evening. The next day she called him and, in her usual way, as if nothing had happened, suggested they go out somewhere.

"No," he said resolutely. "I don't think so."

"What do you mean, Ronsy Ponsy?"

"I just think it's best if we didn't see each other for a while."

She hung up. A few days later, she called him again, still without apologizing. Where did he want to go? He said nowhere—their relationship had gotten out of hand and it was time to end it. Susan did not seem nonplussed.

She was terrified, nonetheless, and when enough time had passed, she let go her pretense of composure and called Ron in a semi-panic.

"I've had enough, I give in," she said. "Let's end this. What do you want? I'll do anything you want. Just come over."

There was a line in one of Susan's films, *Smash-Up*, her first portrayal of an alcoholic: "You have to hit rock bottom before you can come up." That seemed to sum up what was happening to Susan now, a kind of ultimate (and very theatrical) catharsis of self-destruction. Nelson was part of whatever it was, that driving of her psyche into the wind, that wild willfulness that threatened to run boats and people aground. He was part of a kind of "testing" behavior which seemed at first glance to lack purpose. She had never had such a friend before: someone with whom she could strain all the mechanisms of an inter-relationship, spill her guts, display the unattractive residue of a lifetime of playing every part but that of Edythe Marrenner. She vented all the sarcasms and meannesses that were stored, almost as a way of showing a doctor the symptoms in hopes of seeking a cure.

Susan and Ron had a mutual friend who was gay and a man of excellent character. (She had never really decided what she thought of homosexuals, but had, in practice, liked many gay individuals.) One day, in front of this man, she said to Nelson about him, "I don't want to be bothered by that fucking queer." The man was shattered by the gratuitous cruelty. Later, she appealed to Ron: "I have done that all of my life, and I don't like myself when I do that. How can I make it up to him?" Ron said, "The only thing you can do is call him on the telephone and say you're sorry. Tell him what you told me, 'There's only one reason I could have done that, because I'm not a very nice person.'"

Susan did precisely that and she and the man became fast friends again. It was like a learning, or unlearning, process, a kind of therapy, drunken as it became, for all the stoic armor she had acquired. She had never, for instance, been in the habit of saying thank you; it was nearly as foreign as "I'm sorry." Now she sent Nelson frequent thank-you notes, with lines like, "Dear Ron, You wonderful, warm, kind human being. No wonder you work for the Heart Association. You've got the biggest heart in the world. Can you forgive me?"

"I detected a crying need," says Ron. "She had never made friends. She didn't know the value of friendship. She could never be sure that if a friend told you something, you could put it in the damn bank. I walked her all the way to the bank."

In hindsight, it appears that the Fort Lauderdale period was one of tremendous change for Susan, and that the mania was almost a kind of medicine. She was trying to scream quiet, withdrawn Edythe back into existence. The money, the fame: they had finally come. But she was not yet whole. She was still too many disconnected *personae*: the movie star, the sweet Georgian housewife, the beautiful woman with claws, the grieving widow. Yet, ever so gradually, she was starting to face her true self.

"Hey, Hooligan."

It was Marty Rackin calling again, late in 1971, with another job for her. Would she do a cameo opposite her old friend Bill Holden in a low-budget Western that Rackin was filming in Mexico? The strange loyalty and attraction she felt for Marty lingered, and this time, without so much as asking for a script, she gave him a quick yes, and even said she would work for no pay.

Rackin's *The Revengers* turned out to be another clinker. Right after the filming, Marty set up an interview between Susan and a top Hollywood agent, Norman Brokaw. Brokaw remembers: "She sat opposite me on the couch in my office, and I couldn't believe it. I had always represented big stars like Barbara Stanwyck and Loretta Young, but this one looked as if the clock had stopped for her, physically and emotionally, twenty years ago. Knowing her temper as well as her enormous talent, I carefully brought up the fact that television was the big thing now. I mentioned that I had just put together a fine ninety-minute movie-for-television, written by Fay Kanin for Barbara Stanwyck. I said that the movie was a pilot to give Barbara another shot at a successful TV series like 'The Big Valley.' I told Susan I'd like to find another property of that same quality for *her*. Susan just nodded and said, 'Fine.' I couldn't dream that a few days later Barbara Stanwyck would go into the hospital to have her left kidney removed; so, suddenly, the very property I had held up as an example for Susan became available for *her*. It took me about thirty seconds to convince CBS and Metromedia to continue *Heat of Anger* with Susan in the lead."

Susan's extremes of drinking and self-destruction had somehow led to a clearing in the woods of her confusion; the way out was apparent: a true comeback in Hollywood. She worked long, hard hours for *Heat of Anger*, which never became a series but nevertheless impressed the networks. She brought to her role as a lawyer the required stoic maturity, yet tinged with the old Hayward fiery romanticism, a superb combination which encouraged TV producers to request her services to play professionals in other TV movies. Early in 1972, Brokaw scheduled Susan to do two more pilots.

While she was making *Heat of Anger*, she sent Barbara Stanwyck, whom she had never met, three dozen pink roses, with a card, "From one Brooklyn broad to another." Stanwyck was so moved that she insisted the roses be kept in her hospital room, against doctor's orders. Susan, who had always idolized Stanwyck, refused to allow the costumers to remake a wardrobe for her. Her costumes would be the ones made for Stanwyck.

Susan decided to move permanently to Hollywood, where, not coincidentally, Timmy and, of course, Wally lived. Now she needed a house. She was to see one in "Birdland" atop the highest hill in Beverly Hills. She drove up Laurel Way, a peaceful, winding road, finally encountering, beyond an idyllic path embraced by palm trees and Italian cypresses, the two huge oak doors of a magnificent, sprawling, one-level mansion. Enhanced by a swimming pool, a sauna and a two-car garage, the estate was perched on the brink of a startling deep drop, overlooking all of Los Angeles. Susan found the inside of the house just as marvelous. In the middle of an enormous living room was a sunken area, with a cozy round fireplace at its center. She was told the price, which she thought inexplicably low. Investigating, she found that prospective buyers, learning how a former owner had died, would not buy a "jinxed" house. The owner had been homosexual. His gruesome, self-murdered corpse had been found floating in the swimming pool. Susan, with all her superstitions—which even included some little-known ones, such as a fear of walking into a room which had peacock feathers as decoration—brushed aside the jinx idea with a little joke and quickly bought the house.

"Jinx, indeed!" she thought, standing on her new property, literally on top of the world, looking out wistfully over the city she had once owned. She would be happy to have at least part of it back.

CHAPTER 11

Specter

USAN had flown to Georgetown University Hospital in Washington, D.C., in March of 1972, for her annual checkup by Dr. Thomas Kellerer, the internist who had been one of Eaton's doctors. As part of his thorough exam, he injected a dye into a blood vessel to enable him to check for growths, using a sophisticated scanner. She was used to the procedure, although this time it took longer and the physician's manner was more tense. Later, Dr. Kellerer asked her how much she smoked. "Two packs a day." He warned that the habit was dangerous. Another dye test was done. There was no doubt: a tumor was growing on one of her lungs. If a biopsy showed a malignancy, and the odds were that it would, the lung would have to be removed.

When the tremors of the initial shock subsided, she both wanted and didn't want to know details. It was a terrified woman who heard the somber talk of major surgery, the removal of part of her body, the prognosis for total recovery, and that single numbing word: cancer.

She packed her bags and fled Washington for Fort Lauderdale, where she joined Ron Nelson in a long drinking spree. Eventually, she told him what had happened in Georgetown, and when he urged her not to shut her eyes to the problem, she responded: "Well, what have I got to live for, anyway?"

Dr. Kellerer had begged her not to run off, but to deal with the life-threatening tumor. Most likely her life was at stake, and if so, it could be saved by prompt action. After she fled, he sent his findings to another of her doctors, Dr. Davis in Los Angeles, who contacted her in her Laurel Way home but got nowhere. Her most trusted physician in Hollywood, Dr. Lee Siegel, had no better luck.

Wally knew nothing of her condition, for Susan, as she vowed, was simply going on as if she had never spoken to a doctor. Closer to his sister than to another living soul, he was delighted to have her near him. In the middle of 1972, Carole became ill with tuberculosis, serious complications arose and she died rather abruptly. Susan remained with her brother throughout the crisis.

According to Carole's wishes, she was cremated, the ashes to be scattered over the Pacific Ocean. Wally and Susan were in many ways much alike. When the funeral director told them that he had arranged for them to fly over the ocean in a single-engine plane, they both chimed that they weren't going to jeopardize their lives in such a crate, and eventually, at the airport, chose a shiny, sturdy twin-engine Cessna from which to sprinkle Carole's remains. These were in a cloth bag, which, according to safety regulations, the pilot himself had to drop. The pilot, taking the whole thing deadly seriously, turned to Wally and asked if he wanted to hold on to the bag until the very last moment. "Okay," said Wally, adding, "It's just a bag of ashes as far as I'm concerned." Over water, he gave the pilot the bag, it was dropped through a little side window, then blown to oblivion by the wind and propellers.

Dizzying headaches began to bother Susan. She thought they were hangovers from her drinking and told Wally that she had better cut down because her head was always throbbing. She was scheduled to star in her next TV movie-pilot, *Say Goodbye, Maggie Cole*, at the end of 1972. She hoped the "hangovers" would end by then.

When they didn't, she flew back to Georgetown University Hospital for another examination. The news this time was doubly horrifying. X-rays showed growths in her brain as well. Apparently, whatever had started in her lungs had metastasized and spread to the head. By the time she returned to Los Angeles, she had lost weight, was pale and unsteady. Somehow, she made it through the filming of *Say Goodbye, Maggie Cole*, giving a performance which was not only adequate but, under the circumstances, remarkable.

For the next few months, she was in stasis, not knowing what was happening to her body. She continued to drink heavily and to use the painkillers prescribed for her headaches. The first real signs of change were hindered movements. At times, she had difficulty walking. She would drop things. She couldn't light a cigarette.

Susan appeared to face up to the facts with astonishing bravery. She showed no sign of panic or depression when she very coolly told Wally, out of the blue, "Don't you know I am dying?"

"Oh, come on, quit your kidding."

She said she had brain tumors. Wally became silent, as was his habit when he couldn't deal with an emotional shock. Susan was the only person he had left in the world.

"I've got these rocks in my brain," she told Nelson in a joking, biting way.

In April, Susan attended a gala presentation party in honor of Henry Hathaway's seventy-fifth birthday. In front of a crowd of her fellow stars, Susan had her first seizure. Medically, it was much like an epileptic fit; the brain growths had caused a cerebral "electrical storm." To see it was blood-curdling. Her body jerked spastically. Her hands became grasping claws. Her face scrunched, lips twisted, cheek and jaw muscles pulled every which way: one of the most beautiful of filmdom's faces turning to a Halloween mask. When the seizure ended, she went into a deep sleep.

She was taken to Century City Hospital, where rigorous testing uncovered no less than twenty tumors growing at an incredible rate in her brain. Dr. Lee Siegel was told that they were inoperable: too much of the brain was already involved, even if they weren't malignant. Siegel told Susan that only immediate massive chemotherapy and radiation treatments, plus a super-miracle, could keep her from the cold embrace of the Specter of Death; she would not leave the hospital alive without the treatments. Yes, she would endure them. Yes, she was willing to fight for more time.

The nightmare began.

Monstrous machines circled her body, menacing needles jabbed her flesh, pills were shoved down her throat, gadgets stuck to her head with a trillion wire tentacles running to scopes. She had to drink awful potions to kill the things in her brain. She was drugged and nauseous most of the time. She had no appetite and couldn't hold down food.

At times, all the medicines, especially the large amounts of thorazine that were injected, caused extreme disorientation. She began yelling at the nurses, like a crazy (as Dr. Siegel recalls), "Look, I'm Susan Hayward! I'm a big star! You can't do this to me!" After she smashed her hand through a window, she was moved to a psychiatric area and restrained until the violent episodes abated.

By now, rumors that Susan was at the point of death were spreading all over Hollywood, and gossip columns began to print them. The phone in her room would not stop ringing. It seemed everyone in the world knew she was at Century City, practically in her casket, and wanted some "last words" from her. She was secretly moved to Cedars of Lebanon Hospital under the name of Margaret Redding.

Six weeks later, she was released, still alive but looking like a ghost. Her five-foot-one-inch frame held a mere eighty-five pounds.

Lee Siegel informed her frankly that her time was short; there was only the merest glimmer of hope. He told Nelson, who had flown in from Fort Lauderdale fearing the worst, that it could be "a week, a month," but probably she would be gone around the Fourth of July.

The chemotherapy treatments caused all of her gorgeous red hair to fall out.

Wally began to brood—in the daytime going about his chores as a page at the racetrack with a heavy heart, in the evenings spending time with his sister or wandering about his home in a quandary. Susan, when the world became too much for her, could vent her emotions in a loud argument with a waiter, curses over the telephone, drinking binges or, if need be, a good scream. Later, her nerves would quiet down. Wally was not a screamer or a loud drunk. He was an unobtrusively quiet man, preferring to keep his frustrations to himself. It was that quality in Wally which always made Susan feel protective toward him. Now it was she who was fading, and Wally, helpless, couldn't bear it.

On the Fourth of July, two months after Susan was released from Cedars of Lebanon and, so strangely, the very day that was to have found her dead, Wally's brooding over Susan and the loss of his wife helped bring about a heart attack. Ten minutes after he collapsed, he was rushed by ambulance from the Hollywood

Park Race Track to the Intensive Care Unit of Centinela Hospital. His condition was soon listed as stable. Susan, who wasn't permitted to see him immediately, phoned Centinela the next morning, identified herself by her movie-star name and asked to be put through to her brother. Everyone thought it was some kind of joke, since small Wally, the most unpretentious man in the world, looked the furthest thing from a close relative of a cinema queen. After hesitating a moment, the young nurse on duty put her lips to Wally's ear and whispered, so no one else would hear, "Susan Hayward is on the telephone for you...Susan Hayward, the movie star."

"Oh, I'll talk to her," he said. Noticing the look on the nurse's face, he added with a smile, "She's my sister."

Nurses jumped around Wally after that call. Susan came to see him the first day she was allowed and brought with her a small stuffed animal for her older "baby brother." She came many times, in wigs, wobbly on her feet, and each time brought another stuffed animal. She would look after him, she said; he was alone and he needed her. She talked to him like a football coach pepping up a losing team: "Don't let this get you down. When you're on your feet again, you and I are going to take a trip around the world. Just the two of us. We'll show 'em they can't keep a Marrenner down."

Susan began to cling to Wally, and he to her, as in the old days when brother and sister had seen each other through the storms of their own crises and devastating family hardships. Now in middle age they were both weak from illness, but Susan, who possessed a strong drive, needed to be the stronger. Wally said he just had to move out of the old place he had shared with Carole, and, heart attack or no, he wanted to move right away. Susan insisted on helping him. In dark glasses and fur coat, she trekked with him from building to building in search of a new apartment in his old neighborhood. He liked one in a building on Hauser Boulevard. She approved and even oversaw the signing of the lease in the rental office. Soon, she was carrying his things from his old apartment, driving them over to the new place, dumping them onto the elevator and chastising Wally when she thought he was doing too much to help her. Patricia Morison, who lived in the building, met Susan on the elevator and was surprised. Morison hadn't seen her old friend since their early days at Paramount. She heard herself say, at the sight of the supposedly dying woman robustly carrying a shopping bag full of clothes, "Why, Susan, you're looking so well."

"Did you think I wasn't?" asked Susan happily, before beginning to reminisce.

Susan had some of her fine furniture shipped over to Wally's new apartment and he bought a sofa bed for her to sleep on, since they were spending so much time together. They went shopping for groceries at the Farmers Market, not far from his place, she pushing the heavy cart around to save her brother the exertion, he worried that she would lose her balance and injure herself in a fall. They drove around to her old favorite places, like Nate and Al's for corned-beef sandwiches on Beverly Drive, or Señor Pecos for guacamole in Century City near her old Twentieth Century-Fox studio, Howard Johnson's for breakfast, the Tick Tock off Hollywood Boulevard for lunch, and Musso and Frank for dinner. Soaring seagulls, pictured in a framed print, caught her eye, along with some poetry beside the gulls:

> Hold fast to dreams,
> For if dreams die,
> Life is a broken-winged bird,
> That cannot fly.

When she began to lose feeling in her fingers, Wally would light her cigarettes for her. The danger grew that Susan, who smoked as much as before, might drop a lit cigarette on a bed, couch, chair or rug.

A nurse was hired, for, despite Susan's bravado, she needed constant watching over. Carmen, an attractive, sturdy woman with a resolute manner, moved into the house, helped her charge in and out of cars, became a post for Susan to lean on while walking, made sure she took her medication, helped her dress and, in general, devotedly offered the strength that Susan was quickly losing. She accompanied her everywhere.

Human nature is ceaselessly amazing. People tend to shun the average dying person, an upsetting reminder of mortality. A dying celebrity, however, is eagerly sought after; the precious time he has left imparts rarity and value to gatherings. Many people, consciously or unconsciously, wish to be able to say later that they and perhaps only a few others were the last to see the great person alive. While there had been a time when Susan's behavior on sets had caused her to be passed over by Hollywood party-givers, she now found herself on more guest lists than she could handle. Trying to make the most of her time and now always in the mood for company, for loneliness as much as the Specter of Death was becoming her great enemy, she accepted as many invitations as she could. Before going to a party, she spent much time primping to look as she had in the past. She had a large selection of realistic reddish-auburn wigs, made for her by the finest Hollywood wig-makers, and she would choose one to complement a gorgeous gown, often a striking shade of green, which would be set off by dazzling jewelry from her large collection. Makeup to hide her bony paleness was carefully applied.

Pre-party drugs included painkillers and—a must—Dilantin, the epileptic's anti-seizure drug. Any kind of excitement, such as that generated by the buzz-buzz and laughter of a party, could bring on a seizure, which instantly ended the evening for her and was positively petrifying for the guests. Sometimes the Dilantin worked; often it didn't. Susan's drinking, which Carmen was instructed by the doctors to curtail but could not, didn't help. Susan rightly assumed, however, that if the hosts could put up with her seizures, she could continue going to their parties.

On March 30, 1973, Timmy filed a petition with the courts through his lawyers, Gerald Lipsky Inc., to be given control of his mother's cash and property holdings because she was "unable to care for herself or her property." He felt he had to take the action when he discovered that $40,000 in unpaid bills had piled up; he thought that her life had become difficult enough without having to worry about creditors. She had been served with the papers just before her long confinement at Cedars of Lebanon, but had not been lucid and had not at first understood the papers.

Through attorney Charles Beardsley, she challenged the petition for conservatorship and on May 1 Timmy withdrew it. A few months later, feeling now that he had to make some sort of public statement, he gave a quote to the *National Enquirer* which read:

Nobody can hide this any more. She has multiple brain tumors. My mother could live for only a few more days or she could live for another six months. No one can answer that question—not even the doctors. It's in the hands of God. My mother knows but she hasn't accepted it. She keeps telling me she's going to beat it but in her heart she knows.... When I last saw my mother she was alert. But under the circumstances, because you're dealing with a portion of the body that controls everything else, sometimes she's in, sometimes she's out. She fluctuates.

Susan went beyond mere fury when she picked up the July 17, 1973, issue of the *Enquirer*, read Timmy's quotes and saw a photo of herself having a seizure. She complained to Nelson, Carmen and Jay Bernstein, for whom Timmy worked. This was a time of great tension for Susan and her son, but in the end she forgave him; the bond between them was inseparable.

Carmen became deeply attached to Susan and soon grew irreplaceable, for her devotion, emotional commitment and companionship raised her far above the usual paid nurse. Carmen listened to all of Susan's musings and felt them deeply, even when Susan, because of liquor, opiates or her condition, lapsed into temporary incoherence. She held Susan's hand when fear of the Specter suddenly gripped her. Carmen's ears took in Susan's reminiscences of the past, with all of the hurts and joys now so precious. She heard Susan's religious thoughts—that there would be a Hereafter, there had to be—and would reassure Susan. Above all, Carmen shared Susan's longing for an extension of life, telling her that doctors were working night and day and were on the brink of a cure. The radiation treatments had controlled the metastasizing of the brain tumors. Maybe those rocks would just fade away. They do that. And the longer a person lasts, the greater his chances. She would pray with Susan. She bathed her in holy water shipped from Lourdes.

For spiritual comfort, Susan leaned on Nelson, too, when he came to stay at the house in mid-1973. He tried to help her face her dying by facing all her unresolved relationships. "I saw how frightened and troubled she was. I felt it was important for Susan to put to rest some of the demons that were plaguing her. I wanted her to be as at peace with herself as one can be as one faces one's own mortality." They talked about making up for the past, and a lot about Florence, whom Nelson still hadn't met and Susan hadn't seen since 1958. It was almost like a mini-trial, with Susan again saying how badly her sister had treated her when they were small, and Ron playing defense attorney: "I understand the competition that took place between you two girls when you were growing up. I understand the role your mother played in it. I got a mother who's just like your mama. But that, as you say, is 'yesterday's spaghetti,' honey. Jesus Christ, you're old ladies now. You can't do this."

Susan would answer, "Do you think I'm wrong to hate Florence the way I do?"

"Yes, I do."

"But she would have ruined my career at the drop of a hat. And still would."

"She can't hurt you anymore."

It was an ongoing struggle for emotional and familial justice. There were times when Susan would admit that, yes, she had mistreated Florence. Nelson suggested that she consider leaving something to Florence in her will. Susan thought that was a good idea. One evening, he even talked her into letting Florence come to visit, so that he could meet her, but the meeting never came about because Susan didn't know her sister's whereabouts.

Wally was in and out of the house and didn't take well to Ron Nelson, whom he thought of as almost an intruder. He says he just didn't like all the drinking Nelson had done with Susan even before she became ill, all the parties he took her to and the running around they did. Wally felt that Nelson was using his sister. Timmy felt much the same way, although Nelson, who was always helpful around the house, and Timmy developed a certain sort of positive communication. Adding to the irritations, Timmy and Carmen, who both loved Susan deeply but in their different strong ways, were often angry at one another over details of Susan's care. But, in fairness, whatever resentments or disagreements existed around Susan were ultimately aroused by the power of Susan's plight. Not one person in the Laurel Way house failed to sense the horror of Susan's ordeal or to respond with compassion. Even as she was dying, Susan's magnetism was disruptive.

How much Susan sensed the dilemmas and irritations of those around her isn't certain. She was almost totally preoccupied with her own condition, or the denial of it, becoming happy with hope one moment when the pain in her head would subside, and miserable the next when it began again. She had already lived past the death date predicted by the doctors and she summoned courage to seek the answer from the only source she had left.

* * *

Nelson and the nurse helped a thin, drawn, depressed Susan move shakily toward the front door of the home of her old and trusted astrologer friend, Carroll Righter. He was much older but alert as ever, the twinkle in his eye and the sly sense of humor still alive. Susan was aware of the recently published book by Hildegarde Neff (whom Susan knew from *The Snows of Kiliman-jaro*) in which she claimed to have beaten cancer; Neff had given Righter much praise for his support and predictions. He greeted Susan in his reception area. After a few formalities, her companions had to retire to the pool area out of earshot. She began the confessional-like consultation by coming directly to the point.

"Do I have cancer?"

He averted the question at first, saying her chart showed a "professional decline," then: "But I see you will be alive in January 1975."

She was instantly cheered, her whole depressed manner suddenly dissolving into excitement: "I'm going to get well!" In that moment, she knew the doctors to be wrong and Carroll Righter, who had never before failed her (hadn't he instructed her that she, a Moonchild, needed a Taurus, which Eaton was?), to be conversant with far more accurate powers than they.

The "professional decline," she assumed, had to do with her next scheduled TV pilot, which would probably not do well, or would be canceled before filming, but what did she care? She would be alive for another year and a half; maybe for another ten! When she was leaving Righter's, her companions offered to help her down the stairs. "No!" she said happily. "I can do it alone." And she did, quite amazingly, without limping or losing balance. For the first time in months, she removed her sunglasses while walking on a street.

Believing the doctors to have grossly miscalculated the time left to her, perhaps her whole condition, she made plans to have further tests done at Boston's Massachusetts General Hospital, which had different physicians, different equipment and, hopefully, different answers. Ron had already flown back to Fort Lauderdale; Susan promised to meet him there with the "good news" after her testing. She asked Wally to move into her Laurel Way home, feeling that he would be safer, and she, so frightened of dying with only the nurse in the house, would have her brother nearby if her time came suddenly.

It was October 1973 when Susan, with Wally and Carmen, left for Carrollton, before the ordeal of her scheduled testing at Massachusetts General. The trip to Carrollton was really to be a backward glance at the past—her last one, as she must have suspected, despite her desperate hopes.

In Atlanta, the three checked into a Hilton. Susan called Ann Moran's house, reached her daughter, said she was coming over, adding cheerily that Ann had better have her wonderful banana cake ready. Then she called Monsignor Regan and Mary Williams. In a rented chauffeur-driven limousine, Susan and company made the journey toward tiny Carrollton, their eyes fixed on the yellow and sorrel-colored leaves of the great elms that arched prayerfully over the roads and filled the spacious woods. It was a sleepy, timeless town that Susan brought Wally and Carmen to. They got out of the car, Susan wrapped in a fur, and strolled for a while in the post-summer air, still warm yet faintly nippy. Memories were stirring terribly within Susan when, later, the car drove through Main Street, then on through Dixie Street, passing the places she and Eaton had been together—the town's one movie theater, the post office, the courthouse. Wally had never seen any of it, and Susan kept saying, "Look, Wally, there's..." and "Over there, that's..." They passed the old houses, the picket fences, the big lawns, and Wally was truly sorry he had waited until now to see his sister's land of treasured memories. Susan, in her grief over Eaton, had almost forgotten the pure, beautiful, dormant peace of Carrollton.

She wanted to show her brother the big Sunset Boulevard ranch that she and her beloved had owned and run together. They stood before Monsignor Regan's rectory, across the road from the great wood-slatted house which she and Eaton had kept a simple white, while before them spread the cleared, neatly grassy land, almost to the horizon. Susan didn't have to say, "It was all ours." The great house, inhabited by strangers, could not have been easy to look at for very long. She brought Wally and Carmen inside the rectory, and introduced them to affable Monsignor Regan. They walked around, began to talk about all the things that Susan and Eaton had brought from Europe for the rectory and the church, Our Lady of Perpetual Help, right next door. She said she was delighted that her imported statues were at last placed about the church—she had always known they would be. "Wally, that fireplace is exactly the same as the one we had in our house." Susan, who had not forgotten how to act, did not bat an eye at the sight of two huge Irish wolfhounds in the house and, outside, dogs, cats, hamsters, chickens, peacocks and donkeys. She didn't complain, but later hinted that what had happened to the parish was not what she and Eaton had had in mind.

The limousine drove them another five miles to Ann Moran's house. Ann heard the car pull up and waited tensely, excitedly, for Susie, whom she hadn't seen since Eaton died and the ranch was sold. Ann had heard of her illness and was determined that, no matter what Susie looked like, she would not show surprise or sadness. As soon as Susan walked in the front door, bundled in fur and scarf, Ann rushed forward and hugged her. "Oh, Susie! . . . I'm sorry I don't have a banana cake for you," she said, then adding, before Susan could register disappointment, "but I'll bake one for you tonight. If I had known you were coming sooner . . . I have bananas in the refrigerator." Yes, she looked sick and frail but, oh, still so pretty. Ann would do anything for her, if it would make Susie happy.

The two women talked about many things. Susan showed Ann snapshots of the Laurel Way house in Los Angeles, created links for Carmen and Wally with Ann Moran by discussing the old days. Then she told Ann that Wally was living with her because he had had a heart attack and was alone and could get rest and care in her home, and, after all, she was alone, too, except for Carmen. Susan said not a word about her sickness. Before Susan left Ann Moran's, the two friends made a date for them all to meet the next day at Aunt Fanny's Cabin, the restaurant where Eaton and Susan had spent so many hours eating and talking with their bosom buddy Harvey Hester. Ann would bring her banana cake.

But the next day was windy and Ann, without mentioning that she knew of Susan's condition, called her and said she didn't think that Susie should go out in all that wind. "God bless you," said Susan. "I was thinking about that, too, but I just didn't want to renege on the invitation."

"No," said Ann, "you just stay there and eat dinner at the hotel and I'll call Mary Williams and we'll come to the hotel and we'll have coffee and cake." Now Susan knew that Ann knew.

Susan placed fresh flowers on Eaton's grave, where she spent some time reflecting. The wind gusted and memories flooded her mind. She looked at the spot, next to Eaton, where she would join him.

The next day, she flew to Massachusetts General for more tests and the cold, clinical eyes of another team of doctors.

The moment Ron Nelson saw her emerge from a plane at Fort Lauderdale International Airport, he knew what the "good news" in Boston had been. She had waited until all the other passengers had left before attempting to leave the jet with Wally and Carmen. She was in dark glasses and sable, holding on to the nurse, dragging her left foot as she moved. Her face was ashen and stoic. Ron tried to embrace her. "Don't touch me," she spat.

That night, after they were all settled in the house Nelson had rented for Susan, he offered her a glass of Chivas Regal. Carmen, for Susan's good, suggested that she forgo the liquor. "Who the hell says I can't drink?" shot Susan. "I can do anything I please." She was angry and crabby over what had happened in Boston. Ron didn't need to ask for the sorry details.

Susan was in a mood to tie a big one on, but after a couple of drinks she collapsed from exhaustion and had to be put to bed. Nelson could see, as the days passed, that her condition was growing worse, as those rocks destroyed more of her voluntary nervous system. Susan's dragging of her left foot was the result of one of the tumors in her right brain lobe growing large and beginning to paralyze the left side of her body. The right side of her brain, fortunately, was more expendable, since Susan was right-handed and therefore left-brain-oriented. Had that large tumor emerged on the left side, she would have quicly lost her ability to reason and remember; nothing would have remained but her autonomic functions.

Back in her Laurel Way home after three weeks with Nelson in Fort Lauderdale, Susan saw what was happening to her and made the decision not to undergo further chemotherapy and radiation, and she would accept narcotic painkilling drugs only in moderation. The painful, nerve-racking, continuing effort to save her life seemed increasingly futile, robbing her of peace in what had to be her last months. She appeared to be giving up the fight.

"I don't want any more life-saving crap!" she cried out to Wally.

Those closest to Susan praised her for her sanity and bravery. But she wavered constantly between courage and terror, conviction and uncertainty. Despite her brave words, she told Nolan Miller and Wally, in almost the same words, "If I thought it would help, I'd travel anywhere, take anything, even rat poison."

The laetrile frenzy was just beginning in the United States. She begged he doctors to give her laetrile treatments, which were illegal, and she was refused. On her own, Susan arranged for secret injections of laetrile to be given to her on a regular basis.

The prayed-for miracle happened. There was a wonderful remission in the early months of 1974. The rocks were shrinking and the paralysis was halted. Much to the absolute amazement of her doctors, Susan was once again filled with hope.

Nolan Miller, Hollywood's famed designer, received a mysterious phone call from Susan, who said that she wished to come down to the Goldwyn studio to see him but would explain no more.

Sitting alertly before him, with Carmen by her side, she said, "I am going to make a public appearance."

"You're *what*?"

"They asked me to be on the Academy Awards. What should I wear? How do you think I should look?"

Hollywood had learned quickly enough of Susan's remission and in March the Academy had sent her a formal invitation to appear live on television to present the 1974 Best Actress award with David Niven at the Oscar ceremonies on April 2. Her frequent seizures were no secret. The Academy people were well aware of the enormous risk of a grotesque fit in front of millions of viewers, but the spectacular effect of Susan stepping out of her deathbed to make a grand public appearance was, apparently, worth the potential horror. Susan was just as aware of what might happen, yet the idea of giving the Specter one good kick in the shins by appearing whole, perhaps even beautiful, in front of the millions who believed she was all but His, seemed irresistible. She had wavered for a few days, talked with Dr. Siegel, Carmen, felt even more sanguine, then given the Academy a yes.

When Nolan recovered from the shock, he grabbed pencil and

sketching pad, jotted down notes, drew a few lines, then shot at her: "First let's get you the goddamnedest Susan Hayward wig they ever made, lots of red hair. I'll do sketches for the dress. The jewelry..."

"It's all in Fort Lauderdale in a safe deposit box. What can I do?"

Nolan called Van Cleef and Arpels and asked for a loan of jewelry for her to wear to the Awards. "They never do this," says Nolan, "but when Huey Skinner heard her name, he said, 'Bring her over and let her pick what she wants.'"

In no time, Nolan was at the house showing Susan sketches of six gorgeous gowns. She chose one as soon as she saw the sketch. Nolan drove her to Van Cleef, which put out three trays of diamond necklaces, bracelets and earrings. She took her time, picking out pieces that were tasteful but big enough so that no viewer could possibly miss the aura of life and glamour she wished to project. She paid visits to Perc Westmore, a member of the most esteemed makeup-artistry family in Hollywood. She spent many hours working on the details of her big night, nervously preparing, hoping for a mirage that everyone would believe.

At one point, she turned to Nolan and said, "This is the last time the public ever sees me, so I want to look beautiful."

Nolan was devastated by her honesty.

Between the time of her acceptance and Academy Award night, she did not fare well. She underwent seizures and her left side was again becoming paralyzed. What might happen in front of the TV cameras worried her to distraction. The day of the Academy Awards, she told Carmen to call the Academy and tell them she had changed her mind. Instead, someone in Susan's entourage called Katharine Hepburn, who didn't know Susan well but agreed to talk to her.

"Susannah, you must," cajoled Hepburn.

"Why?" said Susan, adding with her old sarcasm: "You never did."

It was true. Hepburn had never appeared at the ceremonies, not even to accept her own awards. This year, she had been invited to give the Irving Thalberg Award to her friend, producer Lawrence Weingarten. Kate said that she was going on, too, and would be backstage to see Susan through the ordeal.

That night, Susan came through the side entrance of the Pantages Theatre wearing her $40,000 black sable. In her dressing room, which Groucho Marx reluctantly abandoned for her, her retinue flitted about her, including Carmen and Nelson; Noreen Siegel and Dr. Lee Siegel, who gave her a big shot of Dilantin to prevent an on-camera seizure; Perc Westmore, doing a last-minute makeup check; Nolan Miller, fussing with her gown; and Katharine Hepburn, who became far more concerned about Susan's big moment than she was about her own first appearance tonight.

The Best Actor award had just been given and the dressing-room tension became nearly palpable as David Niven appeared onstage, ready to introduce Susan: "...and to help me present the award is someone very dear to all of us. She is no illusion. Ladies and gentlemen, Susan Hayward!"

"Don't stop for a moment when you hear that applause," Hepburn hurriedly whispered to Susan, knowing what the applause excitement might do to her, moments before Susan walked out into the hot TV lights.

The Academy people were just as terrified as everyone else of a sudden fit and never once photographed Susan in close-up, keeping her in an odd, inappropriate long shot from the moment she appeared. Nevertheless, people all over the country saw a fabulous Susan Hayward, sheathed in a high-neck, Nile-green gown, with long, tapered sleeves and a full-blown skirt, everywhere splashed with glistening sequins, so that no vestige of her emaciation could be detected.

Noreen Siegel says that she will never forget the sight of Susan bravely walking out on that stage in high heels, straight and sure, holding her head up, as if to say, "I'll show the world." The applause for Susan was not as heavy as one would have expected, for so many people were nearly dumbstruck at the glamorous sight of what was supposed to be a woman only days away from death. It was as if some higher power had kept the applause low; a thundering ovation might have triggered a tragedy.

Susan helped David Niven give the Best Actress award and left the stage as confidently as she had come on. Dr. Siegel gave her some more Dilantin in the dressing room. She took off the thirty-pound gown and the wig. Unabashedly, she looked at herself in the mirror, saw her bald pate, on which some peach fuzz was beginning to grow back, her skinny arms and concentration-camp torso, and laughed, without bitterness, as the others watched her: "If they could only see me now." She had pulled off the greatest theatrical stunt of her career, and, calling it a "miracle of faith," became terribly happy and excited—too much so. Fifteen minutes after she left the stage, she suffered a gruesome seizure. Dr. Siegel did what he could. She was carried out of the Pantages on a stretcher.

Ever since that photo of her had appeared in the *National Enquirer*, Susan had stopped going to parties, for fear of another hidden paparazzo. But she welcomed certain visitors, people who loved her despite her wasted appearance. Katharine Hepburn, Hollywood's great-hearted Earth Mother, had never met Susan before her illness, yet after they met at the Academy Awards she came often to the Laurel Way house. Once, Hepburn followed Wally's car into the driveway. Upon emerging from her 1961 Thunderbird, Kate, in blue jeans and black leather jacket, looked at Wally's KHH on his license plate and laughed and said he had her initials. He opened the front door with his key, and, seeing Kate look askance, said, "Oh, I'm Susan's brother." Wally, and everyone, really, grew to love Kate. She always bought a big bouquet of flowers, and Susan, who could vie with the world's best penny-pinchers, adored it when Kate said: "These are from my own garden, dear. You don't really think I'd pay the prices they're asking in florists' these days." They talked endlessly about directors and films and other actors, telling wonderful on-set stories from the past. Each might just as well have been holding her Academy Award, for they were communicating as could only the few who occupied filmdom's Mount Olympus. Kate was wonderful therapy for Susan.

Barbara Stanwyck had never forgotten the gift of pink roses when she herself was ill, and she began a lively correspondence with Susan, even though they still had not met. Nolan Miller, one of Susan's frequent visitors, became their messenger. He would come to Susan's house, say, "Missy has been asking about you," and then go to Stanwyck and say, "Susan wants to know how you are." This went on for some time. One day, Susan found out that Stanwyck and Miller were going to the Getty Museum. "She asked if she could join us," says Miller. "We said of course. Her limousine arrived ahead. Missy and Susan met and were very casual: 'Hello,' 'Wonderful to meet you,' like that. We did the entire museum. Missy was very concerned about Susan's state and kept saying, 'Susan, are you tired? Susan, do you want to sit down?' After we spent the day there, we had lunch, and then, when we got to the parking lot and the two of them had to part, they were both in tears, hugging and kissing goodbye. You wouldn't believe they had never met before." After that, Susan kept saying to Nolan that she wanted to have him and Stanwyck up to the house for dinner. That never happened. But much later on, Barbara, without telling Nolan, quietly came to visit the desperately ill Susan.

Ruth Gillette was a loyal friend and constant visitor. One time when Ruth and Nelson were at the house, a less welcome guest came: the young actress who had made eyes at Nelson in Las Vegas, to Susan's dismay. The actress arrived at Laurel Way ostensibly to see Ron, but wound up in an audience with Susan. "She came up there," says Ruth Gilette, "and sat on the floor at Susan's feet, crying these crocodile tears, pressing her hand and saying, 'Oh, my beautiful,' 'Oh, my darling,' and so on. I was dying to say, 'Save your performance for the stage.' I had had my fill of her. That night, Nelson asked Susan, who was not always conscious of what was happening, 'Did you know that so-and-so came to see you today?' And Susan said, 'She's full of shit.' That's something, for a woman half dead to get that."

Still handsome, Jess Barker came frequently to the house. He had never remarried. Over the previous few years, he and Susan had had occasion to meet, at first because of the boys but then out of renewed friendship. They had both forgotten all the past bitterness. Susan had had eons to consider their nine years together and had often worried that she had damaged his life. Now, in her twilight months, there was genuine warmth between them. When she felt up to it, they would go out to dinner. He would sit in the house with her, laugh with her, hold her close, play affectionate games with her.

One day, she received another visitor from the past.

Florence hadn't seen her sister in sixteen years and had learned of her illness from the *National Enquirer* and other papers. She was greatly upset at the news. At the age of sixty-two, she was living in Los Angeles with her son, Larry, and her daughter, Moira, now thirteen, and the family was still on welfare, although intermittently. Florence tried to support her children by working as a cook in an old-age home. Anxious to learn more about Susan, she talked about her to a friend; she feared Susan would never have a chance to see her niece. Florence couldn't call her sister, but knew her address, and one day the friend suggested he drive Florence and Moira to the Laurel Way house.

Florence was amazed at all the winding and twisting that the car had to do, while she sat tensely next to her daughter, wondering what Susan would be like. Finally, the car arrived, and she and little Moira rang the front doorbell while the friend waited in his car. To Florence's surprise, Susan herself opened the door. She looked at the two people vacantly. Florence's heart sank.

"I'm Florence, Susan," she said. "This is my daughter, Moira. Can we come in?"

Susan cordially invited them into the living room. A man, who Florence later learned was Susan's accountant, sat nearby. Susan went immediately into the kitchen to fetch cream soda from the refrigerator and offered it to them, and they all sat down. During the conversation, Susan was distant, "as if she was talking to a stranger." She did not appear as ill as Florence had read, but Moira noticed that her aunt repeated herself and seemed not to comprehend everything that was being said. She looked at her pretty, red-headed niece, then at Florence, and said the only thing during the meeting that indicated her understanding that she was talking to family: "You had the girl." (Florence had always believed that Susan had been angry at her for having a baby girl, having wanted one for herself.) Florence told Susan that she didn't have any money and that she was worried that Moira wouldn't have a chance for an education. Susan just nodded, quite coldly, and finally said, "She'll just have to work for it the way I did." Florence realized there was nothing left; there were only blank stares and perfunctory responses from her sister. They never discussed family recollections or the illness. After half an hour, Florence told Susan that she and Moira had to go because her friend was waiting to drive them back. Susan saw them to the door and did not ask them to return. It was the only time Moira Dietrich ever saw her famous aunt and the last time Florence saw her sister.

The coldness toward Florence persisted despite all those drawn-out discussions with Ron Nelson regarding forgiveness for the past. Susan may have forgotten those talks about reclaiming her sister because of the coherency problems; more than likely, her anger was just too deep. Around this time, there came another voice from the past, Benny Medford's, on the telephone, saying to Susan, "Why don't you put Florence in your will? Florence is destitute."

"I should say not," said Susan. There was a moment of silence and then: "I hate her." She was utterly coherent.

In a way, Susan was receiving visitors from all over the world, through the mails. One letter, from Richard Nixon at San Clemente, gave her endless pleasure. She read it over and over. It was cheerful—he admired her "gallant fight" and he was so pleased that word had come to him of her partial recovery. He and Pat were looking forward to her visiting them at San Clemente as soon as she was well enough. Susan was moved by the fact that, despite Watergate and his own health problems, Nixon cared enough to call a mutual Hollywood friend for her address and then wrote to her as if he were a man with his own life in order. If she ever licked this thing, she said, she would visit Richard and Pat.

From her fans, she received a glut of letters enclosing religious artifacts. Wally would read the heartfelt, sometimes hysterical and morbid fan mail to her, but she refused to touch the rosary beads, pictures of saints on medals and cards, booklets and various alleged relics. "I'm sick enough now," she told Wally. "I don't know where all this stuff's been." Besides, she had her own rosary beads and Eaton's black onyx cross, blessed by the Pope, which she wanted to have in her bedroom at an arm's reach at all times, just in case.

The contrast between the glamorous Hayward whom the world saw when she walked out in front of the Academy Award cameras and the "remains" that her friends saw in her dressing room was startling and not lost on her image-obsessed ego. She decided to capitalize on the mirage she projected to millions by having Jay Bernstein and Timmy proclaim to all the columnists that she was not only cured and nearly ready to work again, but had never had cancer in the first place. The *Los Angeles Examiner* and *Times* ran repeated items about her recovery, but what gave Susan the most gratification was a story in the June 9, 1974, edition of the *National Enquirer*, headlined: SUSAN HAYWARD'S MIRACULOUS RE-COVERY FROM THE EDGE OF DEATH. The story quoted Timmy as saying, "My mother is in fine health again. Whatever she may have had she doesn't have now." Bernstein told the *Enquirer* that one of her two doctors had said, "This is sure one for the books. Miss Hayward has had a miraculous recovery and there is no way to explain it. It wasn't cancer as suspected and now all of her symptoms are gone." Even Norman Brokaw got into the exaggeration act by saying: "I think Susan demonstrated just how well she's feeling when she made the presentation of the Best Actress award at the April 2nd Oscar awards. Movie studios are swamping her with offers." The picture accompanying the piece was of a flawlessly beautiful Susan at the Oscar presentation. So effective was the campaign to change Susan's image from that of one who was dying to one who had been victimized by erroneous cancer reports that the TV networks began sending Susan scripts. Then, Susan actually agreed to do a TV pilot to be filmed in 1975. She was beginning to believe her own publicity.

Susan's remission had already ended by the time the "miraculous recovery" items were published. The tumor on the right side of her brain was enlarging again, causing further paralysis of the left side and occasional comas. She had to use a wheelchair, crutches and leg braces to keep the partially paralyzed and wasted leg from breaking under the weight of her body. Wally and a friend built plywood wheelchair ramps over the three steps leading to the living room so she wouldn't have to be carried when she wanted to sit by the fireplace.

June 30, 1974, was to be Susan's last birthday. She had not been feeling well and so it was a surprise when suddenly she announced a great yearning for chocolate cake. After the quiet dinner with Nelson at home, the new cook brought out the chocolate cake, glowing with candles. Susan went at it as if it were a life-prolonging elixir, not a mere cake. When half of it was gone, she stared at it and said that Timmy just had to have a piece, too; they must all just pile into the car and drive over to Timmy and Ilse's with the remains of the birthday cake. It was a strange impulse. During the drive to Timmy's, a great tension was building in Susan. She began to speak of the "awful" neighborhood around them. The cook, sitting in the back seat with the cake, must have picked up on the disturbing mixture of anger and anxiety, for, when the car arrived at Timmy's, she got out of the back seat and dropped the cake upside down on the pavement in front of Susan.

"That stupid woman!" yelled Susan, who was only inches from

the cook. Ron and the rattled cook picked up the cake and scraped off the dirty top. Susan suddenly swung into a new mood and began to laugh at the mess that had been patched up. Timmy and Ilse warmly greeted the bearers of the repaired birthday cake, unaware of the hostility that seethed within Timmy's mother that night.

To celebrate the Fourth of July, Susan wanted a big outdoor party like the ones she, Wally and Florrie had gone to when they were kids on Church Avenue, with fireworks and grilled hot dogs and hamburgers and potato salad and buttered corn-on-the-cob. The guests, besides Ron, included Lee and Noreen Siegel, Marty and Helen Rackin, Stanley Cortez and his wife, Wally, and Timmy and Ilse. Everyone there knew that Susan was failing, that she might never live to have a party like this again, and so there was deliberate excitement. Waves of gleeful applause accompanied skyrockets, which could be seen all over Beverly Hills. Those thundering bursts of fire in the air seemed the soul of all that Susan had been, the very essence of Red's splashy existence for more than half a century. The gaiety, the lights in the sky, the sudden memories put a gleam in her eyes.

On July 11, one week later, she checked into Emory University Hospital in Atlanta. She had already been to just about every other important cancer clinic on the East Coast, each offering the most modern treatments and elaborate methods of detection. However, no biopsy had ever been performed. Her tumors, whether or not they were malignant, were considered beyond surgical treatment, and therefore beyond the need of a biopsy, which would require the penetration of the skull with a needle probe. But Susan's continuing untoward survival, at least a year longer than any reasonable medical expectation, caused some of the doctors to believe that perhaps a medical miracle was taking place. All hopes, including Susan's, began to center around the malignancy question.

On July 18, a neurosurgeon, Dr. George Tindall, performed a biopsy, after telling Susan that if the result was positive there was no hope for prolonged survival. When the biopsy procedure was completed, Nelson sat with her in her hospital room while she quipped about the "rocks in my head that I always knew I had." She seemed amazingly prepared, without any forced aura of bravery. The reports were quickly back from pathology and Dr. Tindall and some associates came into her room.

Susan looked grimly at Ron. "If he's gonna tell me what I think he's gonna tell me, you'd better leave."

Out in the corridor, Ron waited tensely. He heard a piercing, utterly heart-rending scream, followed by a dead silence. The physicians left. He went into the room and tried to get her to talk about what Dr. Tindall had told her, air her feelings, thinking it would be good for her. He was deeply worried that the scream he had heard from the corridor was still taking place inside of Susan; he himself was a nervous wreck.

But Susan wasn't. She cut him off. "There's nothing to talk about. I'm going back to Fort Lauderdale and I'm going to act like nothing happened." After a few more awkward exchanges, Susan got rid of Ron by telling him she had a sudden yen for chicken livers in wine and mushroom sauce and would Ron please go out and get them for her?

Dr. Tindall had given it to her, exactly as she had wanted it, straight. He told her precisely what to expect in the coming months. The comas and seizures would happen with increasing frequency. She would not be able to walk at all. The voluntary and then the involuntary nervous network would deteriorate. She would lose her speech and her memory, the swallowing reflex would go, and then only intravenous feeding could keep her alive.

Her wishes were clear. She told Dr. Tindall and, later, her friends and family that she desired to die in peace and with dignity, and would not be made a monstrous vegetable by being hooked up to machines. She forbade intravenous feeding when the swallowing reflex went. "I don't want anybody to push me over the brink," she would tell Nelson, "and I don't want anybody to hold me back."

By now, there were news stories and rumors which made possible connections between the growing number of people who had worked on *The Conqueror* in 1953 who developed cancer, and the government's atomic testing near the movie's desert location. Dick Powell and Pedro Armendariz had both died a few years before, and Agnes Moorehead had just succumbed. People who lived near the atomic site were getting leukemia. Susan told Nelson that she just couldn't believe that the radiation had caused her condition. She preferred to think it was something hereditary.

She and Carmen spent the whole summer of 1974 with Nelson in his home in Fort Lauderdale. She seemed peaceful enough, though one thing bothered Nelson: she spent her days sleeping and her nights watching television and drinking. He finally asked her why she reversed the normal pattern, and her answer was the title of an Edward G. Robinson movie she had always liked: "The night has a thousand eyes."

"The night frightens you?" he asked.

"Let's put it this way. I feel more secure sleeping in the day-time."

Overall, she did not seem particularly tense or terrified. Ron often stayed up during her night vigils, watching television and drinking with her. Their talk was ordinary, not particularly deep or reflective. She seemed to want to experience life in a quiet, unremarkable way, as if the very moments of time were the most important things, not people or sights or conversational reflections. She didn't seem to need great love or tenderness; in fact, she wished not to be distracted by anything too intense. She seemed to be able to feel these unadorned waking moments as astonishing events unto themselves.

As the weeks passed, Dr. Tindall's frightening predictions were coming true. Her coordination was worsening. Her hands shook so badly that Ron would cut her food for her; she had trouble feeding herself. Even reading became difficult. Cigarettes, dropping from her unfeeling fingers, burned the rugs. Rather than have her use the cumbersome wheelchair, Ron usually carried her from place to place. When she wasn't sleeping in the daytime, he would take her out by the pool, where she would hide her wasted body in a bathrobe as they both lounged in the sun.

"It was just horrible to see her that way. I'd have to fight back tears." He would laugh, joke with her, carry on cheerful conversations while, inside, he also was dying.

By the end of September, Susan became so feeble that further care at Ron's house in Fort Lauderdale was impossible, and she had to be flown back to Emory University Hospital in Atlanta on October 5. On October 17, she went into a coma, and the doctors, certain that she would not regain consciousness, notified the family.

October 21, she regained consciousness. I'm thirsty," she said, quite coherently, as if she had merely waked from a night's sleep. "Bring me a glass of water."

Susan kept amazing the doctors. Her steely spirit refused to submit, even with the world's biggest excrescence exploding inside her head. She refused to give Death a second more than was His due.

She made some quick decisions. No, she told Ron, she did not want to go back to Fort Lauderdale. With only a few months at best, she didn't want to die in the same city where Eaton had. For the first time, the warmth of South Florida, which she had previously seen as life-renewing, had changed to a tombstone chill. She wanted to die in California. There were also practical reasons for the decision. It would be better for the probate of her estate.

Nelson rented a plane to fly her and Carmen back to Los Angeles, in order to ensure privacy. He drove the two of them to Miami for the flight, and there a most remarkable discussion took place. For months, Susan had seemed to be quietly approaching her end without qualms or last-minute dilemmas. She had never put into words what she needed from Nelson in all the death plans, until suddenly, as Susan was leaving him to board the plane, she said to him, "You're in this until the end. When I call you, you gotta come, you know that."

"Of course I will."

"I'll never forget this. I picked you, Ron, to do this with me because, hell, I'm scared. I don't like this one bit. I haven't been a very nice person. I may suffer a lot before and after."

"Look," said Ron, comforting her, "I'll be there. You've done all you can to rectify all the mistakes."

Ron had only recently recovered from mild heart trouble, as Susan knew, and she said something strange, almost in the way of striking a bargain: in return for his pledge to fly to California at the last moment, she would promise to fly to where he was if he should be stricken again and was about to die.

At the beginning of the six-hour night flight to Los Angeles, she was half-conscious, but by the time the plane was over Texas, she was suddenly alert and agitated. The Specter tormented her at night, and, so high above the Earth, He seemed terrifyingly near.

She told the pilot, "Put the plane down and find a restaurant. I'm hungry." And frightened. She was boss, so the pilot landed in the middle of Texas and the crew began searching for an all-night restaurant. They found some fried-chicken-to-go and they all joined her in a midnight snack in the plane. After she wiped her hands and lips, the plane re-ascended.

"Can you hear me, dear? It's Kate.... Have they been sticking your behind full of needles again?"

"Hi, Susan darling. It's Ruth... Ruth Gillette."

From the depths to which her consciousness had descended, she would barely recognize her visitors. Carmen usually carried Susan out into the living room and placed her on a chaise lounge, where she would receive them. She only permitted a handful now: Kate Hepburn, Ruth Gillette, Wally, Jess and her two sons. She hadn't yet asked Nelson to make the final trip to California. Others who had been friends suddenly realized that they were shut out. Helen Rackin tried over and over to see her. "Many times, I would talk to her on the phone (it was difficult for her to talk because of the paralysis) and I'd say, 'Suz, can I come up and see you?' She'd say, 'Fine, Helen, but call first.' But every time I came, I would be told that she was asleep. I would always leave a note for her." One day, Cleo Miller's phone rang and it was Jess Barker, saying, "Cleo, I have someone I'd like to have talk to you." Then Susan took the phone and, oddly, in front of Jess, began telling Cleo how much she had loved Eaton. Cleo, overwhelmed by the call and aware of Susan's condition, begged Susan to let her come to see her, but Susan refused with "I'll let you know." It was the last time the two ever talked.

Most of the time, she was heavily sedated to keep her from going into fit after fit, but it wasn't the shots that kept her from seeing Helen and so many others. Rather, it was a combination of her horror at being seen as she was and a growing lack of interest in the matters of this world.

She called Father Brew in Washington and asked him to visit her. In mid-December, he spent a day at the Laurel Way house. "She was sleeping all the time, because of all the sedation, but we did have a couple of conversations." He already knew that her illness was grave, and so he had come expecting Susan to be filled with spiritual anxieties and was prepared to offer what comfort he could. To his surprise, Susan displayed "no fear, no rebellion" at the thought of her impending death. "She realized and accepted," says the Father, "and in her own way was consoled by the Catholic belief in the life hereafter." Total resignation, a wonderful peace, was setting in.

Her call to Father Brew was not only to see him one last time, but to say goodbye to Eaton as well, for she saw the Father, Eaton's friend and confidant, as the closest link in this world, and possibly the next, to her beloved. She was settling matters.

Around Christmastime, the whole house was decorated with wreaths, plants and a big tree for Susan's grandchildren. Susan couldn't have been less interested.

She called Ron on February 7, 1975, and told him it was time, and he left his job, once again, to be with her at the Laurel Way house.

Susan's poolside bedroom, which she seldom left during her last months, sometimes became the focal point of a hurly-burly of rushing bodies, pounding footfalls, as those about her saw a giant in the final thralls of the Specter and fought it bitterly. There was sometimes a hysterical whisper-shout: "Will you keep quiet and let her die in peace!" There were sudden eruptions. The disagreements between Carmen and Susan's son finally grew to a point where Carmen felt forced to leave. Her departure was most touching. She went into Susan's room and said, "Susan, can you hear me? Can you hear me? I have to leave." Susan moved her head weakly toward Carmen's voice and slowly opened her eyes. She couldn't speak, but, amazingly, understood, for tears began to slide down a cheek.

By late February, no non-family members, aside from Nelson and Katharine Hepburn, were allowed to see Susan. Kate was the last visitor to see Susan alive.

There had been one exception to the no-visitors rule.

A woman dressed in a long black cape, with a hood, came to the door and said that she wished to see Miss Hayward. The nurse who answered the doorbell did not recognize the mystery woman, at first, as Greta Garbo, and replied: "Miss Hayward can't see anyone."

"I think she will see me," Garbo replied, and, when she was recognized, was led immediately to Susan.

The bedroom, in which Susan lapsed in and out of consciousness, reeked of foul odors from the oozing fluids and bowel voidings. She could no longer control her sphincter muscle, and could not turn over in bed for comfort when she was awake, She was cleaned and turned by Carmen's replacement, Sydney Miller, and the relief nurse, Janice Campiformo. Ron kept watch at Susan's bedside, taking his own sleep either alongside her on the same huge bed or in the big armchair placed close to it. His nostrils were so filled with the fetid smells in the room that he became almost impervious to them.

At times, when what was left of Susan became conscious, she would cry out in a way that would tear Nelson apart as he lay next to her, "Mamma...Maaaaa-mma, oh, where are you?" She cried out the same thing while Lee Siegel was in the room. Nelson remembered all those blasé descriptions of how hateful her mother had been, how she had not loved Susan and Susan could not love her back, and all that coldness now seemed trivial as she begged Ellen Marrenner to come back to her. She had loved her mother after all.

How much love there had been in Susan that never had a chance to emerge.

Nelson didn't get much sleep. Lee Siegel prescribed Valium from Schwab's drugstore and gave him the sort of clock that insomniacs like. It flashed the hours and minutes on the ceiling in hypnotic bright-red digits.

He felt tremendous compassion for Timmy, who was showing signs of stress as his mother's body grew unrecognizable, as the last days of Susan's life were clearly approaching. He sometimes looked sick and white and distraught.

Nervous exhaustion was overtaking Ron. He wanted Susan to die quickly and in peace, not to just hang on in this horrible way. Ron pleaded with Dr. Siegel for some knowledge, a physical sign that would tell him when it was all about to end. Dr. Siegel instructed him to check various vital signs, like the pulse of the carotid artery in the neck and the wrists, to listen to breathing. He did all of these things, and the pulse, blood pressure and breathing always seemed as strong as ever.

Ron finally broke down and cried to the doctor: "When, in God's name? When?" The answer was simple: "You'll know."

One tormented night, Ron writhed sleeplessly until 1:30 a.m., then he called Dr. Siegel at his Beverly Hills home, saying he just had to talk to someone. He poured out all of his frustration until 5:00 a.m., while Lee Siegel tried to comfort him.

Susan went into a coma on March 6 and four days later amazed everyone, once again, by coming out of it, not only stronger but able to speak. She phoned Gregory in Jacksonville, Florida. It was to be her last conversation with him.

Although Gregory had known that his mother would soon die and had been flying in to see her, she wanted him to hear it from her own lips.

"You know I'm dying," she said to Gregory.

He spoke affectionately to her. "Is there anything I can do?"

"You're a veterinarian," she joked. "I thought you might be able to fix up this old horse."

He tried to get her to talk about other things as well, but Susan, perhaps because of fatigue, ended the conversation there. "This is my nickel," she said, "so I'm signing off now. I want you to remember something, though... remember that I love you."

Soon afterward, she lost her speech again.

Tuesday, March 11. At night, an old speckled hoot owl perched on the diving board of the swimming pool under Susan's bedroom window. When Ron looked out and saw it, an icy shudder lashed his body. He had never forgotten Susan telling him of the Irish superstition, in which she believed, that the appearance of an owl meant imminent death.

Hooooooooot.

The ululation rent the night's stillness. Would Susan hear? His heart began to beat like a drum. He downed Dr. Siegel's Valium like so many peanuts.

Wednesday, March 12. Susan had been in a stupor all day. Nelson had not gotten any sleep the night before. That night, the same owl, drawn by implacable forces, came back to the pool's diving board. When it began to hoot once again, Ron was beside himself. "I can't let her hear it!" he thought, and he rushed through the darkened house, searching for Susan's old hunting shotgun, found it, ran down to the pool and drew a bead on the owl, which was in ghastly silhouette against a full-moon-lit sky.

The blast from the gun failed to frighten the omen bird from its post, but the horrendous sound did bring in the ever diligent Beverly Hills police. Half out of his mind, Ron tried to explain that a person was dying, and that there was the owl, and it was dreadful, just terrifying. Seeing the man in such a state, the police did not give him a citation, merely warned him not to fire the gun again.

Hooooooooot.

With Susan near him in bed, Nelson, like a madman, watched the owl all night long, perspiring, shaking, hoping that she wouldn't awaken and hear. At dawn, as if called away by the same demons that summoned it, the owl disappeared.

Thursday, March 13. With unflagging promptness, the hooting owl returned to its spot for the third night in a row. "It was meant to be," Ron realized. It hooted its message that Susan would be taken from the living, never more to see or think or feel or be seen. The owl, with its third-time supernatural finality, was now almost comforting. This third night was as bright with moonlight as the previous two, but as the old bird called, Ron could see that clouds had darkened the moon.

Friday, March 14. Ron had been with Susan all morning, while she remained restive. With one clawlike hand, she clutched the black onyx crucifix. Time seemed at a standstill as Ron sat by the bed.

The new nurse, Sydney Miller, walked in and out of the room.

He and Nurse Miller were with Susan when something began to happen. She was aroused from her torpor by a great inner storm, a massive seizure that gripped and whipped and smashed every part of her body. The muscle spasms that scrunched her face and clamped her jaws violently together caused her to bite off the part of her tongue that remained; much of it had been bitten off during countless previous seizures. The tornado of massive muscular upheavals, pounding her body again and again on the bed, lasted only briefly, but seemed endless.

Her head wrenched sharply to an abrupt halt. Nelson, still alone with her, checked the now quiet body. The pulse was gone. The breathing had stopped. The agony was over.

Edythe Marrenner Barker Chalkley, whom the world knew as Susan Hayward, lay peacefully dead.

Uncannily, at what appeared to be the moment of her death, Ron's eyes had been drawn to his insomniac's digital clock. It read 2:24 p.m. He remembered that in the TV movie she had made several years before, *Say Goodbye, Maggie Cole*, Susan, playing a doctor, had to write down the time of her patient's death. The time had been 2:24 p.m. Was it some joke? Was the Creator drawing inspiration from her filmed dialogue in His shaping of her life and her very death? She had won her Oscar for *I Want to*

Live! in which there were many excruciating reprieves from the moment of death. She had played a woman dying of a brain tumor *(Stolen Hours)*. She had played a tormented boozer, a woman on crutches...and on and on.

Nelson picked up the bedroom phone and dialed Lee Siegel. The doctor ordered him not to tell anyone. Just guard the body. And let no one into the bedroom until he got there. He would explain.

Nelson dipped his fingers in the holy water Susan had near her and administered extreme unction, according to the instructions given to him by a priest. He touched his wetted fingertips gently to her forehead, made the sign of the cross, chanting "The Father, the Son, and the Holy Ghost," and sealed her eyelids.

He sat in the armchair near the bed, staring at the little figure wrapped in a pink blanket, right arm stretched out clutching the cross, head turned to the left. She was still beautiful. Somehow, the cancer that had consumed the flesh of her body had not affected her face. Her long lashes, which had so enhanced her vivid eyes, had remained, despite the loss of her scalp hair. He covered the top of her head with a pink chiffon scarf to hide her baldness, reached for his camera and took flash pictures of her.

A quiet tap on the door; Dr. Siegel slipped into the room.

In low tones, Siegel told Nelson his plan. He wanted to have an autopsy done, as soon as possible. He, along with the other doctors, had been wonder-struck that Susan had remained alive for two years after the discovery of malignant brain tumors that medical science decreed should have taken her life within a matter of weeks. In her dead body, said Siegel, might be found some strange cancer-delaying process which might help countless other sufferers. Nelson, made acutely aware of medical detective work through his job with the Heart Association, didn't hesitate in agreeing to the suggestion. He believed Susan would have wanted to "throw out another lifeline."

In order to keep the press from being alerted before Susan's body arrived at the hospital for the autopsy, a benign conspiracy took place. It was as if a scene were being staged for a movie. The corpse was propped in a sitting position in a wheelchair. The pink chiffon scarf hiding the baldness was replaced with one of the plethora of red wigs; dark glasses were slipped onto the lifeless face; and a wrap was pulled over the shoulders. The cadaver, looking quite alive, was wheeled out of the house and into a waiting ambulance, while a neighbor peered from a window, wondering where on earth Susan, looking better than she had for months, was going now.

Nelson called Timmy and told him of his mother's death, and Timmy rushed to the house, taking over the chore of notifications and publicity. Nelson helped with arrangements for the funeral, which was to be held on Sunday in Carrollton, according to Susan's wishes. However, Timmy told the press that the funeral would take place on Monday, hoping to avoid a swarm of reporters and visitors disturbing the services in the little city.

During the break after the first flurry of phone calls, Ron and Timmy stood quietly in the living room of the house. Timmy seemed bitter and shattered. It appeared, in those moments, as if he were reacting to some sort of unforgivable theft: a part of himself had been taken away. Just then, Timmy glanced at the dozens of artifacts on open shelves in the living room, and he suddenly seemed uninterested in anything. He asked Nelson, never Timmy's favorite person, if there was any remembrance of Susan he would like to keep; it would be Ron's last chance, since all would be disposed of at an auction right after the funeral. Ron thought Timmy terribly enigmatic, and in that instant suddenly understood why Susan had loved him so.

Wally was on the freeway driving back from his job at the racetrack when he heard on the radio that his sister had died hours earlier. He was stunned. He had been prepared and he hadn't been prepared. He had loved her, and it had been terribly important to him to be notified the minute anyone thought she was on the brink of death; he had wanted to be with Susan when she left for good, to say goodbye. He had often told Ron, during the past few weeks, "If anything happens to my sister, or if it looks bad, call me right away." Ron, who was leaving all the notifications up to Timmy, didn't do that. Wally felt deeply hurt.

He called the Laurel Way house and was told that Susan's body was being embalmed and they would all be flying to Carrollton that night. Wally had just enough time to return to his apartment and pack a bag.

By the time Susan's body reached the hospital, the autopsy room was prepared. The pathologist's knife found, as had been suspected, that the cancer had developed in the right lung and had spread to the brain. Nothing unusual was discovered to explain her spectacular remissions and length of survival. Dr. Siegel concluded that the answer lay in her incredibly strong constitution and heart, which refused to release her body until the biggest of her multiple brain tumors had snapped the vagus, or cranial, nerve, which originates in the part of the brain that keeps the heart beating. The final massive seizure was, in effect, the breaking of the vagus nerve link.

That night, on a Delta flight, Timmy, Ron and Wally accompanied Susan's body, in the cargo compartment, to Atlanta, from where limousines would take them the fifty miles to Carrollton. During the flight, Ron sat alone, undisturbed in first class, drifting into a Life With Susan reverie. He listened to her cute expressions: "I'll see you in the funny papers," "It's all yesterday's spaghetti"; heard her coarse words, vicious yet throatily intimate: "candy-box crap," "rotten SOB." He had a drink. He recalled all the people she loved, like John Wayne ("a real man"), and didn't love, like Dean Martin ("he's vulgar"). He had another drink. She was a cheapskate (forcing him to reimburse her for the fish she had framed for him!) and a monster, at times. He was getting drunk. He remembered her pouring $400,000 in cold cash on a table, out of a paper bag, and counting it, bill by bill, like an old crazy, watching his dazzled look. When her worst movie, *Where Love Has Gone*, came on the tube, instead of blanching with embarrassment she would say merrily, "Every time they show that, Mama gets thirty-five thousand dollars richer," and force him to watch it. She was the heart-pound of a roller-coaster ride when she was furious. Pure fire when she was passionate. Agony when she was desperate. Even better in real life than on the screen. There would be such painful monotony now without her.

When the plane landed in Atlanta, newspapers announcing SUSAN HAYWARD DEAD had already arrived at the airport magazine stands. The limousines drove the party to the Wedgewood Inn, off the main road not far from town, and took Susan's body to the Almon Funeral Home. Susan had said she wanted to be buried in the gown the public last saw her wearing and to be made up, for the last time, by Frank Westmore. Ron steamed her Academy Award dress, that gorgeous green affair designed by Nolan Miller, and took it to the undertakers.

The next night, at nine p.m., there was a rosary at the Almon

Funeral Home's chapel. Susan had spoken of not wishing to be viewed in a wake, so plans were made to keep the casket closed; but Wally couldn't bear the idea of not being able to see his sister one last time and had demanded that the coffin be opened for him, despite objections that Susan wasn't ready to be seen. Then, at the rosary, Ron demanded that the casket be opened again for him and the others. He had the first view of the fully prepared body. Frank Westmore's work was superb. She looked quite as beautiful as the living Susan Hayward had, except for her bosom, which, because of the autopsy, had been puffed up, looking clumsily stuffed with a pillow. She had always been proud of her breasts and, to hide the fake look, Ron placed flowers over the area. She held a rosary blessed by Pope John.

The others now viewed the body. There was solemn calm during most of the viewing, except for a few moments when Gregory's wife came to the casket, saw Susan's face looking as though alive and broke down, sobbing, saying again and again, "She looks so beautiful." She was led from the coffin.

Nelson had a private moment with her. He looked at the casket and couldn't help recalling something that was typically Susan. The casket was bronze, the same model that Eaton had been buried in. Susan had shopped for it herself. When told the casket would cost her $8000, a whopping $5000 more than she had paid for Eaton's, she hit the ceiling, complaining about the sorry inflation that Americans had to put up with.

Perhaps because the funeral was held in tiny Carrollton, so far from the Coast, and because arrangements had been made quickly and clandestinely, no movie-star floral wreaths (except for Barbara Stanwyck's, enscribed FROM ONE BROOKLYN BROAD TO ANOTHER) or any of Susan's fellow stars, for that matter, arrived for the last service, held on Sunday, March 16, at Our Lady of Perpetual Help, Susan and Eaton's church.

The folk of Carrollton followed tradition and baked cakes and hams that Sunday morning. In the early afternoon, standing in mud and rain, they lined seven miles of highway between the funeral home and the church. The message on the Village Theatre's marquee read: SUSAN WE'LL ALWAYS LOVE YOU. People from the city who knew Susan filled the chapel of Our Lady of Perpetual Help for the services at three p.m. The family, with Nelson, sat in the front pew, near Fathers Danny McGuire and Thomas Brew.

Monsignor Regan gave the eulogy. It was somewhat usual, with many quotations from the Bible and many references to the fact that Christ had promised that death was not the end, and finally some talk about Susan's happiness with Eaton and their generous donation of this very church. The lines that Susan would have appreciated the most came at the end: "This separation is not permanent. God willing, we shall one day be together again in heaven." It was an idea that Susan at first hoped was true, then later wholeheartedly believed.

After the service, mourners filed slowly past the coffin, which was heaped high with yellow roses and white orchids. The local grocery clerk paused and remembered seeing her in pedal-pushers with her red hair tied back and chauffeuring a pick-up truck with CHALKMAR (Chalkley-Marrenner) FARMS painted on the sides. The country woman with a small baby in her arms recalled Susan sitting on the back steps of her home, drinking cold buttermilk and talking about "so many things." A bank teller could picture her waiting quietly, patiently, in line. All classes of people had waved to her and she had always waved back. They knew her as Hollywood had never known her nor could ever believe she could behave.

Before the casket was borne from the church, the mayor *pro tem*, Miriam Merrill, gave Timothy and Gregory a scroll of sympathy on behalf of Carrollton.

In the cold wind and downpour, the afternoon ended with a soft sunlit glow that bathed the hills and smoothed the late-wintry trees in the distance into a serene canvas. Susan's casket was lowered into the red Georgian earth next to Eaton's plot, in the graveyard set in front of the church she and Eaton had built, just across the way from the home they had shared.

When it was over, Susan's party went back to the inn. In the to-do to expedite post-burial matters, there was insensitivity toward Wally; arrangements were made for him to fly back to Hollywood that very night, although the others intended to remain a few days. Wally was doubly hurt when he learned that the airline had been asked to hold a plane in Atlanta in case his limousine arrived late. He had no reason to want to leave Carrollton and Susan so quickly. As soon as he stepped onto the plane, he asked the stewardess for two drinks to soothe him. A morbid foreboding of what would lie ahead of him now, without Susan, ate relentlessly at him. He took momentary comfort in the smile of the stewardess, a stranger. Later, in Los Angeles, he slipped the key into his door and entered a painfully empty apartment.

So many visitors had been coming to Carrollton and asking, "Where is Susan Hayward buried?" that the graveyard attendants and church clerics put up a sign in front of the large, triangular-topped tombstone of Susan and Eaton: GRAVE OF SUSAN HAYWARD CHALKLEY. Ann Moran, who was still a loyal member of the church and a constant visitor to the grave, thought the dreadful sign was the kind put in a zoo—THIS WAY TO THE MONKEYS—and, in a fit of anger to match Susan's temper, took the sign away and smashed it.

Susan would have frowned at the huge mural of her which Ron Nelson never destroyed and still keeps on his living-room wall. Right after Susan's death, Ron gave up drinking—easy without Susan to encourage it—and his heart condition subsequently subsided. He retired from the Heart Fund a few years ago and has since moved from Fort Lauderdale to a small town in Florida where he lives only part of the time, away from the hordes of people he once knew with Susan. He spends most of the year traveling for pleasure (on his own money; Susan left him only memorabilia). A few years back, he converted to Catholicism, under the guidance of Monsignor Regan, and purchased the plot next to Susan and Eaton in Carrollton, where he will one day be laid to rest next to the most important person in his life.

Gregory lives with his wife and children in Neptune Beach, Florida, where he is perhaps the most esteemed veterinarian. Susan had always been proud of him and never doubted that he would have a fine life. Although she worried about Timmy, the concern turned out needless. She would be extremely proud of him today. Well before he and Gregory received their substantial inheritances (a few years ago, on their thirty-fifth birthday), Tim had started his own public-relations firm, Hamilton & Barker, and began to make a fine reputation for himself. In February of 1975, he appeared on "The Merv Griffin Show," just before Susan died to talk about being Susan Hayward's son, and mentioned his mother's terminal illness, which he believed came about from the government's atomic testing in Utah, near the location for *The Conqueror*. (He believed he had been exposed to radiation himself when he and his brother visited Susan on the set in the desert. He and relatives of other cancer victims associated with that film filed a lawsuit against the government.) Since his mother's death, Tim has not encouraged people in Hollywood to make the connection to Susan and has succeeded on his own competence. Today, he has a handful of prestigious clients, who, one hears, are mainly writers. He has married for the second time and has children by both his first wife and his present wife.

Both Gregory and Timmy are still close with their father, Jess Barker, who lives modestly in Glendale, not far from Timothy. Once a year, Jess and Tim go to Cleo's home in Los Angeles for the sort of dinner that they used to have on Longridge Avenue in the days before the divorce, and memories flood back. Susan, despite all her "guilt feelings" about what she had done to him, did not leave him a dime in her will, and, in fact, expressed her wish in that document that the twins not help him financially. Whether the twins have abided by that, only they can say. Jess is described by a friend, Evelyn Lane Dankner, as "a lovely, outgoing man." If he has any bitterness about the past, he never speaks of it, only of his love and admiration for Susan and his pride in his sons.

Florence, too, was left with nothing in Susan's will. At seventy-four and quite healthy, Florence still has great charm and vitality. She lives in Highland Park (very near Glendale) with her son, Larry Zaenglin, and their monkey, Binky. She has no telephone, and travels around Los Angeles by bus, spry as ever, her spirits up, a shopping bag forever in each hand. She reads. She sleeps late. She has not seen Gregrory or Timothy in decades, and seldom sees Wally, for the past continues to control. In the back of her mind, she is always aware of her sister, with mixed feelings of bitterness and a tiny glimmer of affection for the time before the rift occurred. She also knows that she has survived the storm of the past. She says, "Did you hear about Bette Davis' sister who couldn't stand Bette Davis becoming a star and she had to be put in a mental hospital? Now it [Susan's success and subsequent rejection of her] *bothered* me, but I didn't let that happen to me. Susan would have liked that. I'm just grateful to be strong enough to just go on and not let what happened affect my mind."

She is very much wrapped up in her daughter, Moira Dietrich, a pretty, twenty-four-year-old, blossoming actress. For a while, until his recent stroke, Benny Medford was handling Moira's acting career, and believed her even more talented than the twenty-two-year-old Edythe Marrenner. (Every now and then, one looks at Moira, who has creamy skin, a slight, snub-tipped nose and strawberry-blond hair, and the resemblance is stunning. Benny had even wanted to change Moira's name to Moira Hayward.) She works in a Hollywood bank and appears in plays at night. She may have a fine career ahead of her. Her fondest dream is to buy her mother a mobile home in the desert. For herself, Florence's fondest dream is to meet an older gentleman and settle down.

Finally: Wally. He still lives quietly in the same Hollywood apartment and has not remarried. He, too, has had no contact with Timmy or Greg since Susan's death and he often wonders why. Susan left him the perpetual interest from a $200,000 trust fund, on which Wally lives comfortably but modestly. He plays golf, which the doctor encourages to strengthen his heart, and sees a steady woman friend. He thinks of Susan always, and somehow his neighbors sense that he does, for when they see him they remind him that one of her movies will be on television that day or the next and he mustn't miss it, and Wally doesn't. In *Where Love Has Gone* or *I Want to Live!* or *Back Street* or any of the others that he has seen time and again, she comes through the tube to him as though alive again, comforting him. He tries not to be negative and not to think about the obvious injustice of her cruel, early death, but the thought does come to him, anyway, of how hard she worked to insure her future, and his, only to be repaid for her efforts by a fate worse than Job's. It was a terrible way to die.

But then, Susan never felt that her final destiny was unjust, never cursed God. Death was simply one more challenge in a series of obstacles to overcome. The battles had never ceased, from the very onset of her life, and with fire, fury and steel, Red wholeheartedly fought each and every one, especially her last.

FILMOGRAPHY

Girls on Probation, Oct. 1938,* Warner Bros. Director: William McGann. Co-stars: Jane Bryan, Ronald Reagan. Note: Susan was 10th-billed; this was her first billing in a movie.

Comet over Broadway, Dec. 1938, Warner Bros. Director: Busby Berkeley. Co-stars: Kay Francis, Ian Hunter. Note: Susan did not receive billing.

Beau Geste, July 1939, Paramount. Director: William A. Wellman. Co-stars: Gary Cooper, Ray Milland, Robert Preston, Brian Donlevy.

Our Leading Citizen, July 1939, Paramount. Director: Alfred Santell. Co-stars: Bob Burns, Joseph Allen, Jr., Elizabeth Patterson, Gene and Kathleen Lockhart, Charles Bickford.

$1,000 a Touchdown, Oct. 1939, Paramount. Director: James Hogan. Co-stars: Joe E. Brown, Martha Raye, Eric Blore.

Adam Had Four Sons, March 1941, Columbia. Director: Gregory Ratoff. Co-stars: Warner Baxter, Ingrid Bergman, Richard Denning, Johnny Downs.

Sis Hopkins, April 1941, Republic. Director: Joseph Santley. Co-stars: Judy Canova, Jerry Colonna, Bob Crosby.

Among the Living, Aug. 1941, Paramount. Director: Stuart Heisler. Co-stars: Albert Dekker, Frances Farmer, Richard Webb, Harry Carey, Maude Eburne.

Reap the Wild Wind, March 1942, Paramount. Director: Cecil B. De Mille. Co-stars: John Wayne, Paulette Goddard, Ray Milland, Robert Preston, Charles Bickford, Raymond Massey.

The Forest Rangers, Sept. 1942, Paramount. Director: George Marshall. Co-stars: Fred MacMurray, Paulette Goddard, Albert Dekker.

I Married a Witch, Oct. 1942, United Artists. Director: René Clair. Co-stars: Veronica Lake, Fredric March, Robert Benchley.

Star Spangled Rhythm, Dec. 1942, Paramount. Director: George Marshall. Co-stars: Bing Crosby, Betty Hutton, Bob Hope, Preston Sturges, Cecil B. De Mille. Note: 16 Paramount stars played themselves.

249

Young and Willing, Feb. 1943, United Artists. Director: Edward H. Griffith. Co-stars: William Holden, Robert Benchley, Eddie Bracken, Barbara Britton, Martha O'Driscoll.

Hit Parade of 1943, March 1943, Republic. Director: Albert S. Rogell. Co-stars: John Carroll, Eve Arden, Count Basie, Dorothy Dandridge, Freddy Martin, Ray McKinley. Note: Retitled *Change of Heart* for TV, from the Oscar-nominated song.

Jack London, Nov. 1943, United Artists. Director: Alfred Santell. Co-stars: Michael O'Shea, Virginia Mayo, Louise Beavers.

The Fighting Seabees, Jan. 1944, Republic. Director: Edward Ludwig. Co-stars: John Wayne, Dennis O'Keefe.

The Hairy Ape, May 1944, United Artists. Director: Alfred Santell. Co-stars: William Bendix, John Loder, Dorothy Comingore.

And Now Tomorrow, Nov. 1944, Paramount. Director: Irving Pichel. Co-stars: Loretta Young, Alan Ladd, Barry Sullivan, Beulah Bondi, Cecil Kellaway, Helen Mack.

Deadline at Dawn, Feb. 1946, RKO. Director: Harold Clurman. Co-stars: Bill Williams, Paul Lukas.

Canyon Passage, July 1946, Universal. Director: Jacques Tourneur. Co-stars: Dana Andrews, Brian Donlevy, Patricia Roc.

Smash-Up: The Story of a Woman, Feb. 1947, Universal-International. Director: Stuart Heisler. Co-stars: Lee Bowman, Eddie Albert, Marsha Hunt.

They Won't Believe Me, July 1947, RKO. Director: Irving Pichel. Co-stars: Robert Young, Rita Johnson, Jane Greer.

The Lost Moment, Oct. 1947, Universal-International. Director: Martin Gabel. Co-stars: Robert Cummings, Agnes Moorehead, Joan Lorring, John Archer.

Tap Roots, Aug. 1948, Universal-International. Director: George Marshall. Co-stars: Van Heflin, Boris Karloff, Ward Bond.

The Saxon Charm, Aug. 1948, Universal-International. Director: Claude Binyon. Co-stars: Robert Montgomery, John Payne, Audrey Totter, Heather Angel, Cara Williams.

Tulsa, May 1949, Eagle-Lion. Director: Stuart Heisler. Co-stars: Robert Preston, Pedro Armendariz, Chill Wills, Lola Albright.

House of Strangers, July 1949, 20th Century-Fox. Director: Joseph L. Mankiewicz. Co-stars: Richard Conte, Edward G. Robinson.

My Foolish Heart, Dec. 1949, RKO. Director: Mark Robson. Co-stars: Dana Andrews, Kent Smith, Lois Wheeler, Robert Keith, Jessie Royce Landis.

Rawhide, March 1951, 20th Century-Fox. Director: Henry Hathaway. Co-stars: Tyrone Power, Hugh Marlowe, Dean Jagger.

I Can Get It for You Wholesale, March 1951, 20th Century-Fox. Director: Michael Gordon. Co-stars: Dan Dailey, George Sanders.

I'd Climb the Highest Mountain, May 1951, 20th Century-Fox. Director: Henry King. Co-stars: William Lundigan, Rory Calhoun, Barbara Bates, Lynn Bari.

David and Bathsheba, Aug. 1951, 20th Century-Fox. Director: Henry King. Co-stars: Gregory Peck, Raymond Massey, Jayne Meadows.

With a Song in My Heart, April 1952, 20th Century-Fox. Dierctor: Walter Lang. Co-stars: Rory Calhoun, David Wayne, Thelma Ritter, Robert Wagner, Helen Westcott.

The Snows of Kilimanjaro, Sept. 1952, 20th Century-Fox. Director: Henry King. Co-stars: Gregory Peck, Ava Gardner, Hildegarde Neff.

The Lusty Men, Oct. 1952, RKO. Director: Nicholas Ray. Co-stars: Robert Mitchum, Arthur Kennedy.

The President's Lady, May 1953, 20th Century-Fox. Director: Henry Levin. Co-stars: Charlton Heston, Fay Bainter.

White Witch Doctor, July 1953, 20th Century-Fox. Director: Henry Hathaway. Co-stars: Robert Mitchum, Walter Slezak.

Demetrius and the Gladiators, June 1954, 20th Century-Fox. Director: Delmer Daves. Co-stars: Victor Mature, Michael Rennie, Anne Bancroft.

Garden of Evil, July 1954, 20th Century-Fox. Director: Henry Hathaway. Co-stars: Gary Cooper, Richard Widmark, Cameron Mitchell.

Untamed, March 1955, 20th Century-Fox. Director: Henry King. Co-stars: Tyrone Power, Richard Egan.

Soldier of Fortune, May 1955, 20th Century-Fox. Director: Edward Dmytryk. Co-stars: Clark Gable, Gene Barry, Michael Rennie.

I'll Cry Tomorrow, Dec. 1955, MGM. Director: Daniel Mann. Co-stars: Jo Van Fleet, Richard Conte, Eddie Albert.

The Conqueror, March 1956, RKO. Director: Dick Powell. Co-stars: John Wayne, Agnes Moorehead, Pedro Armendariz.

Top Secret Affair, Jan. 1957, Warner Bros. Director: H. C. Potter. Co-stars: Kirk Douglas, Paul Stewart, Jim Backus.

I Want to Live, Oct. 1958, United Artists. Director: Robert Wise. Co-stars: Simon Oakland, Virginia Vincent, Theodore Bikel.

Thunder in the Sun, April 1959, Paramount. Director: Russell Rouse. Co-stars: Jeff Chandler, Jacques Bergerac.

Woman Obsessed, May 1959, 20th Century-Fox. Director: Henry Hathaway. Co-stars: Stephen Boyd, Theodore Bikel, Barbara Nichols.

The Marriage-Go-Round, Jan. 1961, 20th Century-Fox. Director: Walter Lang. Co-stars: James Mason, Julie Newmar.

Ada, July 1961, MGM. Director: Daniel Mann. Co-stars: Dean Martin, Wilfrid Hyde-White, Ralph Meeker, Martin Balsam.

Back Street, Oct. 1961, Universal. Director: David Miller. Co-stars: John Gavin, Vera Miles, Virginia Grey.

I Thank a Fool, Sept. 1962, MGM. Director: Robert Stevens. Co-stars: Peter Finch, Diane Cilento.

Stolen Hours, Oct. 1963, United Artists. Director: Daniel Petrie. Co-stars: Michael Craig, Diane Baker.

Where Love Has Gone, Nov. 1964, Paramount. Director: Edward Dmytryk. Co-stars: Bette Davis, Michael Connors, Jane Greer, Joey Heatherton.

The Honey Pot, May 1967, United Artists. Director: Joseph L. Mankiewicz. Co-stars: Rex Harrison, Maggie Smith, Edie Adams, Capucine, Cliff Robertson.

Valley of the Dolls, Dec. 1967, 20th Century-Fox. Director: Mark Robson. Co-stars: Barbara Parkins, Patty Duke, Sharon Tate.

The Revengers, July 1972, National General. Director: Daniel Mann. Co-stars: William Holden, Ernest Borgnine.

TELEVISION FILMS

Heat of Anger, 1972, CBS. Director: Don Taylor. Co-stars: James Stacy, Lee J. Cobb, Fritz Weaver.

Say Goodbye, Maggie Cole, 1972, ABC. Director: Jud Taylor. Co-stars: Darren McGavin, Dane Clark, Jeanette Nolan, Madie Norman.

INDEX